1,000,000 Books
are available to read at

Forgotten Books

---

www.ForgottenBooks.com

Read online
Download PDF
Purchase in print

ISBN 978-1-331-43984-4
PIBN 10190454

This book is a reproduction of an important historical work. Forgotten Books uses state-of-the-art technology to digitally reconstruct the work, preserving the original format whilst repairing imperfections present in the aged copy. In rare cases, an imperfection in the original, such as a blemish or missing page, may be replicated in our edition. We do, however, repair the vast majority of imperfections successfully; any imperfections that remain are intentionally left to preserve the state of such historical works.

Forgotten Books is a registered trademark of FB &c Ltd.
Copyright © 2018 FB &c Ltd.
FB &c Ltd, Dalton House, 60 Windsor Avenue, London, SW19 2RR.
Company number 08720141. Registered in England and Wales.

For support please visit www.forgottenbooks.com

1 MONTH OF FREE READING

at

www.ForgottenBooks.com

By purchasing this book you are eligible for one month membership to ForgottenBooks.com, giving you unlimited access to our entire collection of over 1,000,000 titles via our web site and mobile apps.

To claim your free month visit:

www.forgottenbooks.com/free190454

* Offer is valid for 45 days from date of purchase. Terms and conditions apply.

English
Français
Deutsche
Italiano
Español
Português

www.forgottenbooks.com

Mythology Photography **Fiction**
Fishing Christianity **Art** Cooking
Essays Buddhism Freemasonry
Medicine **Biology** Music **Ancient
Egypt** Evolution Carpentry Physics
Dance Geology **Mathematics** Fitness
Shakespeare **Folklore** Yoga Marketing
Confidence Immortality Biographies
Poetry **Psychology** Witchcraft
Electronics Chemistry History **Law**
Accounting **Philosophy** Anthropology
Alchemy Drama Quantum Mechanics
Atheism Sexual Health **Ancient History**
Entrepreneurship Languages Sport
Paleontology Needlework Islam
Metaphysics Investment Archaeology
Parenting Statistics Criminology
Motivational

THE

HISTORY OF TENNESSEE,

FROM ITS

Earliest Settlement to the Present Time.

BY

W. H. CARPENTER.

PHILADELPHIA:
LIPPINCOTT, GRAMBO & CO.
1854.

Entered according to Act of Congress, in the year 1854, by
T. S. ARTHUR AND W H CARPENTER,
in the Clerk's Office of the District Court of the Eastern District of
Pennsylvania.

STEREOTYPED BY L JOHNSON AND CO
PHILADELPHIA.

PUBLISHERS' PREFACE.

THERE are but few persons in this country who have not, at some time or other, felt the want of an accurate, well written, concise, yet clear and reliable history of their own or some other state.

The want here indicated is now about being supplied; and, as the task of doing so is no light or superficial one, the publishers have given into the hands of the two gentlemen whose names appear in the title-page, the work of preparing a series of CABINET HISTORIES, embracing a volume for each state in the Union. Of their ability to perform this well, we need not speak. They are no strangers in the literary world. What they undertake the public may rest assured will be performed thoroughly; and that no sectarian, sectional, or party feelings will bias their judgment, or lead them to violate the integrity of history.

The importance of a series of state histories like those now commenced, can scarcely be estimated. Being condensed as carefully as accuracy and interest of narrative will permit, the size and price of the volumes will bring them within the reach of every family in the country, thus making them home-reading books for old and young. Each individual will, in consequence, become familiar, not only with the history of his own state, but with that of other states:—thus mutual interest will be re-awakened, and old bonds cemented in a firmer union.

In this series of CABINET HISTORIES, the authors, while presenting a concise but accurate narrative of the domestic policy of each state, will give greater prominence to the personal history of the people. The dangers which continually hovered around the early colonists; the stirring romance of a life passed fearlessly amid peril; the incidents of border warfare; the adventures of hardy pioneers; the keen watchfulness, the subtle surprise, the ruthless attack, and prompt retaliation—all these having had an important influence upon the formation of the American character, are to be freely recorded. While the progressive development of the citizens of each individual state from the rough forest-life of the earlier day to the polished condition of the present, will exhibit a picture of national expansion as instructing as it is interesting.

The size and style of the series will be uniform with the present volume. The authors, who have been for some time collecting and arranging materials, will furnish the succeeding volumes as rapidly as their careful preparation will warrant.

PREFACE.

PERHAPS the history of no State in the Union contains more events of romantic interest than that of Tennessee. Settled originally by a rough border population, surrounded by vindictive and subtle enemies, upon whose territory they had established themselves in defiance of opposition and in contempt of danger, the long and bloody wars which followed encroachments repeatedly renewed have no parallel except in the annals of Kentucky. Yet this sturdy people, separated from the older States by intervening mountains, not only sustained themselves against the incessant assaults of their adversaries, but righted their own wrongs, assisted to repel invasion, and finally evolved order and prosperity out of tumult and disaster.

Possessing more than ordinary facilities for blending the science of manufactures with the pursuits of agriculture, it is not difficult to imagine the future greatness of a state so happily situated both as respects fertility of soil and variety of climate. At the present period, as the following pages will show, Tennessee ranks first among the States of the Union in the value of her domestic fabrics, fourth in the production of Indian corn, and fifth in the scale of population.

CONTENTS.

CHAPTER I.

Romantic character of Spanish adventure—The Fountain of Youth—Ponce de Leon—Discovery of Florida—Warlike opposition of the natives—Lucas Vasquez de Ayllon—Lands in Carolina—His treacherous conduct to the natives—Second voyage of De Ayllon—Its disastrous termination—Expedition of Pamphilo de Narvaez—Lands in Florida—Attacked by natives—Sufferings and privations of his followers—They reach Apalachee—The village of Anté—They re-embark at Tampa Bay—Successive loss of the flotilla—Captivity of Alvar Nunez—His escape and return to Spain—His mysterious reports—Hernando de Soto—His early career—His marriage—Entreats permission to conquer Florida—Is invested with the government of Cuba—Sailing of the expedition—Arrival at Cuba—Liberality of Vasco Porcallo...*Page* 19

CHAPTER II.

Embarkation of the Spaniards at Havana—Arrival at Tampa Bay—Skirmish with the natives—Capture of Juan Ortiz—His romantic adventures—The march through Florida—The troops constantly attacked by the natives—Take up their winter quarters at Apalachee—Continued hostility of the natives—The march resumed—De Soto reaches the province of Cofachiqui—His reception by an Indian princess—Enters northern Georgia and encamps at Chiaha—Fruitless search for gold—The province of Coosa—The Spaniards welcomed by its chief—The arrival at the province of Tuscaloosa—Haughty speech of Tuscaloosa—He accompanies De Soto to Mobile—The battle of Mobile—Condition of the victorious Spaniards—De Soto returns to Chickasa—His encampment burned by the natives—Discovery of the Mississippi—The Spaniards cross the river into Arkansas—Encamp at the mouth of the Red River—Sickness and death of De Soto—Wandering of the Spaniards under Moscoso—Their return to Mexico.. 31

CHAPTER III.

The Spanish settlements restricted to Florida—French, English, and Dutch colonies in North America—The Jesuit mission in Illinois—Marquette ordered to explore the Mississippi valley—The Illinois entreat him not to venture—His noble reply—Sets out on his journey—How attended, and by whom—Reaches Maskoutens—Rude evidences of Christianity among the natives—Speech of Jolliet—The *voyageurs* descend the Wisconsin—Their reception at the Des Moines villages—Marquette's address—Response of the chief—Description of the monstrous Piasau—The voyage down the Mississippi—False alarm of the travellers—They reach the cotton-wood region—Approach the village of Michigaméa—Hostile preparations by the natives—Rescue of Marquette and his party—Escorted to Arkansas, and hospitably entertained—The return to Canada..........*Page* 48

CHAPTER IV.

Robert Cavalier de la Salle—His emigration to Canada—Becomes a fur-trader—Establishes a trading-post at La Chine—His explorations—Made commandant of Fort Frontenac—Returns to France—Obtains a patent of nobility and a grant of land—Resolves to explore the valley of the Mississippi—Obtains a monopoly of the traffic in buffalo skins—Builds a brigantine on the upper waters of the Mississippi—Crosses the great Lakes to Mackinaw—Sails for Green Bay—Sends back the Griffin to Niagara, freighted with furs—Proceeds to the mouth of the St. Joseph—Builds the fort of the Miamis—Descends the Kankakee—Builds forts—Crevecœur and Rock Fort—Returns to Fort Frontenac—Reappears in Illinois—Again returns to Canada—Prosecutes his voyage to the Mississippi—Reaches the mouth of the Illinois—Descends the Mississippi to the Chickasaw bluff—Loss of a hunter—Builds Fort Prudhomme............ 57

CHAPTER V.

Discovery of Old Virginia by Amidas and Barlow—Attempts at settlement—The James River colony—Its reverses and eventual prosperity—Extension of settlements—The Albemarle region—A patent granted by Charles II. for the province of Carolina—Locke's constitution—Its rejection in Albemarle—Culpepper's insurrection—Governor Sothel—

Ludwell's administration—The Carolinas under separate jurisdictions—Cary's insurrection—Arrival of Hyde—War with the Tuscaroras—Indian war with South Carolina—French in Louisiana—D'Iberville establishes a colony at Biloxi—Its removal to Mobile Bay—Crozat's grant—Charleville's trading-house on the Cumberland—French forts in the Tennessee country—New Orleans founded—Massacre of the French by the Natchez—Province of Georgia settled by Oglethorpe—French expedition against the Chickasas—Its disastrous failure..*Page* 65

CHAPTER VI.

Waning influence of the French—Progress of Georgia—War between England, France and Spain—Virginia boundary extended—Settlements on the Holston, Yadkin and Catawba—French in the valley of the Ohio—Mission of George Washington—Fort Duquesne—Skirmish at Great Meadows—Surrender of Fort Necessity—Arrival of Braddock—His defeat and death—Earl of Loudoun—Forts Prince George, Dobbs and Loudoun built—Campaign of 1758—Capture of Fort Duquesne—Trouble with the Cherokees—Indian negotiations for peace—Conduct of Lyttleton—Massacre of Indian hostages—Cherokee war—Montgomery marches against the Indian towns—Relieves Fort Prince George—Battle of Etchoe—Surrender of Fort Loudoun—Massacre of prisoners—Generosity of Attakulla-kulla—Advance of Grant—Second battle of Etchoe—Peace....................... 82

CHAPTER VII.

Pressure of borderers upon the Cherokee country—Exploring parties in Tennessee—Wallen's hunters—Boone's—Henderson employs Boon to explore Eastern Tennessee—Discovery of Kentucky—Indian complaints—Royal proclamation—Disregarded by the pioneers—Scaggins explores the Lower Cumberland—Remonstrance by the Iroquois—Council at Fort Stanwix—Cession of lands south of the Ohio—Cherokee council at Hard Labour—Settlements on the Holston—The Long Hunters explore Kentucky—Increase of settlers at Watauga—They establish a local government—The commissioners for Watauga—John Sevier—Extension of Virginia boundary—The Watauga lands leased of the Cherokees—An Indian murdered—Danger of the settlers—Heroism of Robertson—The north-western tribes—Troubles with the borderers—The massacre on the Ohio by Cresap and Greathouse—Indian war—Dunmore's campaign—Battle of Point Pleasant—Treaty of peace................... 96

CONTENTS.

CHAPTER VIII.

Cherokee council at Sycamore Shoals—Purchase of the Watauga territory—Other grants—The Transylvania grant annulled by Dunmore—Colonial troubles—Instructions to the royal governors—Seizure of stores at Concord—Battle of Lexington—Difficulties with Dunmore—Patrick Henry marches on Williamsburg—Flight of Dunmore—Action of the Federal Congress at Philadelphia—Spirited conduct of North Carolina—Increased excitement in the province—Flight of Governor Martin—The legislature of North Carolina advocates a declaration of independence—Annexation of the Watauga settlement to North Carolina—Indian hostilities—Skirmish at Long Island—Defence of Watauga Fort—Anecdote of Catherine Sherrill—South Carolina menaced by a British fleet—Provincial expeditions against the Cherokees..*Page* 106

CHAPTER IX.

Washington county established—Liberality of the North Carolina legislature—Special enactment in favour of the Watauga settlers—Increase of emigration—Military service—Assistance sent to Kentucky—Relief of Logan's Fort—Militia disbanded in Tennessee—Lawlessness of the Tories and Refugees—Committee of safety organized—Summary punishment of obnoxious persons—Hostility of the Chickamaugas—The Nick-a-jack towns—Description of the Nick-a-jack cave—Expedition against the Chickamaugas—Destruction of their towns—Jonesborough founded—Sullivan county established—Exploration of the Lower Cumberland—Robertson's settlement on the Bluff at Nashville—Donaldson's remarkable voyage—Joins Robertson at the Bluff.. 120

CHAPTER X.

War of independence—Evacuation of Boston—Declaration of independence—Battle of Long Island—Of White Plains—Washington retreats across the Jerseys—Battle of Trenton—Battle of Princeton—Howe advances on Philadelphia—Battle of Brandywine—Of Germantown—Burgoyne's invasion—His defeat at Saratoga—Conquest of Georgia—Subjugation of South Carolina—Defeat of Gates at Camden—Activity of the mountaineers—Shelby and Sevier join

CONTENTS.

McDowell—Capture of a tory garrison on Pacolet River—Advance of the British and Tories under Ferguson—Battle of Musgrove Mill—Rapid retreat of the mountaineers..*Page* 129

CHAPTER XI.

Mountaineers disbanded—Advance of Ferguson—His message to Shelby—The mountaineers called to arms—Assemble at Watauga—Advance against Ferguson—The latter retires from Gilbert-town—American reinforcement—Conference of the partisan leaders at the Cowpens—Pursuit of Ferguson—Campbell selected to command the mountaineers—Approach to King's Mountain—Order of battle—Sevier comes under fire of the enemy—The attack commenced—Courageous conduct of Ferguson—Effect of his bayonet charges—Resolute perseverance of the mountaineers—Flag of surrender twice torn down by Ferguson—His defiant conduct—His death—Surrender of the British and Tories—Tarleton sent to relieve Ferguson—His recall—Retreat of Cornwallis—His subsequent movements—Battle of Guilford Court House—Capitulation at Yorktown.......................... 138

CHAPTER XII.

Return of the mountaineers—Indian hostilities—Battle of Boyd's Creek—Expedition into the Cherokee country—Destruction of Indian towns—Greene calls for reinforcements—Response of Shelby and Sevier—They join Marion—Capture two British posts at Monk's Corner—Shelby obtains leave of absence—The mountaineers return home—Prosperity of Tennessee—Death of Unatoolah—Alarm of the settlers—A new station constructed—Pacific overtures made to the Cherokees—Council at Gist—Land-office closed by North Carolina—Re-opened—Arbitrary extension of the western boundary—Greene county established—Explorations—Land-office opened at Hillsborough—Rapid sale of land—Expansion of the settlements west of the mountains... 149

CHAPTER XIII.

Recognition of American independence—Difficulties of the federal and state governments—Cession of public lands by North Carolina—Alarm of the mountaineers—Convention at Jonesborough—Declaration of independence—State of

Franklin—North Carolina annuls her deed of cession—The mountaineers form a separate jurisdiction—Proclamation of Governor Martin—Its effect in the western counties—Political antagonisms—Increase of the party favourable to North Carolina—Tipton and Sevier—Outrages committed on both sides—Reactionary spirit—Return to the jurisdiction of North Carolina—Execution issued against the property of Sevier—Its seizure—Rash conduct of Sevier—His arrest—Escape—Election to senate of North Carolina.*Page* 159

CHAPTER XIV.

Robertson's colony on the Cumberland—Increase in population—Hostility of the Indians—Keywood and Hay killed—Freeland's station attacked—The settlers take refuge in block-houses—Cause of Indian hostility—Settlement on Red River broken up—Donaldson's party attacked—Panic among the settlers—Robertson's resolute advice—Freeland's station surprised—Repulse of the Indians—Desultory warfare—Robertson's fort at the Bluff invested—Eight of the garrison killed by a stratagem—Custom of the country—Close of Revolutionary war—Temporary cessation of hostilities—Indian council at the Bluff—Spanish intrigues—Renewal of Indian incursions—Desperate skirmishes—Treaty of Hopewell—Continuance of hostilities—Robertson's expedition—Attack on Hay at the mouth of Duck River—Surprise of Indian village by Robertson, and capture of traders—Capture of French trading boats—Division of the spoils.. 169

CHAPTER XV.

Desultory Indian warfare continued—American attempts at retaliation—Robertson and Bledsoe remonstrate with McGillivray—Death of Colonel Bledsoe—Robertson's negotiations with the Creeks—Hostilities continue—Increase of emigration—Causes which influenced it—State grants and reservations—District of Morgan established—Courts of law—Davidson county established—Nashville receives its name—Partial cessation of hostilities—Road opened through the wilderness—Sumner and Tennessee counties established—Voyage of Colonel Brown down the Tennessee—Massacre of his party by the Chichamauga Indians—Captivity of Mrs. Brown and the younger children—Their release—North Carolina cedes her western lands to the United States.. 181

CONTENTS.

CHAPTER XVI.

Territorial government formed—Blount appointed governor—Difficulty with Spain—Instructions to Mr. Jay—Indignation of the western people—Instructions rescinded—Unpopularity of the Federal government—Intrigues of Spain—Activity of Governor Blount—Indian hostilities—Campaigns of Harman and St. Clair—Restlessness of the Cherokees—Treaty of Holston—Depredations by the Creeks—Knoxville founded—The lower Cherokees declare war—Attack on Buchanan's station—Capture of Captain Handly—Captain Beard surprises Hiwassa—Is court-martialed—Hostile movements of the Creeks and Cherokees—Massacre at Cavet's station—Sevier's expedition—Defeat of the Indians—The Nick-a-jack expedition..................................*Page* 189

CHAPTER XVII.

Organization of a territorial assembly—Congress petitioned to declare war against the Creeks and Cherokees—Colleges established at Greenville and Knoxville—Washington college established—Convention at Knoxville and adoption of a constitution for the State of Tennessee—Sevier elected governor—Blount and Coxe chosen senators of the United States—Their election declared invalid—Subsequent action of the legislature of Tennessee—Andrew Jackson appointed a member of Congress—His personal appearance—Indian difficulties—Blount expelled the senate—Appointment of Jackson to fill the vacancy—Reception of Blount in Tennessee—Chosen a senator of the State—His trial and acquittal—His death—Roane elected governor—Prosperity of Tennessee.. 201

CHAPTER XVIII.

Aaron Burr—His duel with Hamilton—His journey to the West—Account of his projects against Spain and the United States—Co-operation of Blennerhasset—Burr publicly welcomed at Nashville—Becomes the guest of Andrew Jackson—Descends the Mississippi—Returns to Philadelphia—

Intrigues with Eaton, Truxton, and Decatur—Eaton's visit to Jefferson—Reappearance of Burr in the West—Military preparations in the Ohio valley—Burr's correspondence with Wilkinson—Denounced by the latter—Jackson's warning to the governor of Louisiana—Jefferson's proclamation—Arrest of Burr in Kentucky—His acquittal—Suddenly appears at Nashville—Frustration of his schemes—Burr descends the Cumberland—Encamps on the west bank of the Mississippi—His arrest, trial and acquittal—His subsequent fortunes..*Page* 210

CHAPTER XIX.

Difficulties with Great Britain and France—Action of Congress—Increase of popular indignation against Great Britain—Congress declares war—Disastrous issue of the campaign at the north—Naval victories—Wilkinson calls on Tennessee for volunteers—Prompt response—Reach Natchez under Jackson and Coffee—Ordered to be disbanded—Conduct of Jackson—Return to Nashville—Tecumseh—His attempt to form an Indian confederacy—Effect of his visit to the southern tribes—The Creeks become hostile—Massacre of Fort Mimms—Jackson reassembles the militia of Tennessee—Battle of Tallasehatche—Battle of Talladega—Successes of the Georgians and Mississippians............................ 220

CHAPTER XX.

Jackson's difficulties at Fort Strother—Arrival of fresh troops—Jackson marches toward the centre of the Creek country—Battle of Emuckfau—Repulse of the Red Sticks—Return of the army toward Fort Strother—Battle of Enitachopeo—Gallant conduct of Constantine Perkins and Craven Jackson—Defeat of the Indians—Volunteers discharged—Jackson marches from Fort Strother with a new army—Battle of Cholocco Litabixee—Terrible slaughter of the Red Skins—Anecdote of Jackson—Submission of the Indians—Weatherford surrenders to Jackson—His speech—West Tennessee volunteers ordered home... 232

CONTENTS.

CHAPTER XXI.

Jackson appointed a major-general—He negotiates a treaty with the Creeks—The British at Pensacola—Jackson's correspondence with the Spanish governor—His project for the redúction of Pensacola—He calls upon Tennessee for volunteers—Fort Bowyer attacked—Repulse of the British—They take refuge at Pensacola—Jackson determines to attack that place—Arrival of volunteers from Tennessee—Jackson marches upon Pensacola—Unsuccessful negotiations—Americans attack the town—Submission of the Spanish governor—Escape of the British—Indians driven off—Jackson resurrenders Pensacola—He proceeds to New Orleans..*Page* 243

CHAPTER XXII.

Jackson calls again for volunteers—Patriotism of the Tennesseeans—Disaffection at New Orleans—British forces under Packenham threaten that city—Difficulty with the Louisiana militia—Martial law proclaimed—Vanguard of the enemy encamp on the Mississippi—Night attack by Jackson and Coffee—Dilatory movements of the British—Destruction of the schooner Caroline—First repulse of the enemy—Jackson's difficulty with the Louisiana legislature—Battle of the 8th of January—Packenham slain—Final repulse of the British.. 253

CHAPTER XXIII.

Return of Jackson to New Orleans—Opposition of the citizens to the continuance of martial law—Imprisonment of a member of the legislature by order of Jackson—Arrest of Judge Hall—Intelligence of peace—Return of Hall to New Orleans—Arrest and trial of Jackson for contempt of court—A fine imposed—Demonstration of popular sympathy—Dismissal of the Tennessee volunteers—Honours awarded Jackson by Congress—McMimm elected governor—Difficulties with the Cherokees—With the Florida Indians—Jackson ordered to take the field—Tallahassee towns burned—Seizure of the Spanish fort at St. Mark's—Skirmishes with the Indians—Execution of Arbuthnot and Ambrister—Jackson takes possession of Pensacola—Protest of the Spanish minister—Execution of Arbuthnot and Ambrister discussed by Congress—Jackson sustained by the House of Representatives—Florida ceded to the United States..*Page* 267

CHAPTER XXIV.

Statistics of Tennessee according to the census of 1850—Form of government, &c.—Conclusion............................ 278

HISTORY OF TENNESSEE.

CHAPTER I.

Romantic character of Spanish adventure—The Fountain of Youth—Ponce de Leon—Discovery of Florida—Warlike opposition of the natives—Lucas Vasquez de Ayllon—Lands in Carolina—His treacherous conduct to the natives—Second voyage of De Ayllon—Its disastrous termination—Expedition of Pamphilo de Narvaez—Lands in Florida—Attacked by natives—Sufferings and privations of his followers—They reach Apalachee—The village of Anté—They re-embark at Tampa Bay—Successive loss of the flotilla—Captivity of Alvar Nunez—His escape and return to Spain—His mysterious reports—Hernando de Soto—His early career—His marriage—Entreats permission to conquer Florida—Is invested with the government of Cuba—Sailing of the expedition—Arrival at Cuba—Liberality of Vasco Porcallo.

NOTHING in the whole range of history is more singularly romantic than the remarkable series of exploration and adventure which ushered in the sixteenth century. The discovery of an unknown continent by Columbus, and the heroic yet half barbaric exploits of Cortez and Pizarro, extended the dominions of Spain over a vast region, reaching from the Mexican Gulf to the Pacific Ocean, had poured into the royal treasury at Madrid an almost fabulous amount of wealth, and correspondingly enriched all those daring soldiers of fortune, whose ambitious spirits led them to embark in perilous enterprises, the splendid results of which were owing, not less to their great powers of endurance than to their acknowledged courage.

Successes so astonishing, achieved by a mere handful of men, when compared with the numbers by whom they were opposed, animated others to undertake enterprises of a similar character. And though the field of conquest was, at the period to which we refer, confined to the southern shores of the American continent and the islands adjacent, it was already rumoured that to the north of Cuba lay lands as rich in gold and jewels as those over which the Spanish flag already floated, and nations as easy to be overcome.

But it was a more romantic feeling than either the desire of wealth, or the ambition of renown, which led to the discovery of Florida. Juan Ponce de Leon, the aged governor of Porto Rico, a brave soldier in the old Moorish wars, and one who had acquired honour and distinction as a companion of Columbus, had heard from the natives of the Caribbee Islands of a wonderful fountain, which possessed the miraculous property of restoring the aged and the feeble to all the bloom and vigour of early youth.

Stimulated by reports which were confirmed by Indian traditions, and credited at the court of Castile and Arragon, Juan Ponce, in March, 1512, set sail in search of the Fountain of Youth; and after seeking it in vain among the Bahama Islands, sailed to the north-west, and crossing the Gulf Stream, fell in with a beautiful country, whence the soft airs came laden with the fragrance of unknown flowers, and to which, from that cause, and from its having been first discovered on Palm Sunday—*Pascua de Flores*—he gave the name of Florida. Returning presently to Spain, he obtained authority to conquer and govern this hitherto unknown land; but all his glowing anticipations terminated disastrously. He found the natives far more warlike than those of the islands; and in his attempts to subdue them, he received a severe wound, which compelled him to return with the shattered remains of his expedition to Cuba, where he languished for a short time, and then died.

A few years later, a small quantity of silver and gold, brought from the same coast to San Domingo by the captain of a caravel, stimulated Lucas Vasquez de Ayllon, in connection with several other wealthy persons, owners of gold mines in that island, to fit out two vessels, for the double purpose of exploring the country and of kidnapping Indians to work in the mines. A tempest driving these ships northward, to Cape

Helena, in South Carolina, they finally anchored at the mouth of the Cambahee. The guileless Indians had no sooner recovered from their fears than they came flocking on board, bringing with them presents of valuable furs, some pearls, and a small quantity of silver and gold. Their generosity was requited with the foulest treachery. They were made prisoners, and carried to San Domingo. One of the vessels was lost during the voyage, the other returned safely; but the poor captives were found useless as labourers, and pining for their lost liberty, the greater portion of them speedily died, either of grief or voluntary starvation.

In 1520, while Cortez and his companions were marching to the conquest of Mexico, Vasquez de Ayllon undertook a second voyage to Carolina. His largest vessel being blown ashore, a total wreck, he sailed with the other two a short distance to the eastward, where he landed in a delightful country, and was welcomed with such an appearance of frank hospitality by the Indians, that, wholly beguiled of his suspicions, he suffered the greater portion of his men to accompany their entertainers to a large village about nine miles in the interior. After being feasted for three days with the utmost show of friendship, the Spaniards were suddenly assaulted as they slept, and massacred to a man. Early the next morning, Vasquez de Ayllon and the small party left to guard the ships were surprised in like manner, and very few escaped to carry back to San Domingo tidings of the fate which had befallen their comrades.

Undeterred by the fatality which seemed to attend all attempts to subjugate the warlike natives of Florida, Pamphilo de Narvaez, the weak rival of Cortez, gathered about him a large number of resolute spirits, and bearing the royal commission as Adelantado, or military governor of the country, set sail on an expedition of conquest and colonization. With four hundred men and forty-five horses, he landed on the eastern coast of Florida, on the 12th of April, 1528. After taking unmolested possession of the country in the name of his sovereign, he ordered his ships to sail along the coast to the northward, while he penetrated inland in the same direction, attended by two hundred and sixty footmen and forty cavalry.

The progress of the Spaniards did not long remain undisputed. They had scarcely commenced their march before they began to be annoyed by fierce, though desultory attacks from the natives. Brushing these off with increasing difficulty as they proceeded, they resolutely pressed forward through the tangled wilderness; now cutting a pathway through dense canebrakes, now crossing with uncertain footing broad reaches of treacherous swamps, and at times halting on the banks of rivers too deep to ford and too rapid to swim, until rafts could be constructed to carry them over. Though suffering from hunger, debilitated by sickness, and at all times exposed to the arrows of outlying foes, the report of abundance of gold in the province of Apalachee encouraged them to persevere. They well knew that the early sufferings of Cortez and his heroic followers had been compensated by the wealth of Mexico, and in the midst of their sufferings were sustained by the hope of a similar reward. After struggling through the wilderness for fifteen days, they reached the long desired town of Apalachee, which, to their intense mortification, they found to be a mere collection of ordinary Indian wigwams. The inhabitants had fled before the advance of the Spaniards, but they indicated their presence in the vicinity, and their determined hostility, by lurking in the woods and cutting off all stragglers, and by a series of pertinacious assaults, which gave the invaders no rest either by day or night. At this place Narvaez remained nearly a month, recruiting the strength of his weaker companions, and awaiting the return of parties sent out to examine the country for gold. Finding none, and having reports of a more peaceful people nine days' journey to the southward, where abundance of provisions could be obtained, Narvaez departed from Apalachee, and took up his line of march for the village of Aute on the Bay of St. Mark's, which he finally reached after encountering many perils by the way, and suffering considerable loss both in men and horses. On the approach of the Spaniards the village was found to have been abandoned, and the houses burned; but sufficient corn remained in the granaries to satisfy their most pressing wants. Having lost one-third of their number, the disconsolate survivors, broken down by disease, by weary and painful marches, and by the necessity of unintermitted watchfulness, concluded to return to Hispaniola. Too feeble to prosecute their journey by land, they adopted the scarcely less desperate expedient of building a few open barges, in which they proposed to cruise along the shore, until they met with the squadron from which they had disembarked in the spring.

They at once set about their task. With singular ingenuity, they constructed a bellows of deer hide; and by the aid of charcoal and a rude forge, the iron of their spurs, crossbows, stirrups, and superfluous armour, was speedily converted into nails, and such necessary tools as their exigencies required. Trees were felled, and laboriously hewn into shape. For ropes they used the fibres of the palm, strengthened by hair from the tails and manes of their horses. Their shirts, cut open and sewed together, served for sails; while the skins of horses which had been slain for food, were converted into vessels to contain the water required during the voyage.

In six weeks five boats were completed, into each of which from forty to fifty men were crowded. Freighted so heavily that the gunwales of their barks touched the water's edge, Narvaez and his followers quitted the Bay of St. Mark's on the 22d of September, and, bearing westward, sailed for many days along the coast, landing occasionally to do battle with the natives for food and water. The water-skins proving defective, some of the troops least capable of endurance expired of thirst. Others fell by the hands of the savages. Overtaken by a tempest, two of the boats were driven out to sea, and never heard of after. The remaining three foundered subsequently; and of all that gallant company, only Alvar Nunez and four companions, after enduring ten years of captivity among the Indians, succeeded in returning to Mexico. These poverty-stricken wanderers, encouraged by the credulity of their listeners, narrated such marvellous legends of the countries through which they had passed, that when Alvar Nunez crossed over to Spain, bearing with him the first reliable tidings of the fate of Pamphilo de Narvaez, men turned aside from his tale of peril and suffering to question him concerning the reputed wealth of those lands wherein he had remained so long a prisoner.

Conjecturing from his affectation of mysterious secrecy, that Florida was a second Peru; the assertion of another of the wanderers, that it was "the richest country in the world," gained implicit credence, and imaginative minds became easily convinced of the existence of a new region, where daring men might yet win a golden harvest and a glorious renown.

Foremost among those who entertained this belief was Hernando de Soto, a native of Xeres, and a gentleman by "all four descents." As a youthful soldier of fortune, possessing no property beyond his sword and buckler, he had joined the standard of Pizarro, under whom he soon won a distinguished military reputation. Rendered famous by the courage he displayed in the storming of Cuzco, and no less admired for his boldness in action than for his prudence in council, he speedily rose to the rank of second in command. Returning to Spain in the prime of life, with a fortune of one hundred and eighty thousand ducats, he assumed all the magnificence of a wealthy noble. He had his steward, gentleman of the horse, his chamberlain, pages, and usher. Already renouned for those heroic qualities which women so much admire, his riches and his noble person gained for him the hand of Isabella de Bobadilla, a lady of high rank, and connected by blood with some of the most powerful families in the kingdom. Elevated by these advantages, he repaired in great state to Madrid, attended by Luis Moscoso de Alvarado, Nuno de Tobar, and others, his friends and companions in arms, all of whom were gorgeously apparelled, and scattered their wealth on every side with a reckless prodigality.

Rendered more than ordinarily credulous by his previous successes in Peru, De Soto interpreted the vague replies of Alvar Nunez according to his own wishes; and aspiring to increase the fame he had already acquired as a subordinate, by the honours to be derived from an independent command, he petitioned the Emperor Charles V. for permission to conquer Florida at his own expense. It was not difficult to obtain the royal consent to an enterprise which, while it occasioned no outlay to the government, might be the means of bringing great wealth to the treasury. De Soto was appointed civil and military commander of Florida and governor of Cuba. He was also invested with the rank and title of marquis, with authority to select for himself an estate thirty leagues long and fifteen broad, in any of the territories to be conquered by his arms. It was no sooner made known that Hernando de Soto, Pizarro's famous lieutenant, was organizing an expedition for the conquest of Florida, than numerous young Spanish and Portuguese nobles, burning for wealth, adventure, and distinction, sold their possessions, and hastened to join the standard of so renowned a leader. Men of all ranks speedily followed their example; and disposing of houses and lands, of vineyards and olive groves, assembled at Seville, in which city De Soto had taken up his abode to arrange the details of his magnificent enterprise. After being joined at Seville by the Portuguese volunteers, he departed for the port of San Lucar de Barrameda, where he ordered a muster of the troops, for the purpose of enrolling such as were most capable of enduring the privations and hardships with which he knew the adventure would be attended. To this muster the Spaniards came gaudily apparelled in silks and satins, daintily slashed and embroidered; while the Portuguese made their appearance in burnished armour, excellently wrought, and with weapons to correspond. Chagrined that his own countrymen should have presented themselves in attire so wholly unfitted for the purpose in which they proposed to engage, De Soto ordered a second muster, at which all were to attend in armour. The display was still in favour of the Portuguese, who came equipped with the same soldierly care as before; while most of the Spaniards, having spent the greater part of their fortune upon their silken gauds, made their appearance in rusty and defective coats of mail, battered head-pieces, and with lances neither well made nor trustworthy. From the choicest of these, however, De Soto selected six hundred men, with whom he put to sea in six large and three small vessels, on the 6th of April, 1538. This fleet, having also on board twenty-four priests and monks for the conversion of the heathen, reached Gomera, one of the Canaries, on the 21st of April. At this port De Soto remained a few days, the welcome guest of the governor, of whose lavish hospitality all those on board the squadron were likewise made partakers.

Having refreshed his men, De Soto again set sail, and finally anchored off the island of Cuba toward the close of May. His arrival was made the occasion of great festivity and rejoicing. Tilts and jousting matches, feats of horsemanship and skilful displays with sword and lance, revived the gorgeous and chivalric pastimes of previous centuries; while games of chance, bullfights, dances, and masquerades developed in a striking degree a not less peculiar phase of Castilian character. Billeting his men on the inhabitants of the city and surrounding country, De Soto spent a year in arranging the affairs of his government, and in gleaning information respecting the region he had undertaken to conquer. In the mean time he was joined by Vasco Porcallo de Figuera, a wealthy cavalier, of mature age, whose long dormant ambition was again stirred to emulate the younger adventurers in exploits of arms. By the newly-awakened liberality of this ancient soldier, De Soto was supplied, not only with provisions for present use, but with a large herd of live swine to furnish meat to the troops while on their march. Gratified by this evidence of good-will, De Soto appointed Vasco Porcallo his lieutenant-general, a station from which Nuno de Tobar had lately been deposed for certain irregularities which he subsequently most nobly repaired.

CHAPTER II.

Embarkation of the Spaniards at Havana—Arrival at Tampa Bay—Skirmish with the natives—Capture of Juan Ortiz—His romantic adventures—The march through Florida—The troops constantly attacked by the natives—Take up their winter quarters at Apalachee—Continued hostility of the natives—The march resumed—De Soto reaches the province of Cofachiqui—His reception by an Indian princess—Enters northern Georgia and encamps at Chiaha—Fruitless search for gold—The province of Coosa—The Spaniards welcomed by its chief—The arrival at the province of Tuscaloosa—Haughty speech of Tuscaloosa—He accompanies De Soto to Mobile—The battle of Mobile—Condition of the victorious Spaniards—De Soto returns to Chickasa—His encampment burned by the natives—Discovery of the Mississippi—The Spaniards cross the river into Arkansas—Encamp at the mouth of the Red River—Sickness and death of De Soto—Wandering of the Spaniards under Moscoso—Their return to Mexico.

ALL the necessary preparations being at length completed, De Soto embarked his troops on board eleven vessels, amply freighted with provisions and military stores. He set sail from the port of Havana, on the 12th of May, 1539, and on the 25th of the same month the squadron cast anchor in Tampa Bay. Landing his army, increased by Cuban volunteers to one thousand men, he took formal possession of the country in the name of his sovereign, and was immediately engaged in a skirmish with the natives. Foremost in the melee was the aged soldier Porcallo; but being roughly handled, and having his horse killed under him, the veteran became disgusted with an enterprise which promised more hard blows than profit, and entreated permission to return in the ships which De Soto had resolved to send back to Cuba. His request was coldly granted. The first effort of the adelantado was to gain the friendship of the hostile chief whose territories he had so unceremoniously invaded. "I want none of their speeches, nor promises," said the haughty cacique. "Bring their heads, and I will receive them joyfully."

In the midst of these attempts at negotiation, Balthazar de Gallegos, a bold and hardy soldier, was despatched with a body of horse and foot to scour the country in search of guides. While charging a small body of Indians, one of his men was arrested in his career by the voice of a fugitive, who cried out in broken Spanish, "Seville! Seville!" and making the sign of the cross, added, "Slay me not, I am a Christian!" Stout Alvaro Nietro, the trooper thus invoked, immediately dropped the point of his lance, and joyfully mounting his captive behind him, rode off with him to his leader.

The stranger proved to be Juan Ortiz, a gentleman of Seville, who, at the age of eighteen, had joined the expedition of Pamphilo Narvaez. Returning to Cuba with the fleet, he subsequently set sail for Florida with a score of companions, despatched to ascertain the fate of that unfortunate commander. Lured on shore by pacific signs from the Indians, he was taken captive with three others, and carried to the presence of Hurrihigua, the same chief who had lately returned so defiant an answer to the messengers from De Soto. The companions of Ortiz were speedily massacred, and he himself, doomed to a similar fate, was rescued with difficulty by the daughter of Hurrihigua, but condemned to perform menial offices of the most ignominious and revolting character. Several attempts being subsequently made upon his life, his preserver aided him, finally, in escaping to the village of a neighbouring chieftain to whom she was betrothed. Ortiz was kindly received, and under the care of his hospitable protector he remained nine years, having learned, in the mean while, the language of the Indians, and nearly forgotten his own. Exceedingly rejoiced at obtaining so efficient an interpreter, De Soto welcomed Ortiz with great heartiness. He caused him to be divested of his savage garb, and arrayed in garments more befitting his birth and former condition.

Leaving Pedro Calderon, with one hundred horse and foot, in charge of the camp, and a caraval and two brigantines to command the harbour, De Soto commenced his march inland. His troops were cased in armour of plate, or chain mail, the weapons of the cavalry being swords and lances; the footmen were equipped with cross-bows and arquebusses, and further protected by targets. It was a gorgeous yet cruel spectacle to see this army, splendidly arrayed, set out on its wanderings through the swamps and tangled forests of an unknown land, attended by bloodhounds trained to hunt down the savages, and bearing with them chains to fetter the limbs of their captives; implements of torture strangely contrasting with the sacerdotal dresses, the chalices and other ornaments required in their devotional exercises, and with the wine and the wheaten flour consecrated to the solemn service of mass.

But though they went forth thus gallantly caparisoned, and with the assured port of predestined conquerors, they were soon to learn the difference between the prowess of the Indians inhabiting the region north of the Gulf Stream, and the languid courage of the natives of Mexico and Peru.

Day after day, week after week, encumbered with baggage and by a large herd of swine, the troops moved slowly forward, cutting their way through almost impervious thickets, wading with great labour the treacherous morasses; now swimming the numerous streams which intersected their line of route, and now halting to build rafts where the swift rivers forbade any less practicable mode of passage. After wandering for one hundred and fifty leagues through the forests and everglades of Florida, constantly attacked by hordes of ambushed savages, and suffering great loss both in men and horses, the weary and half-famished soldiers reached the fertile province of Apalachee, where, toward the close of October, a camp was formed, and the army went into winter-quarters. More than four months had been consumed in this harassing and perilous march, and, as yet, neither gold nor jewels had been discovered; although the accounts given by their captives of the existence of precious metals, in provinces yet distant, inflamed their hopes, and enabled them to sustain their privations and disappointments with some degree of equanimity.

But the period of repose which De Soto required to recruit the strength of his army was in a great measure denied him. Everywhere his exploring parties were attacked, and stragglers cut off. Even his camp was the scene of constant alarms. But in the midst of their growing disgust with the country and its warlike inhabitants, the troops were again cheered by information received from two young Indian prisoners, of the existence of gold and silver in the greatest abundance in the remote eastern province of Cofachiqui. Breaking up his cantonment in the early part of March, 1540, De Soto put his troops in motion, in search of a region so promising. On his entering the territory which is now called Georgia, he was met by two warriors, who demanded haughtily, "What seek you in our land? Peace or war?" "We seek a distant province," responded De Soto, "and desire your friendship and food by the way." It was granted. Passing through a pleasant and fertile country, the army finally halted on the bank of the Savannah River. Here De Soto was visited by the beautiful princess of Cofachiqui, whose town was on the opposite bank, now known as the Silver Bluff. She came to the water side in a litter, borne by four men, and entering a canoe richly-carved and ornamented, seated herself upon a cushion overshadowed by a canopy. She was attended by six councillors, grave men of mature age, and by a numerous retinue. On reaching the presence of De Soto, the youthful cacique took from her person a long string of pearls, and placed them about the neck of the Spanish leader. Responding gallantly to this courtesy, De Soto drew from his finger a gold ring, set with a ruby, and presented it to her as a memorial of his friendship. The next day the army crossed the river and entered the village. On the 3d of May, De Soto again took up his line of march. Proceeding through northern Georgia, he crossed the Oostanaula; and, at the invitation of its young chief, took up his quarters early the following month in the island town of Chiaha. Here the troops found vessels containing large quantities of walnut and bears' oil, and pots of wild honey.

After spending a month at Chiaha, greatly to the advantage both of men and horses, De Soto marched down by the west bank of the Coosa, and entered Alabama. He had heard of gold and copper in the mountains to the north, and having sent two fearless troopers to explore that region, he waited at the town of Costa until they returned. The hardy adventurers brought back tidings of copper, but could find no gold. The march was now resumed. Passing through the beautiful province of Coosa, De Soto was met, on the 26th of July, by the chief of that region. He came to him, seated on cushions, in a chair of state, sustained by four of his principal men. He was arrayed in a magnificent mantel of marten skins, and wore upon his head a gay tiara of many-coloured feathers. He was attended by a band of choristers and musicians, and by a thousand noble-looking warriors variously plumed and ornamented.

The chief welcomed De Soto with great warmth, invited the troops to partake of the hospitality of his town, and placed all he had at their service. At the capital of Coosa, De Soto remained for nearly a month, after which he proceeded to the southward, and entering the frontier town of Tallase, situated upon the Tallapoosa River, again encamped. Leaving this place, he entered next the province which received its name of Tuscaloosa from a powerful chief whom, the third morning of their march, the Spaniards found waiting for them in state, seated upon the crest of a high hill, overlooking an extensive and lovely valley, and surrounded by his principal warriors, dressed in rich mantles of furs, and ornamented with gayly-coloured plumes. Forty years of age, and of large stature, yet nobly proportioned, the haughty chief of the Mobilians regarded with calm indifference the military display which was intentionally made by the Spaniards for the purpose of eliciting his notice.

"You are welcome," said he to De Soto. "It is needless to talk long. What I have to say can be said in a few words. You shall know how willing I am to serve you."

They resumed their march, accompanied by Tuscaloosa, who, mounted on a strong hackney belonging to De Soto, was detained under the guise of friendship in a sort of honourable captivity. But no fair speeches or courteous attentions could blind the bold chieftain to the fact that his liberty was restrained; nor were his people less indignant. While on the route two of the Spaniards were missed. Suspecting they had been slain, De Soto demanded tidings of them from Tuscaloosa's followers. "Why do you ask us?" said they. "Are we their keepers?"

Apprehensive of some latent design, De Soto sent two troopers in advance to reconnoitre Mobile, a strongly fortified village, which is supposed to have occupied Choctaw Bluff, on the Alabama River. This village contained eighty houses, each large enough to hold from five hundred to a thousand men. It was surrounded by a high palisade, formed of the trunks of trees, bound together with vines, and covered with a smooth coating of prepared clay, so as to resemble a wall of masonry. As De Soto, accompanied by Tuscaloosa, approached the village with his vanguard, consisting of two hundred horse and foot, large numbers of warriors, clad in furs and decorated with feathers and other ornaments, followed by musicians and dancers, and by a body of young and beautiful maidens, came out to welcome them as to a festival. They had scarcely entered within the walls before Tuscaloosa was engaged in earnest conversation with his people. Presently tidings were brought to De Soto, that within the houses immense numbers of warriors were assembled, amply supplied with their usual weapons and missiles of offence. Orders were at once given to the Spaniards to be on the alert.

Desirous of avoiding a resort to arms, if possible, De Soto endeavoured to regain possession of the person of Tuscaloosa. He sent several messages to the chief by Juan Ortiz, inviting him to come and partake of the dinner which awaited him; but the haughty chief disdained to return any reply. At length, one of his principal warriors, wrought to a passionate frenzy by the voices of the Spaniards, rushed from the house in which Tuscaloosa remained surrounded by his people, and fiercely exclaimed: " Where are these robbers, these vagabonds, who call upon my chief Tuscaloosa to come out with so little reverence? Let us cut them to pieces on the spot, and so put an end to their wickedness and tyranny."

An Indian placed a bow in his hand. Giving freedom to his motions by throwing back his splendid fur mantle, he directed the arrow, drawn to its head, against a group of Spaniards assembled in the square. At this moment he fell dead, being nearly cleft in twain by the

sweep of a sword wielded by stout Baltasar de
Gallegos. A fierce tumult immediately arose.
Myriads of armed warriors swarmed from the
houses, and commenced an attack upon the Spaniards with clubs, and arrows, and stones. Taken
at a disadvantage, five of the latter were quickly
slain; and it was with great difficulty that De
Soto and his companions retreated from the
town to where their horses were tied. Some
succeeded in mounting before their pursuers arrived, others were slain before their eyes, without the power to rescue them. All the baggage
fell into the hands of the enemy. It was carried
into the town amid great rejoicings. The mana-
cles of the Indian captives, who had been constrained to bear these burdens, were speedily
struck off, and arms placed in their hands. In
the mean time, the fight was kept up outside the
walls, although the gates were shut. A reinforcement of cavalry from the main body having
at length enabled the foot soldiers to shake off
their thronging foes, De Soto now headed a furious charge, and the Indians were driven into
the town. Assailed from within by a storm of
arrows and other missiles, the Spaniards were
compelled to retire from before the walls. Their
retreat was the signal for another fierce sally.
In this manner the battle raged for three hours
with varying success, the Spaniards fighting in
a compact body, advancing and retreating as one

man. A small detachment within the city, sheltering themselves in a house, defended their post for many hours with a courage bordering on despair. At length the Indians were forced by loss of numbers to retire within their enclosures, and a great portion of the Spanish main body, under Moscoso, coming up at this time, an assault was determined on.

Obedient to the orders of their leader, two hundred of the cavalry, protected by bucklers, sprang forward, and after repeated repulses dashed in the gates with their battle-axes. At the same time others clambered over the wall, by breaking away the mud plastering for a precarious foothold. In the streets, and from the walls and housetops, the Indians, though falling in great heaps, sought desperately, by the crush of numbers, to overwhelm their assailants. None asked quarter, but all fought until they fell. The great pool which supplied the town with water was crimsoned with the blood of the dead and the dying. Yet of this water the Spaniards drank to appease the thirst by which they were consumed, and then, rejoining their companions, continued the battle. To put an end to this fierce and dubious conflict, De Soto mounted his horse, and with lance in hand, and the battle-cry of "Our Lady of Santiago!" hurled himself into the midst of the struggling masses, closely followed by the gallant Nuno de Tobar. De Soto, deeply wounded in the thigh by an arrow, fought standing in his stirrups. Rending through the multitude on every side, trampling some beneath the hoofs of their horses, and thrusting the life out of innumerable others, the two cavaliers maintained their sanguinary supremacy until night and sheer exhaustion terminated the conflict.

At this time the town was set on fire, and the flames extending themselves with great rapidity, enveloped with a burning girdle the hapless Indians who yet held possession of the houses. Conscious of the fate impending over them, those who were at large gathered together, and men and women precipitated themselves upon their foes. But what impression could poorly equipped and ill-disciplined thousands make upon men cased in defensive armour, wielding infinitely superior weapons, and directed by consummate military skill? Piled one upon another, they fell clutching at the arquebusses, swords, and lances, to the last. For nine hours this terrible battle continued. When it ceased, the great town of Mobile was a heap of ashes, and six thousand Indians lay slaughtered around. To the Spaniards it was a victory purchased at a fearful price. Eighty-two of their number were killed, or mortally wounded, two of whom were near kinsmen to De Soto; and not one of the survivors came out of the battle unhurt.

Seventeen hundred dangerous wounds attested alike the courage of the Mobilians and the endurance of the Spaniards. The latter had likewise to mourn the irreparable loss of a large number of mules, besides the destruction of their baggage, which, with the robes of the priests, the consecrated vessels, and other ornaments sacred to their worship, had been consumed in the flames. Tidings of his ships awaiting him at Pensacola Bay reaching De Soto at this time, caused great rejoicing among the troops, many of whom desired nothing better than to abandon the country. Among the cavaliers a scheme was arranged to desert De Soto, and re-embark for their several homes. Indignant at this contemplated treachery, De Soto turned his back upon his vessels, and marching northward, took up his winter-quarters in the province of Chickasa. Finding here a supply of maize, he remained for several months; but the natives, who had for some time feigned a friendship for the invaders, became jealous of their prolonged sojourn, and toward the spring of 1541, in the midst of a dark, cold, blustering night, rushed into the village where the Spaniards were encamped, and set it on fire. Roused suddenly from their slumbers, the troops rushed out and fought in such clothes and with such arms as they could catch up hastily. Forty Spaniards and not less than fifty horses were killed in this sudden onslaught; while most of the garments of the Spaniards were consumed by the fire, which also injured irretrievably much armour and many weapons.

Repairing these disasters as best they might, they resumed their wanderings; and after struggling for seven days through a wilderness alternating with swamp and forest, entered the village of Chisca, whence De Soto beheld for the first time, from the lower Chickasa Bluffs, the mighty waters of the Mississippi. Here, on the confines of Tennessee, and not far from the present city of Memphis, the wearied troops, after traversing a dense forest for several days, halted for three weeks to build piraguas. Embarking in them, they crossed the river in detachments, without opposition, and continuing their march along its western bank, finally took up their quarters for the winter in the province of Pacahas, in Arkansas. At this place died Juan Ortiz, the interpreter. In the spring of 1542, De Soto, now hopeless of finding gold, and changing from his sterner mood to a profound melancholy as he contemplated his losses and continual disappointments, descended the Washita and encamped at the confluence of the Red River with the Mississippi. At this place he commenced the building of two brigantines; sending out, in the mean time, a detachment to ascertain the course of the great river and the distance to the sea. In eight days the troopers returned, and reported the route impracticable, by reason of the swamps and rivers by which it was obstructed.

Hoping to recruit his own failing strength, and that of his followers, in the opposite province of Quigualtanqui, De Soto sent a messenger to the cacique of a tribe whose residence was in the vicinity of the modern town of Natchez, demanding his homage, on the ground that he was the son of the Sun, and as such entitled to worship and obedience. "If he be so," responded the chieftain, "let him dry up the river between us, and I will believe him. If he visits my town in peace, I will receive him in friendship; if as an enemy, he shall find me ready for battle."

Already sick of a mortal disease, De Soto was in no mood to retort upon the chieftain his scornful reply. Tortured with anxiety for the safety of his command, his illness daily increased. Confident that his end approached, he convened his officers, and appointed Luis de Moscoso his successor. The poor remains of his once goodly army were next summoned by detachments to his couch. After taking a solemn leave of them, he humbly confessed his sins, and on the 21st of May, 1542, expired, in the forty-second year of his age.

Mournfully depositing the body of their beloved commander, wrapped in his mantle, in the trunk of an evergreen oak, hollowed out for that purpose, they reverently lowered it, at midnight, beneath the waves of that magnificent river he had been the first European to discover.

Resuming their wanderings soon after, the disconsolate adventurers endeavoured to reach Mexico by way of the Red River. Beguiled by their guides, they reached, by a tortuous and difficult route, the prairies of the west, from whence, after great suffering, and beset by innumerable difficulties, they retraced their steps to the Mississippi; and, constructing brigantines on its banks, sailed down the river to its mouth.

On the 10th of September, 1543, three hundred and eleven haggard men, blackened by exposure, shrivelled by famine, some clad in skins of wild beasts, and others in Indian mats, or in the ragged remains of their former gay apparel, after a voyage of fifty days, entered the Panuco, a river of Mexico, flowing into the Gulf Stream, where they were kindly received, and entertained with unbounded hospitality. They were the only survivors of the famous but inglorious expedition of Hernando de Soto.

CHAPTER III.

The Spanish settlements restricted to Florida—French, English, and Dutch colonies in North America—The Jesuit missions in Illinois—Marquette ordered to explore the Mississippi valley—The Illinois entreat him not to venture—His noble reply—Sets out on his journey—How attended, and by whom—Reaches Maskoutens—Rude evidences of Christianity among the natives—Speech of Jolliet—The voyageurs descend the Wisconsin—Their reception at the Des Moines villages—Marquette's address—Response of the chief—Description of the monstrous Piasau—The voyage down the Mississippi—False alarm of the travellers—They reach the cotton wood region—Approach the village of Michigaméa—Hostile preparations by the natives—Rescue of Marquette and his party—Escorted to Arkansas, and hospitably entertained—The return to Canada.

BUT though a fatality attended all those Spanish adventurers who attempted to obtain a permanent foothold on the northern shore of the Gulf Stream, Spain claimed henceforth the sovereignty of Florida, including within the limits of her new domain the territory on both sides of the Mississippi, extending backward to the prairies of the West. A century and a quarter after the death of De Soto, the only indication of Spanish possession was the small settlement at St. Augustine, founded in 1564 by the bigoted and sanguinary Melendez. But while the colonial possessions of Spain on the North American continent were restricted to a solitary fort and a slender garrison on its southern peninsula, other nations had entered with success upon the field of adventure; and from Labrador to Carolina, the Atlantic coast of the new world was dotted at intervals with thriving colonies. In remote Canada the energetic Champlain had founded a prosperous province. At the East, the sedate, God-fearing men of the New England provinces were indoctrinating a hardy race in the principles of true political liberty. On the banks of the Hudson, the Dutch of New Netherland had lately taken the oath of allegiance to the Duke of York, afterward James II.; while farther to the south, Maryland, Virginia, and the Carolinas were increasing rapidly in wealth and population.

Up to this period all traces of De Soto's great discovery appear to have been lost, and the existence of the Mississippi was only conjectured from imperfect narratives of that unfortunate expedition, and from reports brought by the Illinois Indians to the members of the Jesuit missions, one of whose stations was at the Saulte de Sainte Marie, a little below the foot of Lake Superior. Here the humble but heroic Marquette first heard of a great river flowing through the Illinois country, and tracing its way southward for thousands of miles, until it finally poured its immense volume of waters into an unknown sea.

In 1671 a new missionary station was formed at Point St. Ignatius, to which Marquette was ordered to repair; and here he continued, devoted to the duties of his calling, until 1673, when he was directed by M. Talon, the Intendant in New France, to explore the region westward. These instructions realized the most ardent wishes of the pious father, and he immediately prepared for the journey, "firmly resolved to do all, and suffer all, for so glorious an enterprise." The terrified Indians to whom Marquette had preached, and by whom he was greatly beloved, characterized his attempt as reckless and desperate. They told him he would meet with nations who never spared the stranger; that the great river was full of hidden dangers, and abounded with terrible monsters, who swallowed up men and canoes; that an immense bird, swooping from afar, pounced upon hapless voyagers, carried them to its inaccessible eyrie among the mountains, and there deliberately tore its victims to pieces with beak and talons. And, lastly, they told him of heats that would dry up the very marrow of his bones. Nothing daunted, the good Marquette thanked them kindly for their counsel, but told them "that I could not profit by it, since the salvation of souls was at stake, for which object I would be overjoyed to give my life." And so, in the spring of 1673, father James Marquette, the Sieur Jolliet, a French Canadian, who had already now some local fame as an explorer, and five boatmen, departed from Mackinaw in two frail birch bark canoes, so light as to be easily borne across portages on the shoulders of four men, crossed Lake Huron into Green Bay, ascended Fox River to the portage of the Wisconsin, and reached Maskoutens on the 7th of June. Beyond this no European explorer had ever ventured. The village of Maskoutens was beautifully situated on an eminence, around which spread prairies on every side, "interspersed with thickets, or groves of lofty trees." But what most cheered the heart of the pious Marquette was to behold a handsome cross planted in the centre of the village, and adorned with skins, belts, bows and arrows, the votive offerings of warriors that had seldom sent out war-parties in vain, to the Christian Manitou, whom Father Allouez had taught them thus rudely to worship.

"I am sent by our governor to discover new countries, and the reverend father, by the Almighty, to illumine them with the light of the gospel," said Jolliet; and he requested of his astonished hearers two guides, to put them in their way. It was granted.

Nine miles from Maskoutens, the *voyageurs*, after carrying their boats across the portage, embarked upon the broad shallow waters of the Wisconsin, with its difficult sandbars and its lovely vine-clad islets; and, on the 17th of June, after descending the river for one hundred and twenty miles, entered the Mississippi "with a joy," says Marquette, "that I cannot express."

For fourteen days they floated down the river without perceiving any sign of human life. At length, on the 25th of June, they discovered an Indian trail, leading westward from the water's edge, until at a distance of two leagues across a beautiful prairie it diverged to three Indian villages. Toward one of these, a village standing on the right bank of the river, Des Moines, Marquette, and Jolliet advanced, leaving the canoes in charge of the boatmen. It was a hazardous service, and the two humble yet resolute *voyageurs* evinced their knowledge of the risk they ran, by devoutly commending themselves to God. Halting within sight of the village, they raised a low cry; whereupon, after the confusion occasioned by their presence had subsided, four old men advanced toward them, two of whom bore tobacco-pipes handsomely adorned, and ornamented with many kinds of feathers. "Who are you?" inquired Marquette. "We are Illinois," they responded; and presenting the peace-pipes, invited their visitors to enter the village.

"How beautiful is the sun, O Frenchman! when thou comest to visit us! All our town awaits thee, and thou shalt enter all our cabins in peace."

Such was the greeting which met Marquette as he approached the cabin appointed for his reception; while the crowd which closed respectfully behind the travellers, occasionally cried out, "Well done, brothers, to visit us!"

After smoking the calumet, they were invited to attend a council at the great Sachem's village. Crowds thronged the way, all eager to behold the adventurous Frenchmen, and all eager to do them reverence. Assembled in the council-house, Marquette addressed himself to the hushed multitude. Dividing his discourse into four heads, closing each part with a present, he declared the object of his mission to be one of discovery, and himself the bearer of tidings of peace and goodwill to all the nations on the river. He next preached to them concerning God the Creator, at whose bidding he had come to exhort them to acknowledge and obey him. He spoke also of the governor of Canada; and after telling them that he had vanquished their enemies the Iroquois, concluded by asking for all the information they could give respecting the course of the Great River to the sea, and the nations through which they had yet to pass.

Then the great chief arose, and thanked the *voyageurs* for having visited them. "Never," said he, "has the earth been more beautiful, nor the sun so bright as to-day; never has our river been so calm, nor so free from rocks, which your canoes have removed as they passed; never has our tobacco had so fine a flavour, nor our corn appeared so beautiful." He closed by presenting Marquette with a youthful slave in token of his esteem for the governor, and with a calumet ornamented with feathers of various hues, to protect him during a voyage which he earnestly exhorted him to prosecute no farther.

"I do not fear death," responded Marquette, "and esteem no happiness greater than that of losing my life for the glory of Him who made all." A festival followed, consisting of hominy, fish, buffalo, and dog-meat, served up in succession; but of the last their visitors would not partake. After passing the night in the dwelling of the principal chief, the travellers were accompanied the following day to their canoes by six hundred persons, who took leave of the good father in the kindest manner, and received from him a promise that he would return the next year and instruct them—a pledge which he subsequently redeemed.

Toward the close of June the little party resumed their voyage; and as they coasted the rocks above the present town of Alton, they were startled at beholding, painted thereon, rude representations of the fabled Piasau, a monster "as large as a calf, with horns on the head like a deer, a fearful look, red eyes, bearded like a tiger, the face somewhat like a man's, the body covered with scales, and the tail so long that it twice makes the turn of the body, passing over the head and down between the legs, and ending at last in a fish's tail." The same day they reached the mouth of the Missouri, and, floating downward, passed another beautiful river, known subsequently as the Wabash—the same we now call the Ohio.

It was the middle of July, and as they approached the region of the cane they became oppressed with the intolerable heat and annoyed by swarms of musquitos. An awning formed from the sails of the canoes afforded an indifferent protection both from the insects and the sun. As the *voyageurs* were thus gliding with the current, they perceived a party of Indians standing on the shore, armed with guns. Marquette presented his calumet, and accosted them in Huron, but they replied in what seemed to him the language of defiance. Happily he was mistaken; and after landing and partaking of their hospitality, the adventurous party re-embarked, and descended the river, whose banks presently were found clothed with lofty forests of cotton-wood, elms, and other unknown trees, until, in about thirty-three degrees north latitude, they came within sight of the village of Michigamea. Marquette and his companions were no sooner discovered by the natives than they assembled in great numbers, armed with bows, arrows, axes, war-clubs, and bucklers; and while some kept watch upon the shore, others sprang into their canoes, evidently bent on the destruction of the intruders. In vain Marquette displayed the calumet, and made repeated signals of peace. The danger every instant became more imminent. One war-club had already been hurled at him, and innumerable bows were in the act of being bent, when some of the chiefs on shore recognised the calumet, and commanding their warriors to desist, hastened to throw aside their weapons and welcome the wanderers to their village. The next morning they were escorted by a deputation eight or ten leagues down the river, to the chief village of Akansea, or Arkansa, where they were again entertained with great hospitality, and where, by means of an interpreter, Marquette endeavoured to bring them to a knowledge of the true God.

Here, in the region where De Soto breathed his last, and where Moscoso fitted out his crazy brigantines, the adventurous voyage was terminated. From the answers of his entertainers Marquette discovered that the Great River emptied into the Gulf of Mexico; and fearful of losing the fruit of his discoveries, resolved to return to Canada. Taking leave of their doubtful friends, they proceeded slowly up the river; and after a tedious voyage reached Green Bay in safety toward the close of September, having thus fearlessly accomplished a hazardous journey of more than three thousand miles.

CHAPTER IV.

Robert Cavalier de la Salle—His emigration to Canada—Becomes a fur-trader—Establishes a trading-post at La Chine—His explorations—Made commandant of Fort Frontenac—Returns to France—Obtains a patent of nobility and a grant of land—Resolves to explore the valley of the Mississippi—Obtains a monopoly of the traffic in buffalo skins—Builds a brigantine on the upper waters of the Mississippi—Crosses the great Lakes to Mackinaw—Sails for Green Bay—Sends back the Griffin to Niagara, freighted with furs—Proceeds to the mouth of the St. Joseph—Builds the fort of the Miamis—Descends the Kankakee—Builds forts Crevecœur and Rock Fort—Returns to Fort Frontenac—Reappears in Illinois—Again returns to Canada—Prosecutes his voyage to the Mississippi—Reaches the mouth of the Illinois—Descends the Mississippi to the Chickasaw bluff—Loss of a hunter—Builds Fort Prudhomme.

THE extraordinary success which had attended Marquette and Jolliet in their voyage of exploration opened up a field for commercial adventure, of which one energetic man was prepared to take advantage. This was Robert Cavalier de la Salle, a native of Rouen in Normandy, who had sacrificed his patrimony by entering a religious order, which he subsequently left to engage in enterprises better suited to his restless and energetic nature. To such a mind Canada offered at once a refuge from poverty and the promise of acquiring both fame and fortune. The hope of finding a shorter passage to China and the East Indies was still entertained by many enthusiastic men, and among them the young but resolute La Salle, who presently established a trading-post near Montreal, and indicated the adventurous bent of his thoughts by calling it La Chine. From this centre of his fur-trading operations he undertook various explorations in the region of Lakes Ontario and Erie, and soon became known to Count Frontenac, the governor of Canada, for his intellectual ability and his enterprising spirit. When, therefore, to repress the incursions of the warlike Iroquois, Fort Frontenac was built at the eastern extremity of Lake Ontario, the governor, an excellent judge of men, intrusted its command to La Salle.

But the latter had a larger ambition than could be circumscribed by the log walls of a fortress in the wilderness. In 1675 he repaired to France, where, supported by the steadfast friendship of Frontenac, and countenanced by De Courcelles and Talon, he obtained a patent of nobility, a monopoly of the fur-trade of Lake

Ontario, and a large grant of land around Fort Frontenac, on condition of rebuilding the fort of stone, of erecting a village in its vicinity, and of supporting, at his own expense, a competent garrison, and a mission of Franciscan friars.

These conditions were fulfilled; but difficulties with rival fur-traders constantly thwarted the designs of La Salle; and although a mixed population presently gathered around the armed trading-post, and his possessions rapidly increased, the restless Frenchman* yearned for a life of adventure and an undisputed field of traffic with the Indians. It was at this period that Jolliet's report of the fertile valley of the Mississippi, and its innumerable herds of elk and buffalo, fired La Salle to attempt some enterprise of great magnitude, which should make his name famous through all time.

Embarking for France, he laid his giant scheme of commerce and colonization before Colbert, the prime minister; and patronized by Seignelay, the son of Colbert, at that time minister of marine, he obtained, "with the monopoly of the traffic in buffalo skins, a commission for perfecting the discovery of the Great River."

Returning to Canada in September, he proceeded presently to Fort Frontenac, accompanied by Tonti his lieutenant, and attended by a party of mechanics and mariners, bearing provisions and merchandise, together with such other articles as were necessary to the construction and equipment of a brigantine in the wilderness. By the middle of November a vessel of ten tons was finished and freighted; and on the 18th of the same month his company set sail from Fort Frontenac, and entering, for the first time, the Niagara River, commenced the construction of a fort and trading-house above the falls. A small vessel, intended to ply on the waters of Lake Erie, was now begun; and while Tonti and Hennepin were penetrating the wilderness on trading and exploring expeditions, La Salle was endeavouring to maintain pacific relations with the Iroquois, whose jealousy had already been excited by the malevolent intrigues of rival traders. To quiet the apprehensions of the savages, the building of the fort was suspended, and the trading-house surrounded by palisades instead. But although large supplies of furs were obtained, La Salle had to contend with many difficulties and some reverses, and only waited for an opportunity to extend his discoveries beyond the limits attained by former adventurers, and to reap the advantages to which he was entitled by the royal charter. At length his new vessel, the Griffin, a bark of sixty tons, was completed, and successfully launched on the upper waters of the Niagara River; and on the 7th of August, La Salle, embarking all his company with the exception of a few clerks and labourers, set sail on his great adventure, the exploration of the Mississippi Valley. Prosperous gales speedily carried the daring voyagers across Lakes Erie and St. Clair, but on entering Lake Huron they encountered so severe a storm that, for a time, they gave themselves up for lost. At length, however, they succeeded in reaching Mackinaw, a place "of prodigious fertility," where he ordered a small fortified station to be constructed. Leaving a detachment of his company behind for this purpose, La Salle sailed on the 2d of September for Green Bay, from whence he sent back the Griffin to Niagara, richly freighted with furs. Those of his followers whom he had sent round by the opposite shore, he ordered to rendezvous at the mouth of the St. Joseph. The same directions were given to the faithful Tonti, who had returned to Mackinaw. With the seventeen men remaining, and accompanied by the Recollect missionaries, Hennepin, Membré, and De la Ribourde, La Salle crossed Lake Michigan in canoes, and halted at the appointed rendezvous until his men should join him.

During the month he remained on this peninsula, anxiously waiting for tidings of the Griffin, the men were kept busily employed in erecting another picketed station, which was subsequently called the Fort of the Miamis.

Receiving no intelligence of the Griffin, La Salle resolved to prosecute his voyage. Leaving four men in garrison at St. Joseph's, he crossed, with the rest of his company, some thirty in number, the short but difficult portage to the Kankakee, and descending the river by easy stages, arrived toward the close of December at an Indian village composed of from four to five hundred cabins, each capable of containing several families. Its usual inhabitants being absent on their winter hunt, La Salle took so much of their corn as his pressing need required, and proceeding on his journey, reached, on the 4th of January, the Lake of Peoria, where he fell in with a large camp of Illinois Indians. By a display of his usual spirit and address, he succeeded in forming an alliance with the tribe; but he had the mortification to find himself still followed by the bitter enmity of his rivals, who influenced the Miamis to send a deputation to the Illinois to denounce him as intriguing their ruin. In addition to this source of annoyance, he could gain no tidings of the Griffin with its rich cargo of furs. His men, too, had become mutinous, and six of them, deserting the expedition, returned to Mackinaw. But these multiplied disasters only served to display with greater force and vividness the heroic nature of the man. Under his orders, those who remained faithful to his fortunes commenced the construction of a fort, to which he gave the pathetic name of Crevecœur—broken heart.

Still resolutely bent upon prosecuting his enterprise, he sent Hennepin with a small exploring party to examine the country of the upper Mississippi, and leaving a garrison at Crevecœur, directed Tonti to return to the vicinity of the Indian village, and fortify there an eminence, since known as Rock Fort. In this beautiful region he had determined to found a colony; but as both men and means were wanting, he set out on foot for Fort Frontenac, a distance of twelve hundred miles, attended only by three companions. Of the particulars of this journey there is no record. On reaching his destination, he found his affairs in the utmost confusion. The loss of the Griffin was confirmed, his agents had proved dishonest, his creditors were clamorous, and his enemies unceasing in their attacks. Surmounting all these obstacles, he collected another band of adventurers, and having with him materials to furnish a brigantine, started again, in the summer of 1680, for the Illinois.

On his arrival at Rock Fort, a more terrible disappointment awaited him. During his absence the warlike Iroquois had driven the garrisons from their posts in the Illinois, and compelled them to return to the lakes. Making his way back to Canada, the energetic La Salle spent the following year in trading to Green Bay, and in reorganizing his scattered bands of followers.

This being at length effected, he sent an advance party under Tonti to the Chicago River, where he joined them with the remainder of his company, on the 4th January, 1682. The entire party, consisting of twenty-three Frenchmen, of whom father Membré was one, and eighteen Mohican and Abnaki warriors, now commenced their journey, travelling on foot over the frozen rivers, and dragging after them their canoes, baggage, and provisions. Finding the Illinois navigable in the vicinity of Fort Crevecœur, the whole company embarked in the canoes, and on the 8th of February reached the Mississippi. Fearful of encountering with their frail barks the masses of floating ice which yet encumbered the river, they halted on its banks until the 13th, when they committed themselves to the current, landing occasionally to hunt, or to visit some Indian village. Nothing of interest occurred until the 24th, when they reached the Chickasa Bluffs. Here Prudhomme, one of the hunters, was missed, and apprehensive that he had fallen into the hands of the Indians, La Salle ordered an intrenched fort to be constructed, and sent out parties in search of him. Several Indians were taken prisoners, but nothing was heard of Prudhomme until the ninth day, when he was found by the scouting parties and brought to the fort. Here then, near where De Soto embarked his forces to cross the river, and in the vicinity of the present thriving city of Memphis, arose the first structure erected by European hands on the soil of Tennessee. The subsequent adventures of the unfortunate La Salle, his indomitable perseverance, his singular misfortunes, and his shameful assassination by the hands of his own followers, form no part of this history. The honour of having first stood upon the borders of Tennessee belongs to the chivalric Spaniard and the heroic Frenchman; but its exploration and settlement was left for a people more enterprising than either.

CHAPTER V.

Discovery of Old Virginia by Amidas and Barlow—Attempts at settlement—The James river colony—Its reverses and eventual prosperity—Extension of settlements—The Albemarle region—A patent granted by Charles II. for the province of Carolina—Locke's constitution—Its rejection in Albemarle—Culpepper's insurrection—Governor Sothel—Ludwell's administration—The Carolinas under separate jurisdictions—Cary's insurrection—Arrival of Hyde—War with the Tuscaroras—Indian war with South Carolina—French in Louisiana—D'Iberville establishes a colony at Biloxi—Its removal to Mobile Bay—Crozat's grant—Charleville's trading-house on the Cumberland—French forts in the Tennessee country—New Orleans founded—Massacre of the French by the Natchez—Province of Georgia settled by Oglethorpe—French expedition against the Chickasas—Its disastrous failure.

ONE hundred years before La Salle descended the Mississippi, from the mouth of the Illinois river to the gulf, Amidas and Barlow, with two ships fitted out by Sir Walter Raleigh, set sail from England, and after exploring the coast of North Carolina and the islands adjacent, returned home with an account of their discoveries. To the country thus visited, Elizabeth, then queen of England, gave the name of Virginia. Various attempts at settlement were subsequently made, but none of them succeeded until 1607, when the first permanent English colony was established on a peninsula formed by the James River, and thirty-two miles above its mouth. After many reverses, the province of Virginia overcame all the obstacles to its progress, and increasing steadily in population, numbered, in 1671, forty thousand inhabitants. Consisting principally of planters, who drew their supplies from England, the settlements, during this period, had been extended to the Potomac on the one hand, and to Albemarle Sound on the other. The delicious climate and fertile soil of the region occupied by the southern pioneers, speedily attracted attention in England, and on application to Charles II., a grant was readily obtained of "all the country, from the Atlantic to the Pacific Ocean included within the thirty-first and thirty-sixth parallels of latitude."

In 1665 a second patent was issued, which largely extended the former territorial limits;

and as the Albemarle region already contained quite a number of inhabitants, it was organized into a county. The terms of the patent restricting the lords proprietaries from enacting any laws without the consent of the freemen of the new province, the first grand assembly of the county of Albemarle met soon after, and adopted such regulations as the condition of the people required. Some exertion having been made to encourage emigration, the population of Albemarle, in 1674, numbered some four thousand souls; and as the settlements now extended southward to the banks of the Ashley River, all the freemen of Carolina were summoned to meet at old Charlestown to elect their colonial representatives. Six years later the present Charleston was founded at the junction of the Ashley and Cooper Rivers, and was presently declared the capital of Carolina.

The constitution framed at the request of the lords proprietaries by John Locke, so well known as the author of the celebrated treatise on "the Human Understanding," being utterly unsuited to the wants of the people of Carolina, the inhabitants of Albemarle refused to adopt it; and finally evinced, in 1677, their abhorrence of its complicated provisions, by breaking out into open rebellion, imprisoning Millar, president of the council, and the proprietary officers, seizing the royal revenue, and setting up an independent government. At the head of this new organization was placed Culpepper, the chief insurgent, who retained his office for two years. The escape of Millar from durance, and his departure for England, led Culpepper thither also to defend his conduct. He was successful with the lords proprietaries; but, at the instance of Millar, he was arrested on a charge of treason. The influence of Shaftesbury procured his acquittal. In the mean time Sothel, a new proprietary, had been appointed governor; but being captured on the high seas by corsairs, he did not arrive in Albemarle until 1683. The object of Sothel, like that of most of the colonial governors in those days, was to enrich himself as speedily as possible at the expense of the inhabitants, and for five years his exactions were borne with more or less patience; but at the end of that time the assembly rose against him, and passing a sentence of deposition, compelled him to depart from the colony. After an interregnum of two years, Philip Ludwell was appointed governor of Albemarle, and the following year his sway was extended over Southern Carolina also. Unable to control the reckless and independent spirits over whom he had been placed, Ludwell vacated his office in 1693, and the government of the provinces was again divided—that of Albemarle, or North Carolina, being assumed by Thomas Harvey. Under his administration, and that of his immediate successors, the colonists continued to prosper in wealth and increase in numbers. At length, in 1708, Deputy-Governor Cary, who had been removed by the proprietaries for malfeasance in office, stirred up the people to revolt; and, deposing Glover, the president of the council, again assumed the administration of affairs. This violent conduct was productive of numerous feuds in the colony, which Hyde, newly commissioned as governor of the Carolinas, was despatched from England, in 1710, to compose. Denounced presently by the assembly of Albemarle, Cary, who had previously been willing to defer to the authority of Hyde, now became alarmed, and summoning his adherents, prepared for war. In this emergency Hyde called upon Spotswood, the governor of Virginia, for assistance; at the approach of which, Cary and his chief abettors fled, first westward, but returning presently to Virginia, were arrested and sent prisoners to England.

Soon after this disturbance was quelled, North Carolina became engaged in war with the Tuscarora Indians. At the commencement of hostilities the frontier settlements suffered greatly; but by the prompt aid of a detachment of South Carolina militia, and the assistance of a large auxiliary force of friendly Indians, the Tuscaroras were besieged in their place of refuge during the winter of 1712, and compelled to submit to terms of peace. These terms being violated by the conquerors, the Tuscaroras again resumed the hatchet; but a similar expedition being organized against them during the winter of 1713, eight hundred were made prisoners and sold into slavery. The remainder of the tribe, finding themselves harassed without intermission, fled northward and joined the Iroquois.

Scarcely were the frontiers relieved from the presence of the Tuscaroras before the confederated tribes, who had aided in their expulsion, were themselves at war with South Carolina.' Many barbarities were committed at the outset, and a large amount of property destroyed; but at length, by the enterprising conduct of Governor Craven, the allied warriors were signally defeated at Salkehachie, the Yemassees driven into Florida, and the Creeks, Cherokees, and Catawbas induced to open negotiations for a peace.

In the midst of these provincial fluctuations, the French government had been steadily encouraging the settlement of a colony at the mouth of the Mississippi. Although the disappointment arising from the failure of the magnificent schemes with which La Salle had dazzled the French ministry, in conjunction with the disastrous death of that enterprising adventurer, had checked for a season the progress of southern colonization, the project of connecting the territory of the lakes with that of the Mississippi, by a chain of military posts, had never been abandoned.

Accordingly, soon after the close of the second French war, Lemoine D'Iberville, an intrepid Canadian officer, was authorized to found a colony at the mouth of the Mississippi. Selecting the shores of the Bay of Biloxi as the site of his new settlement, he landed his colonists, some two hundred in number; and after erecting some dwellings and a fort, left his brothers Bienville and Sauvolle to carry out his plans, while he returned to France for supplies.

But the malaria swept off the settlers almost as fast as they arrived. Sauvolle, the governor, died; and the surviving colonists, with the exception of a few stragglers, fled from the pestilent vapours of the Mississippi, and established themselves at the head of Mobile Bay. Even there the work of colonization did not prosper; and in 1712, Louisiana did not contain more than three hundred French inhabitants.

It was at this time that Crozat, a wealthy merchant, obtained a grant of the whole province, together with a monopoly of trade; and under his auspices trading-houses were presently established on the Mississippi, Alabama, and Red Rivers, and enterprising Frenchmen, traversing the country of the Chickasas and Choctas, successfully competed with the English traders from Carolina.

In 1714, Charleville, coming up from New Orleans, built himself a trading-house on the Cumberland River, not far from the present site of Nashville. Two years later, forts were erected on the Mississippi near Natchez; on the Alabama near Montgomery; at the mouths of the Tennessee and Cumberland Rivers; and at various points inland where the protection of a garrison seemed necessary. Crozat's returns falling far short of his expenditures, he resigned his patent in 1717, which was transferred, the same year, to the Mississippi Company. Eight hundred emigrants were immediately sent out to colonize a country of which the most glowing descriptions were circulated throughout France.

The choice of governor fell upon Bienville. Long resident in Louisiana, and thoroughly acquainted with the region of the lower Mississippi, he set to work with his accustomed alacrity to lay the foundation of a great commercial city on the left bank of the river, and about one hundred miles from its mouth. The labour of clearing the swamp was performed by convicts; and to the cluster of rude cabins which soon after arose, Bienville gave the name of New Orleans.

From this period the province of Louisiana commenced to flourish. At the close of 1721 it contained six thousand inhabitants, one-tenth of whom were negro slaves, imported direct from Africa.

In the meanwhile, the traders of the two nations were striving for the monopoly of the Indian traffic. Through the influence exerted by Bienville and his agents, the Chocta, Arkansa, and Natchez Indians inclined to the French interest; but the more powerful Chickasas, Creeks, and Cherokees were in alliance with the English.

By the disastrous failure of the gigantic but visionary financial scheme under which the association had been organized, the Mississippi Company became greatly embarrassed in its commercial operations. Three commissioners were, however, presently sent to Louisiana to supervise the condition of the colony, and under their auspices the seat of government was removed to New Orleans, still an insignificant village, containing a church, a magazine, a hundred cabins, and about twice that number of inhabitants.

But the greatest check to the prosperity of the province was yet to come. Bienville, after having passed twenty-five years in the service of the colony, was removed from his government, and ordered to answer in France the aspersions of his enemies. The influence of the latter prevailed for a season. Not only was Bienville deprived of his office, but his nearest kindred also.

The new governor appointed by the crown was Perrier, an officer of considerable ability, but without that influence with the Indian population which was possessed by Bienville. In 1727, the year after his arrival, the encroachments of the Carolina traders, and their lucrative traffic with the Chickasa Indians, forms the burden of a despatch to the minister. "The English," he writes, "continue to urge their commerce into the very heart of the province. Sixty or seventy horses, laden with merchandise, have passed into the country of the Chickasas, to which nation I have given orders to plunder the English of their goods, promising to recompense them by a present."

Fortunately for the English, the suggestion was not accepted. The Chickasas remained faithful. The massacre of the French by the Natchez during the winter of 1729, and the fearful retaliation which followed, bound the Chickasas still closer in alliance with the English, at whose request they accorded protection and a home to such straggling bands of the Natchez as had escaped the war of extermination.

While Governor Perrier was seeking, by every means in his power, the total destruction of the Natchez, James Oglethorp, an English officer who had served under Prince Eugene, sailed up the Savannah River, landed a party of English colonists on Yamacraw Bluff, and, concluding treaties with the neighbouring Indians, organized the territory thus acquired into the new English province of Georgia.

Alarmed at this innovation, and at the hostile aspect of the Indian nations, the Mississippi Company, preferring a lucrative commerce with the East Indies to the doubtful prospect of eventual profit from Louisiana, surrendered that province, in 1732, to the crown of France.

It was now resolved that a vigorous effort should be made to restore French supremacy in the valley of the Mississippi, by organizing a large army for the purpose of chastising the hostile Indians, and especially the Chickasas, who, being in alliance with the English, were liberally supplied by them with arms and munitions of war. The services of Bienville were again called into requisition; and invested with chief command in the province, that officer arrived at Mobile in the spring of 1735, after an absence of eight years. He was received with great joy by the alarmed colonists, who, reassured by his presence among them, eagerly assisted in promoting his plans for chastising an enemy of whom they had so long lived in dread.

But it was not until the spring of 1736 that all his preparations were completed. Having previously despatched orders to the younger D'Artaguette, at that time commanding the French troops in Illinois, to descend the river and meet him in the Chickasa country, on the 10th of

May, with all the forces that could be mustered in the north-west, Bienville put his southern army in motion in two divisions, one of which embarked at New Orleans in thirty boats, and sailed for the appointed rendezvous some time during the month of March; the other division leaving Mobile for Tombigby in a similar manner during the early part of April.

D'Artaguette, accompanied by Vincennes, a brave young Canadian; by father Sénat, a Jesuit; one hundred and thirty French soldiers and volunteers, and three hundred and sixty Indian warriors, descending the Mississippi to the lowest Chickasa bluff, marched slowly to the sources of the Yalobusha, among which he encamped on the 9th of May, as by previous agreement with Bienville. For eleven days he remained at this place, expecting either to form a junction with Bienville, or to receive reinforcements from other detachments which were known to be on their way. Weary with waiting, and unable any longer to restrain the impatience of his Indian allies, who, representing that the nearest Chickasa town was inhabited by refugee Natchez, demanded to be led to the attack or suffered to return home. Reluctantly yielding to what appeared to be the general wish, D'Artaguette ordered an advance, and on the 20th of May the army arrived within a mile of the Indian village. Leaving his baggage at this point, in charge of thirty men,

D'Artaguette pressed rapidly forward with the remainder of his command. The impetuosity of his attack promised at first the most brilliant success. The Chickasas, driven from their outposts, fled across a neighbouring eminence, closely followed by the French, who suddenly found themselves drawn into an ambush, and exposed to the concentrated fire of five hundred Indians, rendered still more effective by the support of some thirty English traders. Thrown into disorder by this unexpected attack, the conflict was fierce but brief. A large number of the French officers had fallen at the first fire. D'Artaguette, himself badly wounded, made a desperate attempt to retrieve the fortune of the day; but the greater part of his allies had already taken to flight, and finding those who still fought boldly at his side gradually becoming fewer in number, he reluctantly ordered a retreat to his camp. By extraordinary exertions, a part of his troops succeeded in cutting their way through the enveloping ranks of the enemy; but the chivalric D'Artaguette, Lieutenant Vincennes, two other officers, and nineteen men were taken prisoners. The Jesuit missionary, Father Sénat, who could have made his escape, voluntarily shared the captivity of his companions, believing it his duty to remain.

Retarded by unavoidable delays, the forces under Bienville did not reach the upper waters of the Tombigby until two days after the defeat of D'Artaguette. Disembarking in the vicinity of the place now known as Cotton Gin Port, nearly two more days were consumed in erecting a picketed station for the reception of the artillery and baggage; and it was not until the evening of the 25th that the army encamped on the prairie within three miles of the principal Chickasa village. The original determination of Bienville was to avoid, for the present, this village, and by a circuitous route fall suddenly upon the one inhabited by the Natchez, which lay a short distance beyond. But this design being overruled by his Chocta allies and the eagerness of his own officers, he ordered his nephew, the Chevalier Noyan, to advance at the head of some three hundred men, and commence an attack.

In the gray dawn of the following morning this strong detachment, accompanied by a large number of Chocta warriors, approached silently the clustering huts of the Chickasas, over which, to the great surprise of the French, floated easily the English flag in the fragrant summer air. Within those rude walls also were Englishmen, traders, under whose directions the Chickasas had strongly fortified their position. Thus palisaded and intrenched, and animated to increased daring by the recent success of the Natchez, the crouching warriors awaited the coming of the French, who, under cover of a line of negroes, protected by mantelets, were moving steadily to the assault. At the first fire from the intrenchment the negroes fled; but the French dashing forward, led by the grenadiers, entered the village, carried several cabins, and wrapped others in flames. This brilliant exploit had not been achieved without great loss. De Contrecœur and De Lusser, two brave and accomplished officers, had been shot dead; and the greater portion of the troops, becoming alarmed at the thinning of their ranks, sought shelter within the houses they had taken. Finding it impossible to prevail upon these men to renew the attack, De Noyan gathered around him a few brave spirits, and with the assistance of his gallant officers determined to make a desperate assault upon the principal fort. The arrangements were scarcely completed before a terrible fire from behind picketed intrenchments, from loop, and door, and angle, was poured upon the assembled ranks, which wounded nearly all the officers and a number of the men. De Noyan, himself wounded, still endeavoured to maintain the ground he had won; but having lost control of his own soldiers, and being wholly unsupported by the lukewarm Choctas, he was constrained to throw himself into the cabins on the outskirts of the village, while he sent to Bienville for relief. A reinforcement of eighty men was immediately forwarded; but even this force scarcely sufficed to extricate the French from the difficulties by which they were surrounded. In the midst of their success the Chickasas acted prudently. Fully conscious that they could not hope to succeed in an attack upon the French on the prairie, they wisely remained behind the cover of their fortifications, and suffered De Noyan to retreat to the camp without further molestation.

The next morning the French beheld the mutilated fragments of their unfortunate countrymen suspended, in barbarous derision, upon high poles within the Chickasa intrenchments; and had not Bienville been justly doubtful of the fidelity of his Indian allies, another attempt would have been made to capture the place. Oppressed with grief and indignation, he ordered litters to be prepared for the wounded; and as soon as these were ready, the troops set out on their return to the Tombigby. Hastily dismantling the stockade at this place, and sinking his artillery in the river, Bienville dismissed the Choctas, and descending the stream with the remainder of his command, reached Mobile about the 3d of June.

The retreat of Bienville sealed the fate of D'Artaguette and his companions. Up to this period their wounds had been carefully tended, and their wants hospitably provided for; but no sooner did the French flotilla descend the shallow stream of the Tombigby, than the Chickasas and Natchez, brought D'Artaguette, Father Senat, the brave Vincennes, and fifteen others, to an open space adjoining their village, and binding them to stakes, burned them slowly and deliberately to death.

Smarting under two disgraceful defeats, and inflamed with indignation at the cruelties practised upon their gallant but unfortunate friends, it was not long before the French people projected another expedition against the Chickasas.

Three years, however, were suffered to pass away before the troops destined for this enterprise were assembled at Fort Assumption, on the bluff where Memphis now stands, and already made famous by remembrances of De Soto and La Salle. Here, gradually wasting away under the diseases common to a southern climate, they remained inactive until the spring of 1740, when a weak fragment of what had once been an imposing army of thirty-seven hundred men, was directed to march once more against the Chickasa towns; but being met by deputies suing for peace, Celeron, the commander, eagerly seized the opportunity of concluding a treaty upon more favourable terms than he had the power to enforce. Henceforth the Chickasas remained in undisputed possession of their country. Notwithstanding the peace, war-parties of refugee

Natchez still continued to cut off the French traders, whenever an opportunity occurred, until the latter, finding themselves left unprotected by their government, were forced to abandon their stations between the Cumberland and the Mississippi, and at length none but an Indian foot traversed the region of Tennessee.

CHAPTER VI.

Waning influence of the French—Progress of Georgia—War between England, France and Spain—Virginia boundary extended—Settlements on the Holston, Yadkin and Catawba—French in the valley of the Ohio—Mission of George Washington—Fort Duquesne—Skirmish at Great Meadows—Surrender of Fort Necessity—Arrival of Braddock—His defeat and death—Earl of Loudoun—Forts Prince George, Dobbs and Loudoun built—Campaign of 1758—Capture of Fort Duquesne—Trouble with the Cherokees—Indian negotiations for peace—Conduct of Lyttleton—Massacre of Indian hostages—Cherokee war—Montgomery marches against the Indian towns—Relieves Fort Prince George—Battle of Etchoe—Surrender of Fort Loudoun—Massacre of prisoners—Generosity of Attakulla-kulla—Advance of Grant—Second battle of Etchoe—Peace.

WHEN it became known that the warlike Chickasas had been able to resist, successfully, all the forces which France was capable, at that time, of bringing against them, the neighbouring tribes preferred courting an alliance with the prosperous governments of Carolina and Virginia, rather than with their weaker European neighbours.

Georgia, too, though struggling under the usual embarrassments incidental to a new settlement, had already advanced her outposts to Augusta, where, in 1740, a fort was erected, and where a village presently sprung up, which speedily grew into importance as a trading station.

Another reason which led to the neglect of Louisiana, arose from the necessity of protecting the more important dependency of Canada. The war which broke out in 1740 between England and Spain, involved, in 1744, France also as an ally of the latter power; and although, with the exception of the capture of Louisburg by the New England troops, neither of the belligerents displayed much energy or military skill, the danger which menaced the French possessions in the north prevented the government from affording that assistance to its southern province which its precarious condition so much needed.

In 1748 this war was terminated by the peace of Aix-la-Chapelle. In the mean time Virginia had extended her western boundary by purchasing from the Iroquois their right, as conquerors, to the territory beyond the mountains; and, in

1749, a joint commission, authorized for that purpose by the respective legislatures of Virginia and North Carolina, continued the boundary line between the two provinces to the Steep Rock on the Holston River. The rapid increase of population had rendered this step imperatively necessary. Already a few resolute Virginians had cleared small tracts of land on the borders of the Holston; and a few years later several hardy families of pioneers from North Carolina, settled upon the fertile lands between the Yadkin and the Catawba.

But while the tide of population was slowly advancing toward the borders of Tennessee, and English traders were acquiring almost a monopoly of the traffic with the southern Indians, the French continued to claim, by right of discovery, the fertile regions watered by the Ohio and Mississippi. To perfect their title to the valley of the Ohio, Galissoniére, governor-general of Canada, despatched an officer and a party of soldiers, during the summer of 1749, to bury leaden plates engraven with the arms of France at the mouths of the principal rivers, and to take possession of the country in the name of Louis XV. Four years later, when the incorporation of the Ohio Company became known, a further effort was made to restrain the advance of the English into the north-western territory, by building forts at Erie, on French Creek, and on the banks of the Alleghany River. Alarmed for the safety of the frontier settlements, Governor Dinwiddie of Virginia, purchased of the Indians that piece of land upon which Pittsburg now stands; and while waiting permission from England to build a fort there, despatched the youthful George Washington to hold a conference with the Ohio Indians, and to demand of the French commander at Fort le Bœuf, on French Creek, the withdrawal of his forces, and their return into Canada. This dangerous mission was successfully accomplished; but, as the French refused to retire, a detachment of men was presently sent to the forks of the Ohio, to construct a fort at that place. Being driven off in the spring of 1754 by the advance of a French flotilla, they retreated up the Monongahela, while the invaders proceeded to complete the unfinished works, to which they presently gave the name of Fort Duquesne.

In the mean while, Washington, commissioned as lieutenant-colonel, was hastening to the Ohio at the head of three companies of Virginians. He had scarcely reached Wills Creek before he received tidings of the advance of the French, and their possession of the works he was hastening to defend. A skirmish followed soon after, at Great Meadows, in which a French detachment was defeated and its commander, Jumonville, killed. Washington being reinforced, threw up a stockade fort at Great Meadows, into which he was compelled to retire by the advance of a superior force of French and Indians. After a spirited, but unavailing defence, honourable terms of capitulation were proposed and accepted, and the Virginians, marching out with their arms and baggage, retired across the mountains to Wills Creek.

Provoked by these encroachments, and by subsequent acts of hostility, Great Britain, previous to declaring war against France, despatched General Braddock to America, in the spring of 1755, as commander-in-chief of the royal and provincial forces. The French government was equally active. While advancing against Fort Duquesne, the English troops were drawn into an ambush, and routed with great slaughter. Braddock himself was mortally wounded. Two days after the battle, he was buried by the wayside, in the vicinity of the Fort at Great Meadows. The following spring, war was openly declared; and in July, the Earl of Loudoun assumed command of the British forces in America.

Hostilities were no sooner commenced than French emissaries scattered themselves among the Indian tribes friendly to the English, and endeavoured to detach them from their alliance. Fully conscious how much the safety of the scattered settlements on the western frontiers depended upon the fidelity of the neighbouring tribes, Governor Glen, of South Carolina, attended in person a grand council of the Cherokees, and, renewing with them a treaty of peace, obtained at the same time a cession of considerable territory. Not long after the conclusion of this treaty he erected Fort Prince George, on the head-waters of the Savannah River, and in close proximity to the Indian town of Keowee. Fort Dobbs was also constructed about the same time, under directions from the governor of North Carolina, as a security to the settlers on the Yadkin; to which Loudoun presently added another fort on the Tennessee River, twenty-five miles south of the present town of Knoxville. Under the protection of its garrison, consisting of two hundred British regulars, commanded by Captain Demere, clustered the cabins of the first Anglo-Saxon inhabitants of Tennessee.

The wisdom and energy displayed by the elder Pitt in providing for the campaign of 1758, inspired the provincials with new hopes, and induced them to second his efforts with more than ordinary unanimity.

While Abercrombie marched against Crown Point and Ticonderoga, General Forbes was directed to cross the mountains, and, with a mixed command of regulars, provincials, and Cherokees, attempt the conquest of Fort Duquesne. The attack of Abercrombie was signally repelled by the active and courageous Montcalm; but the brilliant exploit of Colonel Bradstreet in surprising Fort Frontenac, cut off the supplies of the French garrisons in the valley of the Ohio, and led to the abandonment of Fort Duquesne on the approach of General Forbes.

But the prospect of peace which the possession of Fort Duquesne seemed to promise to the inhabitants of the frontiers, was rendered more remote than ever by an incident which grew out of its capture. The Cherokee warriors, who had accompanied the army during its march to the Ohio, finding themselves coldly regarded now that their services were no longer needed, resolved to return to their homes. While travelling through the wilderness of western Virginia, they carried off with them a number of horses belonging to remote settlers, to replace those they had lost during the expedition. The backwoodsmen armed themselves and followed in pursuit; and in the skirmishes which ensued, several of the Cherokees were killed. War parties were immediately organized to retaliate; and the families of the borderers, driven from their homes, were compelled to take refuge in forts and block-houses. Two soldiers at Tellico, and several belonging to the garrison at Fort Loudoun, were surprised and slain. Notwithstanding this sanguinary outbreak, a considerable portion of the Cherokee nation remained friendly to the English; and toward the close of the year a deputation, consisting of six chieftains, proceeded to Charleston to negotiate for a peace. They were answered by a proclamation from Governor Lyttleton, calling out the militia. While hopes were yet entertained that tranquillity would be restored, the fierce anger of the upper Cherokees was again aroused by a demand which was make upon them for the surrender of their chiefs, and by the arbitrary conduct of Coytmore, the commandant at Fort Prince George, in intercepting supplies. No discrimination being made in favour of the friendly towns, the latter sent a remonstrance to Lyttleton, who returned a haughty reply, and, in opposition to the more prudent judgment of the Carolina legislature, continued his preparations for war.

Still anxious to compose the existing differences without a resort to arms, a deputation of thirty chiefs from the upper and lower towns, headed by Occonostota, one of their most renowned warriors, presented themselves before Lyttleton and proffered friendship. "I love the white people," said Occonostota; "they and the Indians shall not hurt one another. I reckon myself as one with you."

"I am going with a great many of my warriors to your nation," replied Lyttleton, "in order to demand satisfaction of them. If you will not give it when I come to your nation, I shall take it." He closed by offering the chieftains safe conduct by the way. False to his promise, he had no sooner reached the Congaree, where his troops were assembled, than he arrested the deputies and carried them prisoners to Fort Prince George. At this place he liberated Occonostota; but to give some colour of plausibility to his dishonourable breach of faith, he obtained the signatures of six of the captive chieftains, to an agreement that the rest of their companions should remain as hostages at Fort Prince George, until twenty-four Indians should be surrendered for execution, or otherwise, in retaliation for the lives which had been sacrificed during the outbreak. Congratulating himself upon the success of his duplicity, he returned to Charleston and disbanded his army. He had scarcely left Fort Prince George before hostilities recommenced. Burning for revenge, Occonostota immediately placed himself at the head of his indignant warriors, and investing the fort decoyed Coytmore, by a stratagem, beyond the reach of its guns, shot him dead, and severely wounded the two lieutenants by whom he was accompanied. Expecting an immediate assault, the alarmed garrison attempted to put the hostages in irons. The chieftains resented this indignity, and in the struggle that followed stabbed three of the soldiers, upon which the companions of the latter fell upon the prisoners and put them all to death.

The whole Cherokee nation, now no longer divided, declared at once unanimously for war. Large parties of warriors immediately spread themselves along the frontiers, leaving sanguinary tokens of their presence wherever they went. Supplied with arms and ammunition from Louisiana, and calling in the assistance of the neighbouring nations, they cut off all communication with Fort Loudoun, and laid desolate all the frontier settlements with the crimson tomahawk and the burning brand.

Unable singly to cope with the mountain warriors, whose implacable hostility had been provoked by the treachery of Lyttleton, messengers were hastily despatched to Virginia and North Carolina for assistance, and to Amherst at New York for a detachment of British regulars. Twelve hundred of the latter were immediately embarked for Charleston, under the command of Colonel Montgomery, who received orders to chastise the enemy, and return in time to assist in the invasion of Canada. Hastening to the rendezvous at the Congaree, Montgomery formed a junction with the provincial forces. By an expeditious march from that place, he entered the Cherokee country, during the early part of June, 1760, surprised the town of Keowee, put nearly all its male inhabitants to the sword, and pushed forward the same night to Estatoe. After burning the town, which had been abandoned by the inhabitants, he proceeded to Qualatchee and Conasatchee, which with every other village through which he subsequently passed he reduced to a heap of ruins. Having thus laid waste all the settlements of the lower Creeks, he marched to the relief of Fort Prince George. When this was successfully accomplished, he despatched messengers to the upper and middle Creeks, offering to treat of peace. Receiving no response, he crossed the mountains to relieve Fort Loudoun, which Occonostota had closely invested, and entering the valley settlements on the Tennessee River, proceeded, on the morning of the 27th of June, against the town of Etchoe. Within five miles of the town his course lay parallel with the stream, which at this point meandered through a plain, covered densely with brushwood, and flanked on both sides by rugged hills. At an order from Montgomery, the rangers advanced to scour the thickets, when a heavy fire from a large force of Cherokees, concealed in ambush, killed Captain Morrison and wounded several of his men. The grenadiers and light companies were immediately ordered to advance, supported on their right and left flanks by the Royal Scots and the Highlanders. These three divisions pressed steadily forward, and after a severe conflict, which resulted in the loss of ninety-seven men in killed and wounded, finally succeeded in routing the enemy. Moving cautiously in pursuit, Montgomery continued his march toward Etchoe, which he reached about midnight. Finding himself in the midst of a country admirably adapted for defence, and with a repulsed but unconquered enemy hovering in large numbers around him, Montgomery was forced to abandon the attempt to relieve Fort Loudoun, and return with his wounded to Fort Prince George.

Cut off from all hopes of succour by the retreat of Montgomery, the half-famished garrison at Fort Loudoun sent Captain Stuart to Chote, a neighbouring Indian town, with a proposal to capitulate, on condition that all who were within the works should be permitted to retire, under the safe conduct of an escort, to Fort Prince George. The terms being agreed to, the fort was evacuated on the 7th of August. Accompanied by Occonostota, and a large detachment of warriors, the soldiers and refugee settlers, to the number of two hundred, set out on their journey. Deserted at Tellico by their Indian guards, they were attacked the next morning by a large force of Cherokees, led by Occonostota, which killed Demere, two other officers, and twenty-three privates, in retaliation for the treacherous murder of the imprisoned chieftains at Fort Prince George. The rest of the garrison were taken prisoners and carried back to Fort Loudoun.

When the aged chieftain Attakulla-kulla heard that his friend Captain Stuart was among those whose lives had been spared, he hastened to the fort and purchased him of his captor, at the expense of his rifle, his clothes, and every thing he could command. Learning soon after that Occonostota had threatened to burn all his prisoners unless Stuart would consent to work the artillery at the contemplated siege of Fort Prince George, the generous-hearted old chief carried off his prisoner, under the pretence of hunting, and plunging into the forest, travelled with him rapidly for nine days, through a wilderness rarely trodden by the foot of man, until they reached the Holston River, where they encountered a party of Virginians advancing to the relief of Fort Loudoun.

Encouraged to persevere in their hostilities by the presence of French emissaries, the Cherokee war parties continued to lay waste the frontiers until the spring of 1761, when the reduction of Canada enabled Amherst to respond to the call of the southern provinces for military assistance, by despatching Colonel Grant with a large body of regulars to co-operate with the provincial levies.

With this mixed force, amounting in the aggregate to twenty-six hundred men, Grant marched from Fort Prince George on the 7th of June; and on the 10th discovered the enemy posted upon the hill-sides and among the thickets of the narrow defile where Montgomery had purchased so severe a victory the previous year. After three hours hard fighting the Cherokees were driven from the ground, and the army, pushing forward into the heart of the territory, remained there for thirty days, burning the villages and destroying the granaries and cornfields. Grant then returned to Fort Prince George, where Attakulla-kulla, accompanied by a number of chiefs, presently arrived to sue for a peace. Honourable conditions were offered and accepted, and the southern borderers were once more at liberty to return to their farms and pursue their accustomed labours.

CHAPTER VII.

Pressure of borderers upon the Cherokee country—Exploring parties in Tennessee—Wallen's hunters—Boone's—Henderson employs Boone to explore Eastern Tennessee—Discovery of Kentucky—Indian complaints—Royal proclamation—Disregarded by the pioneers—Scaggins explores the Lower Cumberland—Remonstrance by the Iroquois—Council at Fort Stanwix—Cession of lands south of the Ohio—Cherokee council at Hard Labour—Settlements on the Holston—The Long Hunters explore Kentucky—Increase of settlers at Watauga—They establish a local government—The commissioners for Watauga—John Sevier—Extension of Virginia boundary—The Watauga lands leased of the Cherokees—An Indian murdered—Danger of the settlers—Heroism of Robertson—The north-western tribes—Troubles with the borderers.—The massacres on the Ohio by Cresap and Greathouse—Indian war—Dunmore's campaign—Battle of Point Pleasant—Treaty of peace.

But the expeditions of Montgomery and Grant were productive of more serious consequences to the Cherokees than the burning of their villages and the loss of a small number of their warriors. By these inroads the hardy and restless population of the frontiers obtained a knowledge of a fertile region of which they were not slow to profit. Traders with trains of pack-horses, whose jingling bells sounded strangely musical in the heart of the primeval forest, were the first to reap advantage of the peace, by bartering their merchandise for the rich peltries of a territory abounding in game. Hunters and trappers followed; and presently came armed bands of explorers, from Virginia and Carolina, who, entering the Cherokee country, gave the earliest English names to the mountains and rivers, and returning to their homes encumbered with the spoils of the chase, infused a similar spirit of adventure into the hearts of others.

Immediately on the close of the Cherokee war, a company of nineteen men from Virginia, among whom were Wallen, Cox, and Scaggs, crossed the northern boundary of Tennessee, and hunted for eighteen months upon Clinch and Powell Rivers. Encouraged by their success, they extended their range during the two following years to the banks of the Cumberland.

Contemporaneous with them a party from the settlement upon the Yadkin was exploring the country between the two forks of the Holston, under the guidance of young Daniel Boone, who had hunted upon the Watauga the preceding year. The local reputation of Boone as a daring and successful pioneer, led to his being employed, in 1764, to explore a country which was already beginning to attract the attention of emigrants. This commission emanated from an association of land speculators, at the head of which was Richard Henderson, a man of great ambition, who had risen from an humble station in life to the dignity of associate chief-judge of North Carolina. Attended by his kinsman, Samuel Calloway, Boone traversed the northeastern party of Tennessee, and ascending a spur of the Cumberland Mountains, saw, with mingled astonishment and delight, the numerous herds of buffalo which thronged the plains of Kentucky. In a burst of irrepressible enthusiasm, Boone appropriated them all. "I am richer," said he, "than the man mentioned in Scripture, who owned the cattle on a thousand hills—I own the wild beasts of more than a thousand valleys." But the time for taking advantage of these discoveries was not yet come. The Indians had already complained of repeated intrusions upon their hunting grounds; and to quiet their apprehensions, a royal proclamation had been issued, forbidding the provincials from making any settlements upon lands west of the mountains, and claiming for the crown the sole right to purchase territory from the Indians. At the same time, Captain Stuart, the friend of Attakulla-kulla, was appointed to the office of Indian agent for the southern district. But the royal mandate was little likely to be respected by men who had passed their lives on the borders of the wilderness. They had discovered that the whole of that vast tract of country stretching from the Cumberland Mountains westward to the Mississippi, and northward to the Ohio, was entirely uninhabited, and caring nothing for vague titles of ownership, pressed resolutely forward to take possession. They too had their claims, for many of them had been soldiers in the war which had stripped France of all her North American possessions with the exception of a small portion of Louisiana, and were authorized by their respective provinces to occupy these lands under their military warrants.

The favourable reports brought back by Boone influenced Henderson to make further explorations, and under his directions, Henry Scaggins, and other hunters, examined the country as far as the Lower Cumberland. In 1766 a small party, led by Colonel James Smith, thoroughly explored the country between the Tennessee and Cumberland Rivers, from Stone's River to the Ohio. Other exploring parties speedily followed, while the border population, pressing forward, began to open settlements on the Kanawha and the Holston. Against these continued encroachments upon their hunting grounds, the southern Indians repeatedly complained, but could obtain no redress; but when the Iroquois, who laid claim to the territory by right of conquest, formally remonstrated, the question became one of too serious a nature to be slighted. Sir William Johnson accordingly received orders from England to treat with the northern confederacy for the purchase of their lands; and at a council held at Fort Stanwix, toward the close of October, 1768, the Iroquois ceded to Great Britain all their claim to the country south of the Ohio River. Ten days before the delegates assembled at Fort Stanwix, the Cherokee Indians met Stuart at Hard Labour in Carolina, and agreed to extend the south-western boundary of Virginia, from the Holston River to the mouth of the Kanawha. Companies were immediately organized for the purpose of purchase and settlement; and while these were disputing among themselves concerning the invasion of each other's rights, a number of pioneer families quietly crossed the boundaries of North Carolina and founded, on the banks of the Holston, the first permanent settlement in Tennessee. These were followed so rapidly by others, that within a period of six weeks all the choicest lands on the north fork of the Holston were taken up. One daring adventurer, Captain William Bean, advanced still deeper into the wilderness, and built his station on Boone's Creek, a tributary of the Watauga. In the spring of 1770, a band of hunters, led by Colonel James Knox, assembled from the valleys of the Clinch and the Holston, and traversing the sources of the Cumberland, explored the middle and southern regions of Kentucky. Returning in 1771, these men, known as the Long Hunters, gave such glowing accounts of the mildness of the climate and the fertility of the soil, that surveying parties were sent down the Ohio to locate lands upon its southern border.

In the mean time, owing partly to local disturbances in the Carolinas, and partly to the growing difficulties between England and the provinces on the question of taxation, the population on the Holston and Watauga had increased so rapidly that, in 1772, the settlers assembled in convention and established a local government. By general agreement five commissioners were chosen, in whom were vested legislative, judicial, and executive powers. The chairman of the committee was Colonel John Carter, a native of Virginia. His associates were James and Charles Robertson, Zachariah Isbell, and John Sevier. The latter was of French extraction, the original name of the family being Xavier. His ancestors being Huguenots, were driven by persecution to seek a refuge in London, where Valentine Xavier, the father of the Watauga commissioner, was born. Emigrating to the colonies early in the eighteenth century, he first settled in Virginia, where, in 1740, on the borders of the Shenandoah, John Sevier was born. In 1769, the latter, already the head of a family consisting of a delicate wife and six children, migrated to the banks of the Holston, where, with his father and brother, he presently took up his abode, the permanence of which, henceforth, was only broken by occasional visits to his family in Virginia. With a better knowledge of men than of books, for his learning was scanty; active, fluent, bold, and generous, the " portly young stranger from Williamsburg" was not long in acquiring the esteem of the rough borderers, among whom he presently rose to the rank of a leader, and rivalled James Robertson in popularity.

By a treaty, which was ratified in 1772, the boundary of Virginia was considerably extended; but as the settlement at Watauga was still beyond provincial jurisdiction, and was an admitted encroachment upon Indian soil, the inhabitants were ordered by Cameron, the deputy superintendent, to retire across the borders. But pioneers, when once in possession of a country, were never known to retrace their steps; and a mandate so imperative might have been productive of serious results, if the Cherokees had not consented to lease, for a term of ten years, the lands already occupied. Unhappily, the ratification of the treaty led to the commission of an outrage which, for a time, threatened to involve the people of Watauga in the horrors of an Indian war. During the sports and festivities which marked the occasion, an Indian was slain by a party of lawless men from Virginia. This cold-blooded assassination, so atrocious and unjustifiable, created the greatest commotion among the settlers, who apprehended, and not without reason, that a sanguinary retaliation would follow. The danger was, however, averted by the courage and heroism of Robertson; who, at the risk of his own life, immediately set out for the principal Cherokee town, and succeeded in exonerating his people from any participation in the murder.

But if the southern Indians were content for a season to maintain pacific relations with the whites, it was far otherwise with the tribes of the north-west. The Shawanese and Mingoes had long viewed with irrepressible feelings of indignation the numerous parties of pioneers which, floating down the Ohio, traversed the territory on its borders, as surveyors or hunters, and marked out the choicest lands for subsequent occupation. Occasional collisions, in which blood was spilled on both sides, increased their hatred of the intruders; but no general declaration of war took place until 1774, when armed detachments of lawless frontiersmen, under Cresap and Greathouse, wantonly attacked, on two separate occasions, a number of inoffensive Indians, and indiscriminately massacred the whole. Logan, a celebrated Mingo chief, whose family Greathouse had exterminated, instantly flew to arms, and being joined soon after by roving bands of Iroquois, Shawanese, Delawares, and Wyandots, commenced a sanguinary and destructive warfare upon the inhabitants of western Virginia.

To afford a temporary check to these alarming inroads, Governor Dunmore despatched a body of troops under Colonel McDonald, against the Indian towns on the Muskingum. This expedition producing no beneficial results, Dunmore prepared to take the field in person. His army consisted of twenty-seven hundred men, organized into two divisions, one of which was composed of levies from southern and western Virginia, and the other of regular troops and volunteers from the northern and eastern counties. In the first division, commanded by General Andrew Lewis, was a company of volunteers from east Tennessee, the captain of which was Evan Shelby; his son, Isaac Shelby, the future governor of Kentucky, serving under him as lieutenant. Among the orderly sergeants were James Robertson and Valentine Sevier.

Quitting, on the 11th of September, the place of rendezvous in the valley region of Green Brier, General Lewis marched his division, through a rugged and untrodden wilderness, to Point Pleasant, at the mouth of the Kanawha, where he expected to form a junction with the forces under Dunmore; but finding the flotilla of the governor had not yet arrived, he halted his men and encamped. On the 9th he received instructions from Dunmore, who was then at the mouth of the Big Hockhocking, to cross the Ohio with his division, and join him at the

Shawanese towns on the Scioto. The following morning, while the troops were in the act of breaking up their encampment, Robertson and Sevier brought intelligence of the approach of an Indian force, which was subsequently ascertained to have numbered a thousand warriors, led by the brave Shawanese chief Cornstalk.

General Lewis immediately ordered his brother, Colonel Charles Lewis, to advance with a strong detachment, and reconnoitre the position of the enemy. Within four hundred yards of the camp, a fire from ambushed Indians mortally wounded Lewis, and disabled Fleming the second in command. The suddenness of the attack threw their men into disorder; but, supported by reinforcements under Colonel Field, they rallied and returned to the attack. From this time the contest was maintained on both sides with indomitable courage and resolution. After lasting nearly the whole day with varying success, it was finally terminated in favour of the Americans through a secret movement, accomplished by the companies of Shelby, Matthews, and Stuart, who succeeded in gaining the flank of the enemy. Placed between two fires, and impressed with the belief that Lewis had been joined by reinforcements, the Indians, who had hitherto fought with great coolness and deliberation, began to waver, and finally breaking up into confused masses, fled precipitately across the Ohio. This important victory led to negotiations for peace; and the chiefs of the hostile Indians having met Dunmore in council, agreed to a treaty, by which they transferred to Great Britain all their claims to lands south of the Ohio River.

CHAPTER VIII.

Cherokee council at Sycamore Shoals—Purchase of the Watauga territory—Other grants—The Transylvania grant annulled by Dunmore—Colonial troubles—Instructions to the royal governors—Seizure of stores at Concord—Battle of Lexington—Difficulties with Dunmore—Patrick Henry marches on Williamsburg—Flight of Dunmore—Action of the Federal Congress at Philadelphia—Spirited conduct of North Carolina—Increased excitement in the province—Flight of Governor Martin—The legislature of North Carolina advocates a declaration of independence—Annexation of the Watauga settlement to North Carolina—Indian hostilities—Skirmish at Long Island—Defence of Watauga Fort—Anecdote of Catherine Sherrill—South Carolina menaced by a British fleet—Provincial expeditions against the Cherokees.

ALTHOUGH the Cherokees were not a party to to the cession of lands exacted by Dunmore at the treaty of Camp Charlotte, they evinced, soon after, a willingness to dispose of a portion of their own sylvan possessions. In March, 1775, they assembled in council at the Sycamore Shoals, on the Watauga River, and, in consideration of the sum of ten thousand pounds sterling, transferred to Henderson and his associates all their hunting grounds between the Kentucky and the Cumberland Rivers. An immense concourse of Indians being present on this occasion, the people of Watauga seized the opportunity thus afforded them to convert their leasehold titles into titles in fee simple. By the payment of two thousand pounds sterling, they obtained a deed for all the lands lying on the waters of the Watauga, Holston, and Kanawha, beginning on the Holston, six miles above Long Island, and terminating at the sources of the Great Kanawha. Two other deeds were obtained by individuals on the same occasion. The store of Parker & Carter had previously been robbed by Indians; and as a compensation for the losses thus sustained, and in consideration of an additional sum which a third partner, Robert Lucas, agreed to pay, they obtained a grant of Carter's Valley, "from Cloud's Creek to the Chimney-top Mountain of Beech Creek." Jacob Brown also obtained grants for lands on both sides of Nolachucky River, adjoining the Watauga purchase. Henderson immediately proceeded to organize a form of government for the new province of Transylvania, notwithstanding his title was declared invalid by Governor Dunmore, within whose jurisdiction the territory in question was at that time supposed to lie. Four days subsequent to the treaty of Watauga, and before its stipulations were complied with, Dunmore issued a proclamation, warning all persons against Henderson and his associates; and, subsequently, the legislature of Virginia declared the purchase null and void. But, as a compensation for the services rendered by the Transylvania association in opening the wilderness, they were granted a tract of land twelve miles square on the Ohio, below the mouth of Green River.

But at this period the prerogatives of the crown were in far more danger within the body of the provinces than in the valley of the Ohio. The resolution of the English ministry to tax the American colonies had been met by a spirit of resistance which was rapidly approaching a crisis. Non-importation agreements had failed to procure redress of grievances. Petitions from the Provincial Congress had been received with contempt. The indignant spirit of the confederated colonies now becoming fully aroused, volunteer corps were organized, and arms and ammunition industriously collected in anticipation of the coming struggle. A considerable force of British troops had already landed at Boston; and early in the spring of 1775, the royal governors received instructions to seize upon all military stores which might be found in possession of the patriots. In obedience to this order, Governor Gage, of Massachusetts, despatched a party of regulars to take possession of some cannon and other *materiel* of war which were known to be secreted at Concord. The tidings immediately spread; the minute-men collecting in great numbers embarrassed the retreating regulars, and the battle at Lexington was the commencement of the War of Independence. This event took place on the 19th of April. Three days afterward, Governor Dunmore ordered the gunpowder in the magazine at Williamsburg to be secretly conveyed on board an armed vessel at anchor off Yorktown. So soon as the abstraction of the powder was made known to the volunteers of the vicinity, they armed themselves, and proceeding in a body to the governor, demanded its restitution. While the dispute was still pending, tidings arrived of the battle of Lexington. Fifteen hundred men from the eastern slopes of the Alleghanies presently collected at Fredericksburg, in readiness for any emergency. In the county of Hanover, Patrick Henry placed himself at the head of his company of volunteers, and marched at once upon Williamsburg. By constant accessions of armed militia, the force under his command was speedily increased to five hundred men. Sixteen miles from the city, Henry was met by a deputation who had prevailed upon Corbin, the king's receiver, to indemnify the province for the loss of the powder. Having thus succeeded in his purpose, Henry returned to Hanover, and on the 4th of May disbanded his company. A few weeks later, Dunmore fled from Williamsburg, and took refuge on board the Fowey man-of-war. The royal government of Virginia had ceased to exist.

Long before this, however, in all the Anglo-American provinces, committees of safety had been organized, local conventions held, and a general Congress, composed of deputies from all the colonies, had been in session at Philadelphia. The new Congress, which met on the 10th of May, promptly sustained the previous action of Massachusetts, by providing for the organization of an army, and the defence of the United Colonies.

On the 17th of June, only two days after the unanimous election of George Washington as commander-in-chief of the American forces, was fought the battle of Bunker Hill.

But though Congress recognised the existence of war, the provinces generally were not yet prepared for a declaration of independence. North Carolina, alone, by her Mecklenburg manifesto, evinced a readiness to throw off all allegiance to Great Britain. Already the freemen of that province had twice elected delegates to a local convention in opposition to the protests of Governor Martin. By a happy unanimity on the part of the electors, those whom they had chosen as members of the convention, were also elected members of the regular provincial legislature, met at the same time and place, and vesting the offices of president of the assembly and moderator of the convention in the same person, combined the functions of legislators recognised by the crown, with the duties of delegates expressly chosen to uphold the cause of the people.

The Watauga purchase had been declared illegal by Governor Martin, but the inhabitants paid no heed to his proclamation. His more strenuous efforts to prevent all action, on the part of the provincial convention, was equally unsuccessful. After the battle of Lexington, and the passage of the Mecklenburg resolutions, the popular effervescence increased to such a degree that Martin began to tremble for his personal safety. The valour displayed by the continentals at the battle of Bunker Hill, increased the influence of the patriotic party in North Carolina, and rendered the position of the royal governor still more precarious. Taking council of his fears, he followed the example of Dunmore, and sought the protection of an English armed vessel, at that time anchored in the Cape Fear River. On the 20th of August, the provincial legislature met at Halifax, and adopted an independent form of government. At the coming session, which took place on the 4th of April, 1776, this patriotic body anticipated the action of the Federal Congress by instructing its delegates to concur with the other colonial delegates in a formal declaration of independence. Laws were also passed constraining loyalists to take an oath of allegiance to the new government, providing for an issue of treasury bills, and for the military organization of the state.

Up to this period the inhabitants of the Watauga settlement, had been living peacefully under the regulations they had voluntarily imposed upon themselves. But though they had disregarded the proclamation of Governor Martin, making void the purchase of their lands, they were not insensible of the difficulties to which they were exposed by their isolated condition, nor regardless of the odium which attached to them, when, as population increased, large numbers of lawless men took refuge among them, to evade the demands of their creditors, or to shelter themselves from criminal prosecutions. Finding their simple code of laws too weak to control these restless desperados, and earnestly desirous of aiding the provinces in the war of independence, they solicited permission to place themselves under the jurisdiction of North Carolina, to which state they petitioned to be annexed under the title of "Washington District." Their prayer was granted, and John Carter, John Haile, and John Sevier were elected delegates to the provincial legislature which met at Halifax on the 12th of November, 1776.

The annexation of the community on the Watauga to the province of North Carolina was productive of the most beneficial results. Outcasts from society were now rendered amenable to the laws. Committees of safety were organized, and Tory refugees and suspected loyalists compelled to swear fealty to the American cause. Companies of volunteers were organized, and every preparation was made for taking part in the revolutionary struggle, as well as to protect the inhabitants from the effects of Indian hostilities.

The measures for local defence were dictated by a wise forecast. It was well known that Cameron, the Indian agent, had been tampering with the Cherokees; some disturbances had already taken place, and information, derived from authentic sources, put them in possession of the fact that Henry Stuart, the deputy Indian agent under Cameron, was instigating the Tories to assemble in arms in the Cherokee nation; and that the latter tribe, in conjunction with the Shawanes, Mingoes, and Delawares, were preparing for a general attack upon the inhabitants of the frontiers.

These alarming tidings roused even those who had hitherto been lukewarm to attach themselves to the common cause. Everywhere the border population deserting their homestead, came flocking into the forts, and picketed stations, bringing with them their wives and children, and their portable effects. Rumours of the intended invasion hourly increased, and the people actively exerted themselves to meet it. The forts were strengthened, arms and ammunition collected, and messengers despatched to various quarters for such assistance as could be afforded. Five companies of Virginians receiving intelligence that seven hundred Cherokee warriors were marching, in two divisions, upon the Holston and the Watauga, hastened to Eaton's station on the south fork of the Holston, for the purpose of protecting that advanced post. They had scarcely reached it, before their reconnoitering parties reported the approach of the enemy. Reinforcements arriving soon after, it was concluded to leave a small garrison in charge of the fort, while the remainder of the armed detachments, to the number of one hundred and seventy men, should march out in search of the enemy. In the vicinity of the Long Island the scouts encountered and defeated a small party of warriors; but as pursuit was difficult, by reason of the rugged character of the ground, it was deemed most prudent to return to the fort. During this retrograde movement, their rear was fired on by the enemy in numbers equal to their own. But the men, though taken by surprise, sustained the shock with great courage, baffled the attempt of the Indians to outflank them, and finally, after a severe contest, which was for the most part hand to hand, succeeded in routing them with considerable slaughter. Another war party of the Cherokees, marching by the Nolachucky trace, drove in the garrison at Gillespie's station, and made a sudden assault upon the fort of Watauga. Of this station James Robertson was commandant. His effective force did not exceed forty men, but it proved sufficient to beat back the enemy, who, after suffering a signal repulse, and losing a considerable number of warriors, contented themselves with investing the fort until the siege was raised by a reinforcement of cavalry under the gallant Colonel Shelby.

It was while assisting in the defence of Watauga Fort, as second in command to Robertson, that an incident occurred which gave to Lieutenant John Sevier a romantic introduction to his future wife. In the midst of the alarm produced by the approach of the Cherokees, Sevier "discovered a young lady, of tall and erect stature, coming with the fleetness of the roe toward the fort, closely pursued by Indians, and her approach to the gate cut off by the enemy, who doubtless were confident of a captive, or a victim; but turning suddenly, she eluded her pursuers, and leaping the palisades at an unexpected point, fell into the arms of Sevier. Catherine Sherrill, the dashing heroine of this remarkable feat, whose beauty, activity, and natural gracefulness were for many years the theme of border praise, became, in 1779, the happy consort of "the portly young stranger from Williamsburg," and, through a long and eventful life, shared with him his varying fortunes, proving herself under all circumstances his wisest counsellor and dearest friend.

Notwithstanding the defeat at Long Island, and the repulse before Fort Watauga, other detached parties of warriors were successful in penetrating the frontiers of Virginia, and carrying desolation and dismay to many an isolated household.

The appearance off Charleston of the British squadron under Sir Peter Parker, diverted for a season the arms of the Cherokees from the Watauga settlement, and precipitated them, as if by previous concert, upon the frontiers of South Carolina. Moultrie's admirable defence of Sullivan's Island frustrated the designs of the British commander; and with the repulse of the fleet, the sanguinary activity of the savage warriors slackened also.

Now it was that the four southern provinces, being freed from the alarm of immediate invasion by sea, determined to break the power of the Cherokee nation, by sending separate expeditions to make a simultaneous attack upon the lower, middle, and upper towns. Those who resided on the Tugaloo, were defeated by the Georgian troops. The militia of South Carolina, under General Williamson, after dispersing a mixed force of Indians and Tories at Oconoree, laid all the towns of the middle Cherokees in ruins, destroyed their growing crops, together with the contents of their granaries, and, subsequently, defeated a second body of Cherokee warriors with considerable loss.

While Williamson was devastating one portion of the middle settlement, General Rutherford, marching from North Carolina with an army increased by accessions to two thousand men, crossed the Blue ridge at the Swannanæ Gap, and falling upon the towns on the Tennessee and Hiwassee Rivers, destroyed them without opposition.

Virginia undertook to chastise the mountain Cherokees, those brave and haughty warriors inhabiting the overhill towns, who, by their remoteness and the difficulties of the route, had escaped unharmed the earlier expeditions of Grant and Montgomery. Authority having been given to Colonel William Christian to organize an army at the expense of the state, he speedily found himself at the head of a large number of frontier men, who had moved by companies and detachments to the rendezvous on the Great Island of Holston. Here also Christian was joined by a reinforcement of several hundred men from North Carolina. Volunteers from the Watauga joined him a few days later; and with this army, amounting in the aggregate to eighteen hundred men, he took up the line of march for the overhill towns, two hundred miles distant. At the crossing-place of the French Broad, the Indians were reported to have stationed themselves, to the number of three thousand warriors, with the avowed resolution of disputing the passage. Deceiving the Indians by a stratagem, Christian threw a strong detachment over the river under cover of the night; and having thus secured a landing-place on the opposite shore, crossed securely over the next morning with his main body. One thousand Cherokee warriors, who had previously assembled at the Big Island of French Broad, seized with a panic at the resolute advance of Christian, abandoned all thought of resistance, and hastened back to their towns to provide places of security for their families in the recesses of the mountains. Along the route, thus unexpectedly opened to him, Christian moved with as much rapidity as consisted with prudence, until he reached the Tennessee River, where he expected the inhabitants of the towns on the opposite bank would make an obstinate stand. To his great surprise he found those habitations also deserted. The Great Island town, in the midst of its fertile meadows, was soon in possession of the invaders; and here it was, surrounded by abundance of provisions, that Christian established his head-quarters. The detachments sent out from this point laid waste all the villages inhabited by the hostile warriors, who, under old Abram of Chilhowee, the Raven, and the Dragging-Canoe, had threatened previously the Holston and Watauga settlements, and wreaked their vengeance on the borders of Virginia. The towns inhabited by such Cherokees as had remained neutral were wisely spared. After having thus effectually humbled the pride of the mountain warriors, Christian offered to entertain negotiations for a peace. The proposal was eagerly accepted, and an agreement was soon after drawn up, by which the Cherokees bound themselves to send delegates from all the tribes to meet in council at Long Island the following May, for the purpose of formally ratifying a treaty. Having thus satisfactorily accomplished the object of the expedition, Christian returned to Long Island, where he disbanded a portion of his army, retaining only a sufficient number through the winter to construct and garrison Fort Patrick Henry. Thus closed the most important expedition that had ever penetrated into the Cherokee country of East Tennessee. The success which had attended it increased largely the flood of emigration to the waters of the Holston, and the

Watauga, and though a few of the hostile chiefs declared their determination to continue the war, their threats produced no further effects than to render the settlers more watchful and prepared.

CHAPTER IX.

Washington county established—Liberality of the North Carolina legislature—Special enactment in favour of the Watauga settlers—Increase of emigration—Military service—Assistance sent to Kentucky—Relief of Logan's Fort—Militia disbanded in Tennessee—Lawlessness of the Tories and Refugees—Committee of safety organized—Summary punishment of obnoxious persons—Hostility of the Chickamaugas—The Nick-a-jack towns—Description of the Nick-a-jack cave—Expedition against the Chickamaugas—Destruction of their towns—Jonesborough founded—Sullivan county established—Exploration of the Lower Cumberland—Robertson's settlement on the Bluff at Nashville—Donaldson's remarkable voyage—Joins Robertson at the Bluff.

In November, 1776, the legislature of North Carolina changed the name of Washington district into that of Washington county, and assigned for its bounds the limits of the present State of Tennessee. At the same session a law was passed, establishing a land office in the new county, the price of lands being fixed at forty shillings the hundred acres. Each head of a family was allowed to take up six hundred and forty acres for himself, one hundred acres for his wife, and the same quantity for each of his children. By a special enactment in favour of the Watauga settlers, payment for the lands they occupied was not to be exacted until after the 1st of January, 1779. Great numbers of hardy and energetic men hastened with their families to take advantage of this liberality. Many of whom, by enrolling themselves as militia in the service of the State, were enabled during the year to pay for the lands they had taken up, while, at the same time, they afforded protection to the industrial population from roving bands of hostile Cherokees. But the inhabitants of Tennessee did not confine themselves merely to the defence of their own territory. They no sooner learned that Kentucky was suffering an Indian invasion, and that Boonesborough, Harrodsburg, and Logan's Station were invested by large parties of warriors, than forty-five riflemen from the Holston hastened to reinforce the beleaguered garrisons. These proving insufficient, one hundred additional riflemen, bearing with them supplies of provisions, promptly responded to the personal appeal of Captain Logan, and after a march of two hundred miles through the wilderness, entered the fort, the siege of which the enemy hastily abandoned at their approach.

But while the pioneers of Tennessee were generously aiding to promote the security of the scattered population of Kentucky, they grew careless with regard to their own. Believing that the storm of war had rolled to the northward, and that they were now sufficiently strong to dispense with the services of the militia, the greater part of the latter were disbanded in 1778. This measure was soon found to have been an impolitic one; for, although there was but little danger to be apprehended from the Indians, bands of Tories and desperate men had settled on the frontiers, whose numbers enabled them to defy the laws and to pursue their career of rapine and bloodshed with insolent impunity. The power of the judiciary being found inadequate to curb this ruffianly domination, the older settlers determined to take the affair into their own hands. A committee of safety was appointed, with unlimited authority to execute summary justice upon all offenders. Under the direction of this committee, sixty mounted riflemen, divided into two companies, were speedily organized for the purpose of patrolling the whole of the country. These rangers were empowered to " capture and punish with death all suspected persons who refused submission, or failed to give good security for their appearance before the committee. Slighter offences were atoned for by the infliction of corporeal punishment; to which was superadded, in cases where the offender was able to pay it, a heavy fine in money. Leaders in crime expiated their guilt by their lives. Several of these were shot; some of them at their execution disclosed the names and hiding-places of their accomplices. These were in their turn pursued, arrested, and punished; and the country was, in less than two months, restored to a condition of safety." Among the members of Captain Bean's company were Lane, Sevier, and Robertson, men foremost in settling the wilds of Tennessee, and always ready, at the hazard of their own lives, to promote the welfare of its industrious population. This exercise of despotic power can only be justified by the plea of necessity. Self-protection is the first law of man's nature. When those regulations in which he has acquiesced fail to provide for the security of his person and property, he has a right to resume the functions he had transferred into the hands of others, and to adopt such other measures as may be required for his own security and the general welfare of the community in which he resides. In the brief period during which the administration of justice was entrusted by the popular voice to the committee of safety, some obnoxious persons may possibly have been hardly dealt with; but if such cases did occur they were few in number, while the evil thus inflicted was greatly overbalanced by the benefit which accrued to the whole settlement from the prompt and energetic action of those who had been active in the restoration of law and order.

It will be remembered that a few of the Cherokees refused to treat with Colonel Christian or to send delegates to the council at Long Island. They were principally Chickamaugas, a tribe which originally "occupied the borders of Chickamauga creek, but afterward extended their villages fifty miles below, on both sides of the Tennessee." Establishing themselves in what were subsequently known as the Nick-a-jack towns, they carried on so successful a predatory warfare upon parties of emigrants descending the dangerous rapids of the Tennessee River, that their numbers were rapidly increased by roving bands of Indians from other tribes, and by the addition of lawless white men, who had fled from the provinces to evade the penalty of their manifold crimes.

This community of desperadoes were able to send out, on their various incursions against the frontier settlements, one thousand armed men, whose favourite place of resort, either in times of danger, for the storing of their plunder, or for more sanguinary purposes, was the Nick-a-jack Cave, an immense subterranean formation which, piercing the end of the Cumberland Mountain, has its principal entrance upon the Tennessee River. "At its mouth it is about thirty yards wide, arched overhead with pure granite, this being in the centre about fifteen feet high. A beautiful little river, clear as crystal, issues from its mouth. The distance the cave extends into the mountains has not been ascertained. It has been explored only four or five miles. At the mouth the river is wide and shallow, but narrower than the cave. As you proceed from thence up the stream, the cave becomes gradually narrower, until it is contracted to the exact width of the river. It is beyond this point explored only by water in a small canoe."

The excesses of these hostile Indians and their confederates keeping the border population of Virginia and North Carolina in a condition of continual uneasiness, the forces of the two provinces were combined for an effective descent upon the Chickamaugas and the destruction of their towns.

The command of this expedition, which comprised one thousand volunteers and a regiment of twelvemonths' men, was given to Colonel Evan Shelby. From the rendezvous at the mouth of Big Creek in Hawkins county, the troops embarked in piraguas and canoes, on the 10th of April, 1779, and descending the Holston, fell suddenly upon the enemy, who, taken completely by surprise, offered no resistance, but instantly took refuge in their mountain fastnesses. After killing, during the pursuit, some forty warriors, the troops returned and burned the towns, destroyed the granaries and stores of provisions, and made prizes of large herds of cattle, which, by an overland march, they brought in safety to the settlement. This expedition humbled the spirit of the Chickamaugas and their allies for a season, and effectually prevented them from forming a coalition with the north-western tribes which Hamilton, the British commandant at Detroit, had strenuously exerted himself to promote. For the important service rendered by the Shelbys on this occasion, Colonel Evan Shelby was raised to the command of the Virginia militia, with the rank of general, while in 1779 his son Isaac was appointed, by Governor Caswell of North Carolina, colonel-commandant of Washington county. The acts of the legislature during this year embraced the appointment of commissioners to run the boundary between Virginia and North Carolina, the erection of the new town of Jonesborough into the seat of justice for Washington county, and the establishment of a new county out of part of Washington, which was named Sullivan, in honour of the revolutionary general of that name.

In the mean time parties of enterprising men were exploring the Lower Cumberland; but with the exception of a few families who resided in a picketed station at Bledsoe's Lick on the Sulphur fork of the Red River, and a French trading post lately established on the Bluff at

Nashville, no settlers had as yet ventured to occupy any portion of middle Tennessee. At length, in the spring of 1775, a small party under James Robertson left Watauga for the purpose of testing the fertility of the lands on the Cumberland River, preparatory to the removal of their families. Their report proving favourable, other emigrants, to the number of three hundred, accompanied them in the fall of the same year to the French lick, the principal part of whom crossed over to the south bank of the Cumberland and commenced the erection of blockhouses on the Bluff, now occupied by the city of Nashville. The situation of these adventurers, in the midst of a wilderness, surrounded by swarthy foes, and at a distance of three hundred miles from their friends upon the Holston, called for constant vigilance and an ever ready system of defence. To add to the discomforts of their condition, the first winter they passed upon the Cumberland was one of extraordinary severity. Their cattle died; their provisions became exhausted; game was scarce, and while the river remained frozen, it was impossible to obtain supplies from the older settlements. Toward the close of April the colony at the Bluffs was largely increased by the arrival of a flotilla of emigrants under Colonel Donaldson. These intrepid voyagers descended the Holston from Fort Patrick Henry, and entering the Tennessee River, committed themselves to its current. The danger to their frail and heavily laden barks from the rapids and whirlpools which impede the navigation of this river, was nothing in comparison to the perils by which they were beset from sanguinary bands of the Chickamaugas, who, travelling by both banks of the river, fired into the boats whenever an opportunity offered, and were successful in killing one company of thirty persons, besides wounding a number of others. The voyage was, however, resolutely continued to the Ohio, where most of the boats took a southerly direction. Donaldson's company, however, ascended the river, and entering the mouth of the Cumberland reached Robertson's settlement at the French lick on the 24th of April, 1780, after a weary and most eventful voyage of four months.

CHAPTER X.

War of independence—Evacuation of Boston—Declaration of independence—Battle of Long Island—Of White Plains—Washington retreats across the Jerseys—Battle of Trenton—Battle of Princeton—Howe advances on Philadelphia—Battle of Brandywine—Of Germantown—Burgoyne's invasion—His defeat at Saratoga—Conquest of Georgia—Subjugation of South Carolina—Defeat of Gates at Camden—Activity of the mountaineers—Shelby and Sevier join McDowell—Capture of a Tory garrison on Pacolet River—Advance of the British and Tories under Ferguson—Battle of Musgrove Mill—Rapid retreat of the mountaineers.

For the most perfect understanding of the important services which were rendered by the riflemen of Tennessee, during the War of Independence, it will be necessary to trace briefly the progress of events in the united colonies from the outbreak of the war to the defeat of Gates in South Carolina. In March, 1776, General Washington succeeded in forcing Lord Howe to evacuate Boston; and during the following June, it will be remembered that the British fleet signally failed in an attack upon Charleston, through the admirable defence of Moultrie. On the 4th of July, Congress adopted the Declaration of Independence. At this period, the continental army under Washington was encamped in and around New York, which was closely invested by the military and naval forces of Great Britain. The defeat of the American troops on Long Island toward the close of August, compelled Washington to evacuate New York and retreat to White Plains, where, on the 28th of September, a battle was fought, which induced Washington to break up his camp at White Plains, and cross the Hudson into New Jersey. Fort Washington being captured soon after by the British, and Fort Lee abandoned by the Americans, the advance of the enemy compelled Washington, who, with his army diminished to three thousand men had moved southward to Newark, to retreat through the Jerseys. In the midst of the almost universal gloom and despondency he passed over into Pennsylvania, and went into winter-quarters on the right bank of the Delaware. Reinforced by some militia, and the regulars under Lee, Washington recrossed the Delaware on the night of the 25th of December, captured at Trenton a thousand Hessians under Rahl, and after eluding the superior forces of the enemy, which were soon in motion, fell suddenly upon the British rear-guard at Princeton, routed two regiments, captured nearly the whole of a third, and obliged Cornwallis to fall back upon New Brunswick. Through the remainder of the winter the American army was encamped at Morristown.

During the summer of 1777, General Howe,

sailing up the Chesapeake with sixteen thousand men, marched from the head of Elk toward Philadelphia, the capture of which had been made the principal object of the campaign. Washington hastened to oppose him; but losing the battle of Brandywine on the 11th of September, was obliged to retire before the victorious columns of Howe, which took possession of Philadelphia without any further molestation. On the 11th of September, Washington made a serious attack upon the British advanced post at Germantown, in which the Americans again suffered a severe repulse. In the mean time, however, General Burgoyne, descending from Canada upon New York, had gradually involved his army in a network of difficulties from which there was no escape. The defeat of Baum at Bennington by the militia of Vermont under Stark, was followed by the battles at Saratoga, and the surrender to General Gates of the entire army of Burgoyne. The following year France formed an alliance offensive and defensive with the united colonies of North America, and General Howe thought it prudent to evacuate Philadelphia and retreat to New York. The British commander now turned his attention to the southern provinces, and succeeded with but little difficulty in making a complete conquest of Georgia. In 1779, General Lincoln, assisted by a French squadron under Count D'Estaing, made a bold but ineffectual attempt to recapture Savannah, and drive the British from the province. At the north, the capture of Stony Point by Wayne was hailed as a brilliant and daring achievement, though productive of no more than a temporary triumph, as it soon after fell again into the hands of the enemy.

In 1780, Sir Henry Clinton, who had succeeded Howe as commander-in-chief, set sail from New York, and investing Charleston, which was defended by the southern army under General Lincoln, succeeded in forcing the latter to capitulate. The garrison numbering five thousand men became prisoners of war.

Leaving Cornwallis to complete the reduction of the province, Clinton returned to New York. Undismayed by the loss of Charleston, and the capture of the southern army, a new force was speedily organized under the direction of Congress, the command of which was given to General Gates. Less fortunate than when opposed to Burgoyne, Gates suffered a severe defeat at Camden on the 16th of August, by which the whole of his army was broken up and dispersed.

So complete at this period did the subjugation of South Carolina and Georgia appear to be, and so little resistance did Cornwallis anticipate in North Carolina, that he projected a junction, at an early day, with the British forces already ravaging Virginia under Phillips and Arnold, while some of the more ardent loyalists calculated upon the reduction of all the States south of the Hudson before the close of the campaign.

But the activity of the mountaineers of Virginia and North Carolina was destined to turn the scale of victory, and to afford time for a general arming of the Whigs. On the approach of the British to Charleston, General Rutherford of North Carolina summoned the militia of the state to arm in defence of the common cause. The requisition was promptly met by John Sevier, as lieutenant-colonel of Washington county, and by Isaac Shelby in the adjoining county of Sullivan. In the absence of Rutherford, who had hastened with the main body of the militia to join the forces at this time collecting under Gates, the command in North Carolina devolved upon Colonel McDowell, who directed Sevier and Shelby to meet him with all the mounted riflemen they could collect at his camp in South Carolina, near the Cherokee ford of Broad River. These orders were promptly responded to. Five hundred mounted men from the Holston and the Watauga, led by Sevier and Shelby, crossed the Alleghanies, and presently made their appearance in the camp of McDowell. To this rendezvous also repaired Colonel Clark, a daring refugee officer from Georgia.

At this period the British troops occupied all the important posts in Georgia and South Carolina. The steady and uninterrupted advance of Cornwallis inspirited the Tories on the borders of North and South Carolina to place themselves under the command of Colonel Patrick Moore of Tryon county, who, with a detachment of ninety-three men, proceeded to Pacolet River, and took possession of a strong fort which had been built there during the Cherokee war.

As this post was but little more than twenty miles distant from the camp of McDowell, the latter despatched Shelby, Sevier, and Clarke, with six hundred men, to attempt its surprise. The enterprise was completely successful. Summoned by Shelby to surrender, Moore at first resolutely refused; but when he saw the mountaineers preparing to carry the post by storm, he consented to capitulate "on condition that the garrison be paroled not to serve again during the war." By this bloodless exploit the victors obtained two hundred and fifty stand of arms, and a small but welcome supply of ammunition.

The effect of this bold and decisive movement not only led the Tory inhabitants of the Carolinas to repress their exultation, but to reflect more seriously upon the risks to which they exposed themselves by joining the British standard. The forces under General Gates were also at this period rapidly increasing in numbers. While Cornwallis was marching to Camden to reinforce Rawdon against the approach of the American army, he directed Colonel Ferguson, a brave, popular, and energetic officer, to proceed with a detachment of regulars to Ninety-Six, and summon to his assistance the loyalists of the adjoining provinces. Being presently joined by two thousand disaffected Americans, exclusive of a small troop of horse, Ferguson made several ineffectual attempts to surprise McDowell in his camp. Shifting his rendezvous frequently, and keeping Shelby and Clarke with six hundred mounted men on the constant watch for detached parties of the enemy, McDowell was not only enabled to baffle the designs of Ferguson, but frequently to cut off his foragers. A skirmish of this kind occurred on the 1st of August, when Ferguson's advance, seven hundred strong, encountered the mounted men under Shelby and Clarke, who, though forced from the field of battle by the approach of the main body under Ferguson, succeeded in carrying off with them as prisoners, two officers, and fifty rank and file.

While lying at Smith's ford of the Broad River, McDowell learned that a body of Tories were collected at Musgrove's Mill, on the south side of the Enorée, and distant from his camp about forty miles. Although Ferguson with his whole force lay midway between, Shelby, Clarke, and Williamson of South Carolina, whose respective commands amounted in the aggregate to six hundred mounted men, determined by a rapid night march to evade the vigilance of Ferguson's patrols, and fall suddenly upon the Tory camp beyond. Taking a circuitous route through the forest, during the night of the 18th of August, they reached the vicinity of the enemy before dawn the following morning, drove in the outposts, and were preparing for a general assault when they were informed by a countryman that the Tories had been reinforced the previous evening by six hundred regulars commanded by Colonel Innes. To retreat with horses already fatigued from hard riding would have laid the mountaineers open to a successful attack from a vigorous and superior foe, while to advance was equally dangerous. In this emergency it was decided to throw up a rude breastwork of logs and brush on the edge of a thick wood, facing a narrow lane, and in this position await the approach of Innes. Captain Inman was thrown forward with twenty-five men to skirmish with the enemy at the crossing at the Enorée. In obedience to previous orders, he kept up, for a short time, a sharp fire, and then retreated. Supposing that the whole force of the Americans had been routed, the British and Tories followed in pursuit, until they came within range of the American rifles, when a deadly and destructive fire opened upon them, which was kept up for more than an hour. The dragoons and mounted militia, after being repulsed in an attempt to force the American lines, fell back in disorder upon the regulars, who, being confined within the limits of the narrow lane where they had not room enough to form, were borne back in confusion. While they were thus huddled together, the rifles of the mountaineers proved terribly destructive. Sixty-three of the enemy, including all the officers with the exception of a single subaltern, were either killed or wounded. Hawzey the Tory leader was among the former. Innes himself being also disabled, his troops became disheartened, and at length giving way on all sides, sought safety in flight. The gallant Inman pursued them to the crossing of the Enorée, where he fell mortally wounded in a hand-to-hand conflict. The loss of the British, in killed, wounded, and prisoners, was two hundred and twenty-three. The American loss was four killed and nine wounded. Flushed with their recent success, Shelby and his associate partisans resolved to proceed at once against the British post at Ninety-Six; but in the midst of their preparations a messenger, despatched by McDowell, placed in the hands of Shelby a letter from Governor Caswell, containing a brief account of the defeat of Gates at Camden, and advising the confederated officers to disband their respective corps until a better opportunity should offer for successful resistance. An immediate retreat across the mountains now became necessary.

Mounting his prisoners behind his men, one to every three, and shifting them alternately, Shelby set out on his return, marching all night, and all the next day, without waiting for refreshments. This saved the troops and secured the prisoners, for the next day Ferguson sent out a strong detachment in pursuit; but baffled by the superior activity of the mountaineers, Dupoister, the officer in command, after a chase which was continued until the evening of the second day, returned to the British camp.

CHAPTER XI.

Mountaineers disbanded—Advance of Ferguson—His message to Shelby—The mountaineers called to arms—Assemble at Watauga—Advance against Ferguson—The latter retires from Gilbert town—American reinforcement—Conference of the partisan leaders at the Cowpens—Pursuit of Ferguson—Campbell selected to command the mountaineers—Approach to King's Mountain—Order of battle—Sevier comes under fire of the enemy—The attack commenced—Courageous conduct of Ferguson—Effect of his bayonet charges—Resolute perseverance of the mountaineers—Flag of surrender twice torn down by Ferguson—His defiant conduct—His death—Surrender of the British and Tories—Tarleton sent to relieve Ferguson—His recall—Retreat of Cornwallis—His subsequent movements—Battle of Guilford Court House—Capitulation at Yorktown.

AFTER the brilliant exploit at Musgrove's Mill, the mountaineers were disbanded and retired to their respective homes. The prisoners captured by Shelby were sent for safe keeping into Virginia, in charge of Colonels Clarke and Williams. The success of Cornwallis at Camden, and the subsequent disaster of Sumpter, had so thoroughly paralyzed all effort on the part of the Whigs, that, for a short period, the hope of recovering Georgia or the Carolinas from British domination seemed utterly futile. Gates was indeed striving to reorganize the scattered remnant of his army; but in this desperate condition of affairs it was with great difficulty that the militia could be persuaded to report themselves for service.

At this period the main army under Cornwallis lay at Charlotte, North Carolina. Ferguson, with two thousand regulars and loyalists was at Gilbert Town, in Rutherford county. The position of the latter was such as enabled him to overawe the surrounding Whigs, while keeping a sharp watch upon the movements of the mountaineers. Exasperated by the capture of Pacolet fort, and the defeat of Innes at Musgrove's Mill, he had drawn his forces nearer to the mountains; and, on the return of the detachment sent out to recapture the prisoners taken in the last-named battle, he despatched a messenger to Washington and Sullivan counties, threatening, "that if the officers west of the mountains did not cease their opposition to the British arms, he would march his army over, burn and lay waste their country, and hang their leaders."

Shelby received this insolent missive toward the close of August, and immediately rode from fifty to sixty miles to concert with Sevier a new plan of action. After an earnest conference, it was resolved to call in the assistance of Colonels Campbell and McDowell, and with the forces thus hastily raised in North Carolina and Virginia, to make a rapid march across the mountains and surprise Ferguson in his camp. On the 25th of September, one thousand and forty men, in obedience to the summons of their respective commanders, assembled at Watauga. The following morning they commenced their march. On the 30th of September, after traversing the difficult defiles of the mountains, they were joined by Colonel Cleaveland and other refugee officers, with three hundred and fifty volunteers from Wilkes and Surry counties.

Fully advised of the danger by which he was threatened, Ferguson broke up his camp at Gilbert Town, and despatched a messenger to Cornwallis, soliciting aid. Calling at the same time upon the loyalists for reinforcements, he fell back on the 4th of October to the Cowpens. The following day he crossed Broad River to Tate's Ferry, recrossed the river at that point, and encamped about a mile above. On the 6th, he marched by way of the Ridge Road to King's

Creek. Passing the gap, he ascended King's Mountain and encamped upon its summit. Using an impious expression, he is said to have declared that here was a place from which he could not be driven. After being reinforced by the volunteers under Cleaveland, the mountaineers moved with great expedition to Gilbert Town, from whence Ferguson had already retreated. Here a council of officers was held, at which it was decided that the mounted men should hasten in pursuit, leaving the foot and weaker cavalry under the command of Major Hendon to follow after. In accordance with this arrangement, between five and six hundred picked men, mounted on the best horses, left Gilbert Town on the morning of the 6th of October. Fortunately for this advance party, they were reinforced on the way by additional volunteers from North Carolina, and by some South Carolina troops under Colonel Williams. At the Cowpens they halted for a short time to refresh; but learning that a large body of Tories was collecting at Major Gibbs's, with the intention of forming a junction with Ferguson the following day, they broke up their meal, and hurried off to bring Ferguson to an engagement before his reinforcements should arrive.

Learning that he was encamped near the Cherokee ford of the Broad River, thirty miles distant from the Cowpens, they pressed forward all night, in the midst of a heavy rain, and crossing Broad River early the next morning encountered, soon after, two men fresh from Ferguson's camp. The information obtained from these men revived the drooping spirits of the detachment. Notwithstanding their fatigue and exhaustion from muddy roads, hunger, cold, and wet, the officers, after holding a brief consultation on horseback, determined to form their men in four columns, and proceed at once to the attack. The right wing, commanded by Colonels Winston and Sevier, was composed of the troops brought into the field by those officers and of the battalion of McDowell. Colonels Campbell and Shelby's regiments formed the centre, while the left was made up of Cleaveland's regiment, and the volunteers under Colonels Williams, Lacy, Hawthorne, and Hill, led by Cleaveland in person. By courtesy the command of the whole was given to Colonel Campbell of Virginia. Keeping the locks of their rifles dry by covering them with bags, blankets, and hunting-shirts, they took up the line of march until they approached the base of King's Mountain, when "the two centre columns deployed to the right and left, pushed forward to attack the enemy in front, while the right and left wings were marching to surround him."

Leaving their horses in charge of a few guards, the respective columns, led by men already familiar with the ground, proceeded with alacrity to take up the several positions assigned them. The right column was the first to come under the fire of the enemy. The action immediately commenced. Shelby, with a part of his men, dashed up the ravine in the direction of Ferguson's camp, while the remainder of the column ascended by a circuitous route to the summit of the mountain. The heaviness of the firing, and its destructive effects, obliged Ferguson to send Dupoïster with a part of the regulars to the other end of his line, for the purpose of making a charge upon the American right. Thus reinforced by the regulars and the tories, they succeeded in driving the right column of the Americans to the foot of the mountain. But at this moment the left column under Cleaveland reached the opposite extremity of the encampment, and opened so destructive a fire upon the British troops in that quarter, that Ferguson was compelled to recall his regulars from their successful charge, and the Americans who had retreated before them returned with increased ardour to the attack.

On their way back to repel the assault of the left column of the assailants, the regulars suffered severely from the fire of the riflemen led by Williams. Their disorder was however speedily remedied, and by a dashing charge they drove the Americans on this side also to the foot of the hill. In the meanwhile the mountaineers under Sevier and Winston, having regained their former position, commenced plying their rifles with so much effect that Ferguson ordered a second charge to be made upon them by his regulars. But the latter had already become so much shattered that, although supported by a number of Tories with butcher-knives fitted to the muzzles of their guns, they failed in accomplishing the desired effect.

By this time the central columns of the Americans had reached the plateau, and the British forces being now completely surrounded, were exposed on all sides to an incessant fire from enemies who were themselves protected from injury by intervening trees, and by the rugged slope of the hill. To free himself from this desperate strait, Ferguson resorted to a succession of charges with the bayonet, but as one part of the American line receded another advanced; and when these were assaulted in their turn, those who had previously retreated, relieved from the pressure of the enemy, reascended the mountain and became in their turn the assailants.

Finding that a resort to the bayonet made no more than a temporary impression, and that at the close of each charge the mountaineers succeeded in restricting his efforts to a narrower circle, Ferguson determined upon making an attempt to break the lines of his adversaries with his cavalry. But his men were no sooner seated in their saddles than they were picked off by the unerring rifle, and the design was presently abandoned. Still undaunted, Ferguson rode "from one exposed point to another of equal danger, encouraging his troops to prolong the conflict. He carried in his wounded hand a shrill sounding silver whistle, the signal of which being universally known in the ranks, was of immense service throughout the battle, and gave a kind of ubiquity to his movements." Keeping close under the crest of the hill, the American riflemen, with that accuracy of aim which had already made them famous, maintained the ground they had won with the utmost coolness and daring. At length, alarmed at the manner in which their ranks were ceaselessly swept away on every quarter, some of the Tories raised a white flag as a sign of surrender. It was instantly torn down by Ferguson. "A second flag was hoisted at the other end of the line. He rode there too and cut it down with his sword." Dupoister, the next officer in command, counselled him to surrender, but he indignantly spurned the advice. Cheering those nearest him with voice, mien, and example, and rousing the faltering confidence of those more distant by the shrill notes of his whistle, he succeeded in infusing a portion of his own indomitable spirit into the breasts of all under his command; and the contest was contined with a sort of blind, confused, reckless desperation, until Ferguson fell dead from his horse, pierced by a bullet from the rifle of some unknown mountaineer.

The Americans now advanced upon the plateau, and closed more firmly around the struggling masses of the enemy. Although suffering a considerable loss by this more perfect exposure of their persons, they vigorously followed up their success until Dupoister, losing all hope of extricating his men, raised a flag of surrender and cried out for quarter. Along some portions of the assaulting line the firing was immediately suspended; but as it still continued in other quarters, under the impression that the surrender was not general, Shelby shouted to the enemy to throw down their guns; and this being done, the attack immediately ceased. After the confusion incident to the surrender had subsided, the prisoners were ordered from their arms and marched to another part of the plateau, where they were securely surrounded by a double guard. The loss of the British and Tories in this well-fought battle was two hundred and thirty-five in killed, one hundred and eighty in wounded, and seven hundred made prisoners of war. Fifteen hundred stand of arms, with a large amount of baggage and plunder, fell into the hands of the victors. The loss of the Americans was twenty-eight killed, and sixty wounded. The principal officers who fell on this occasion were Colonel Williams and Major Chronicle. The latter was struck down early in the action, the former in the moment of victory; Like Wolfe, he lived just long enough to express his satisfaction at the signal triumph of his countrymen, and died with a smile upon his lips.

Three days after the battle of King's Mountain, and while yet ignorant of the defeat of Ferguson, Cornwallis ordered a powerful detachment under Tarleton to proceed to his relief. It was ascertained soon afterward that all succour came too late; and as the patriots were everywhere rising in arms, Tarleton was recalled, while Cornwallis himself, dismayed at this sudden and unexpected reverse, broke up his encampment at Charlotte, and hastily retreating to Winnsborough in South Carolina, remained inactive at that place until reinforcements from New York under Leslie enabled him once more to resume offensive operations. A new southern army under Greene was at this time in process of being organized. Early in January, 1781, Cornwallis ordered Tarleton to disperse the division under General Morgan, which held the Tories in check in the western part of South Carolina. The opposing forces met at the Cowpens on the 17th of January, where Tarleton was completely routed with the loss of eight hundred men. Cornwallis with the main army immediately proceeded in pursuit of Greene, who retreated before him to Guilford Court House, where a battle was fought on the 25th of March which resulted unfavourably to the Americans, although their loss was less than that of the British. Greene retreated across the Dan, but presently returned and marched into South Carolina before Cornwallis was aware of his presence. Leaving Rawdon to defend South Carolina against Greene, Cornwallis proceeded to invade Virginia, where he formed a junction with a strong force under Phillips and Arnold. After marching down the James River, closely followed by Lafayette, whose army was too inferior in numbers to admit of his making a battle, Cornwallis crossed over the peninsula to Yorktown, where, under instructions from Sir Henry Clinton, he proceeded to fortify himself. At this place, on the 6th of October, he was besieged by the combined forces of America and France, commanded by Washington, assisted by a naval squadron under the Count De Grasse, and on the 19th of the same month was compelled to surrender his whole force, consisting of seven thousand men, together with their arms, ammunition, and one hundred and sixty pieces of artillery.

CHAPTER XII.

Return of the mountaineers—Indian hostilities—Battle of Boyd's Creek—Expedition into the Cherokee country—Destruction of Indian towns—Greene calls for reinforcements—Response of Shelby and Sevier—They join Marion—Capture two British posts at Monk's Corner—Shelby obtains leave of absence—The mountaineers return home—Prosperity of Tennessee—Death of Unatoolah—Alarm of the settlers—A new station constructed—Pacific overtures made to the Cherokees—Council at Gist—Land-office closed by North Carolina—Re-opened—Arbitrary extension of the western boundary—Greene county established—Explorations—Land-office opened at Hillsborough—Rapid sale of land—Expansion of the settlements west of the mountains.

AFTER the battle of King's Mountain, the riflemen under Sevier and Shelby returned to their respective homes and were disbanded. But Sevier had scarcely crossed the frontiers before he found himself compelled to organize an expedition against the Cherokees, who had already murdered two traders, and were preparing for more extended hostilities. While this force was assembling, Sevier determined to strike a blow at such armed bodies of Cherokees as were known to be advancing; and for this purpose set out to meet them with about one hundred men, "principally belonging to the companies of Captains

Russell and Guess." After encamping on the second night of the march, his advance encountered a considerable body of Indians, with whom a brief skirmish took place. The detachment presently returned to the camp, and Sevier being reinforced during the night by seventy men under Captain Pruett, set out the next morning in pursuit of the enemy, but did not come up with them until early the following morning, when they were discovered in ambush in the vicinity of Boyd's Creek. Drawn under the fire of the main body of the Americans by the feigned retreat of the detachment sent out to reconnoitre, they were speedily thrown into disorder, and lost a considerable number of their warriors before they could effect their escape into the adjoining swamp. In this battle the Indians lost twenty in killed. Of the Americans not a single man was killed, and only three seriously wounded. Among the latter was Major Tipton. When the Cherokees were effectually dispersed, Sevier returned to Big Island until his reinforcements should arrive. In a few days he was at the head of seven hundred men, part of whom consisted of Campbell's regiment of Virginians, and a party of volunteers from Sullivan county under Major Martin. With these troops Sevier again set out in search of the enemy; but the latter fell back as the Americans approached, and suffered them to enter the old beloved town of

Chota without opposition. Chilhowee, deserted by its inhabitants, was presently burned; and, soon after, "every town lying between the Tennessee and Hiwassee Rivers was reduced to ashes, the Indians flying before the troops." The Americans next advanced against Tellico; but, upon meeting proposals for peace, consented to spare that settlement, and proceeded to retaliate upon the Chickamaugas the numerous injuries they had received at their hands. Finding these towns also deserted, they were burned by the troops, "who killed all the cattle and hogs which could be found, and spread over the face of the country a general devastation from which the Indians could not recover for several years. The march was then continued down the Coosa; and when the villages upon its banks, and the country around had been laid waste, the army returned to Chota, where a peace was agreed upon, and the prisoners given up who had previously been taken by the Indians. A desultory warfare, however, was still kept up by some of the middle Cherokees. As these had hitherto escaped punishment, Sevier, in March 1781, collected a small force of volunteers, and by a rapid march to the head waters of the Little Tennessee, fell suddenly upon the town of Tuckasigah, slew fifty warriors, and captured as many women and children. A number of other towns were burned, and their granaries destroyed. An expedition sent to the Clinch River the following month failed in bringing the Indians to an engagement.

Notwithstanding these reverses, parties of Cherokee warriors continued to harass the settlements. With one hundred men Sevier marched against these, surprised one of their camps, killed seventeen men, and effectually dispersed the remainder. He had scarcely disbanded his men before he received a letter from General Greene, calling upon him for a reinforcement of riflemen to assist in cutting off the communication of Cornwallis with South Carolina, in the event of his attempting to retreat southward before the combined American and French forces assembling at Yorktown. A similar message being sent at the same time to Shelby, both these partisan officers presently crossed the mountains at the head of all the troops they could collect. Learning, however, that Greene had already driven Rawdon from his position at Camden, and that the British outposts had been successively driven in, they concluded that their services were no longer necessary, and retraced their steps homeward, after notifying Greene of their intention.

Receiving soon after another requisition from Greene, they again summoned the mountaineers to arms, and in a short time were on their march; Shelby with his regiment from Sullivan, and Sevier with two hundred men from Washington county. After the surrender of Cornwallis, the riflemen, who had enlisted only for sixty days, desired to be dismissed; but were finally induced to join the corps of Marion on the Santee. They reached the camp of that enterprising officer early in November, and were presently ordered, in conjunction with the forces of Colonels Mayhem and Howe, to make an assault upon the British post at Fairlawn, near Monk's Corner, where a garrison of one hundred and fifty Hessians had been stationed. When the commandant was first summoned to surrender, he firmly refused; but becoming alarmed soon after by the personal representations of Shelby, he finally agreed to capitulate. The Americans next advanced against a second post, some six hundred yards distant; a brick house, strongly built, well fortified, and protected in front by an abbatis. A momentary disposition to resist was manifested by its garrison; but their courage failed as the assailants advanced, and they consented to surrender themselves prisoners of war.

Toward the close of November, Shelby, who had been elected a delegate from Sullivan county to the legislature of North Carolina, obtained leave to absent himself from his command for the purpose of attending the session then approaching. Sevier remained with Marion for some time longer; but as the war was in effect closed, though the British did not evacuate Charleston until the middle of December, he finally concluded to return home and disband his men, whose term of service had expired.

From this period until the ratification of peace in 1783, the prosperity of Tennessee was marked by a large increase of emigration. The district of Salisbury was presently divided, and a new district, named after General Morgan, was formed of Washington and Sullivan counties. Some slight disturbances took place with the Indians, in one of which a Cherokee chief named Unatoolah, or Butler, lost his life at the hands of Major Hubbard, a courageous but reckless borderer, the whole of whose manhood had been devoted to revenging upon the Indians the losses he had sustained at their hands.

The American settlements had extended to the French Broad; and during an interval of peace with the Cherokees of the Upper Towns, and of scarcity among the settlers, Colonel Hubbard, accompanied by a fellow-soldier, ventured into the Indian nation in quest of a supply of corn. Already famous in border warfare, it was his fortune in one of the later encounters to unhorse Unatoolah, the chieftain among the Upper Cherokees, who immediately lost caste and command among his followers. Smarting to retrieve this disgrace, Unatoolah no sooner learned that

Hubbard was approaching the town of Citico, than he took with him a single companion and went out to meet his enemy. In a little while the two warriors came within sight of the Americans, advancing on foot and leading their horses by the bridle-rein. Unatoolah, or Butler, as he was called by the whites, immediately rode up and demanded, in an insolent manner, the purpose of their visit. Hubbard responded with great calmness, that the war being over, he had brought into the Indian country some clothing to exchange for corn, and carelessly exhibiting the contents of his sack, invited the Indians to drink of the whiskey, which he produced at the same time. He sought still further to disarm them of their resentment by depositing his rifle against a tree, yet not beyond the reach of his hand. But Butler and his companion received these pacific overtures with increasing sullenness. Both still remained seated in the saddle. After some manœuvering on the part of the Americans, who desired to avoid hostilities lest it should involve the frontiers once more in a general war, Unatoolah endeavoured to thrust himself between Hubbard and his rifle. This design was soon penetrated by the latter, who resolved to defeat it. For this purpose he carelessly suffered his hand to rest on the muzzle of his rifle, but still allowed the butt to remain on the ground, keeping at the same time a watchful eye upon his cunning and vindictive adversary. Frustrated in his original scheme, Unatoolah became excited, and after aiming a blow at Hubbard, which was avoided by the latter, he suddenly levelled his gun and fired. The ball narrowly missed piercing Hubbard to the brain, the hair being cut from his temple. Though stunned for a moment, he presently recovered, and although the retreating Indians were by this time eighty yards distant, a bullet from his rifle brought Unatoolah to the ground, mortally wounded. His companion continued his flight. When the Americans came up with the dying warrior they placed him, at his desire, against a tree, and then inquired of him whether his nation was for peace or war. "They are for war," replied the bleeding chieftain; "and if you go any farther, they will take your scalp." A coarse and abusive dialogue succeeded, during which Unatoolah vented upon Hubbard the most insulting invectives. At last the hot blood of the borderer could bear it no longer, and with one blow from his rifle he dashed out the brains of his antagonist.

Apprehensive that retaliatory measures would be attempted by the mountain Cherokees, the settlers drew closer together, and constructed a station at Henry's, near the mouth of the Dumplin, to which they could retire in case of emergency. Nevertheless, they did not neglect endeavouring to preserve the peace. They sent a message to the upper towns deploring the loss of Unatoolah, and proposed that a council should be held at Gist's, now Henry's, for the adjustment of the difficulty. To this proposition the Cherokees assented; and although the number of those who attended was small, the conference resulted in the preservation of the existing truce.

The great increase of emigrants into the Tennessee territory led to a rapid extension of the frontier settlement, and to renewed jealousies, complaints, and apprehensions on the part of the Cherokees. In a vain endeavour to keep the restless border population within their present bounds, the assembly of North Carolina closed the office for the sale of lands in the summer of 1781, but re-opened it in May, 1783, "for the purpose of paying the arrears then due the officers and soldiers of that part of the continental line which was raised in North Carolina, and of extinguishing the national debt."

About the same time, by an arbitrary enactment, and in direct contempt of the Indian claims to the territory, the western boundary of North Carolina was extended. A portion of their old hunting-grounds were however reserved to the Cherokees, the lines of which were clearly and distinctly defined. During the session the governor was authorized to meet the Cherokees in council, and endeavour to effect a treaty with them. Joseph Martin was also appointed Indian agent. A portion of the county of Washington was detached and formed into a separate county, which received the name of Greene.

Explorations still continued. General James White, accompanied by Colonels Love, Ramsey, and others, " explored the Tennessee country as low as the confluence of the Holston and Tennessee." Some few Indian excesses still continued, but they were not of a character to deter settlers, many of whose lives had been passed in the midst of pressing dangers. An act of the general assembly designated the district within which the bounty land given to the North Carolina soldiers, who had formed a part of the continental line, were to be located; and, on the 21st of October, a land office was opened at Hillsborough for the sale of lands not included in the previous reservations. Within six months large quantities of land was taken up, either by speculators or actual emigrants; and the following year the rude log cabins of adventurous pioneers were to be found scattered along the banks of the Big and Little Pigeon, and on Boyd's Creek south of French Broad.

CHAPTER XIII.

Recognition of American independence—Difficulties of the federal and state governments—Cession of public lands by North Carolina—Alarm of the mountaineers—Convention at Jonesborough—Declaration of Independence—State of Franklin—North Carolina annuls her deed of cession—The mountaineers form a separate jurisdiction—Proclamation of Governor Martin—Its effect in the western counties—Political antagonisms—Increase of the party favourable to North Carolina—Tipton and Sevier—Outrages committed on both sides—Reactionary spirit—Return to the jurisdiction of North Carolina—Execution issued against the property of Sevier—Its seizure—Rash conduct of Sevier—His arrest—Escape—Election to senate of North Carolina.

THE general burst of joy which, in 1783, succeeded the recognition by Great Britain of the independence of the United States had scarcely subsided, before it was followed by a period of gloom and depression which fostered a spirit of anarchy among the malecontents, and threatened finally to end in a dissolution of the confederacy.

The chief source of difficulty was the immense debt which had been contracted to carry on the war, both by the states individually and by the general government. After many plans had been devised, without success, to meet this pressing exigency, Congress was constrained to call upon such states as held vacant lands to cede them to the United States, in order that the money arising from their sale might be applied to the liquidation of the national debt. Among the states thus appealed to was North Carolina. Virginia had already consented to cede the large body of lands held by her; and during the legislative session of 1784 North Carolina followed her example.

But the western pioneers of the latter state, who had won their homesteads by constant vigilance, active warfare, and a condition of suffering unknown to the people of the sea board, were indisposed to see themselves placed once more beyond the pale of the law, and to have to support the whole weight of Indian hostilities during the two years which had been allowed by North Carolina for Congress to accept the terms of the cession.

They accordingly met in convention at Jonesborough, on the 23d of August, 1784, and after choosing John Sevier, president, and Langdon Carter, clerk, adopted a resolution forming themselves into a separate and distinct state, independent of North Carolina. By a subsequent resolution, the government of the new state was vested in commissioners until such time as a constitution was adopted by a second convention, which was appointed to meet at the same place, on the 16th of September. For some cause, however, this convention did not hold its session until November; and in the mean time the legislature of North Carolina becoming alarmed at the sturdy method by which the mountaineers proposed to redress their own grievances, sought to hold them to their allegiance by retracting the cession previously made to the general government, and by providing, in a more efficient manner, for the military and civil government of the western counties. In the convention held at Jonesborough in November, differences of opinion arose among the delegates respecting the policy of separating from North Carolina at that time, which resulted in a disorderly adjournment. The tidings which Joseph Martin brought soon after across the mountains of the recent action of the legislature—the formation of the western counties into a judicial district, the grant of a general court, and the organization of their militia into a separate brigade, of which Sevier was appointed brigadier-general—would, it was at first supposed, arrest the tide of popular disaffection; but when the convention again met on the 14th of December, it was resolved to secede from North Carolina, and a constitution was adopted for the state of Franklin, leaving it to be ratified or rejected by the people, whose delegates were to meet for this purpose at Greenville, on the 14th of November, 1785. This body accordingly met at the time and place appointed; the constitution was ratified. After this the members formally organized themselves into a legislative assembly, by the election of Langdon Carter as speaker of the senate, and William Cage speaker of the House of Commons. John Sevier was chosen governor; David Campbell, judge of the superior court; and Joshua Gist and John Henderson, assistant judges. Various acts were subsequently passed for the purpose of facilitating the operations of the new government; and, before the assembly adjourned, the speakers of both houses were directed to notify Governor Martin, of North Carolina, of the formation of the counties of Washington, Sullivan, and Greene, into a separate sovereignty, styling itself the state of Franklin.

On the reception of this "Declaration of Independence," Governor Martin summoned a meeting of his council; and on the 25th of April issued a proclamation, in which he contended that, as the grievances of the mountaineers had already been redressed, the revolt was a rank usurpation of the authority of North Carolina, and only tended to the injury of the people of Franklin, and the dishonour of the country. He called upon the mountaineers to return to their allegiance; and assured them that any grievance of which they yet complained, if presented by their representatives in a constitutional manner, should be met by the next legislature with a prompt and efficient remedy. If they were still bent on separation, he proposed that it should be on terms honourable to both parties; but if, on the contrary, they were determined to continue in their present course, they might be assured that the spirit of North Carolina was not so damped, or her resources so exhausted, "but that she may take satisfaction for this great injury received, regain her government over the revolted territory, or render it not worth possessing."

This able state paper was not without its effect among those to whom it was especially addressed. It made converts of many who, led away by the enthusiasm for independence, had neither done justice to the efforts which North Carolina had really made to satisfy the complaints of her western counties, nor had seriously contemplated the consequences which were likely to arise from their sanction of an independent government. But although the minority which had always opposed a separation from the present state was considerable strengthened, there yet remained a large portion of the community in favour of maintaining a separate jurisdiction.

To manifest still further the desire of North Carolina for a peaceful termination of the existing difficulties, the legislature, which assembled at Newbern in November, 1785, passed an act to bury in oblivion the conduct of the people of

Franklin, on condition that they returned to their allegiance, and sustained, in the execution of their duty, the officers already appointed by North Carolina. But although the adherents of the latter state, supported by Colonel Tipton, gradually gained ground in the new commonwealth, a majority still clung to Sevier, and refused to recognise any government but the one they themselves had organized.

In this opposition of parties, disorders sprang up which presently degenerated into lawlessness. Both governments claimed jurisdiction, and both sought to exercise it. The consequence was that both became inefficient. Party quarrels ensued; old friends became enemies; Tipton and his followers openly supported the claims of South Carolina; Sevier sought to maintain his authority as the executive officer of Franklin. This antagonistic spirit led to the commission of various outrages. In 1786 a party, headed by Tipton, entered Jonesborough, the capital of Washington county, dispersed the justices of the court at that time in session, and took possession of their papers. Sevier retaliated by ejecting, in a similar manner, an officer appointed by North Carolina. Acts of this character speedily became more frequent, and the followers of Sevier and Tipton more imbittered against each other. The principals themselves met, not long after, at Greensboro, and were presently engaged in a personal conflict, which was brought to a close, without injury to either of the belligerents, by the timely interposition of their respective friends.

But in the midst of these inglorious quarrels, Governor Sevier did not neglect to defend from Indian aggressions the state over which he had been called to preside. Outlying bands of hostile Cherokees had already committed several murders on the Holston, and driven in a number of the settlers who had opened farms in the neighbourhood of Beaver Creek. Collecting a hundred and sixty mounted riflemen, he pushed forward into the heart of the enemy's country, destroyed three of the valley towns and killed fifteen warriors. The assembling of the Cherokees in overwhelming numbers prevented Sevier from following up the advantages he had gained; but the promptness and energy he had already displayed had the desired effect of restoring the extreme frontier to a state of comparative security.

He was far less successful, however, in giving peace to the distracted state of Franklin. The continuance of intestine dissensions, and the nice balance of parties which took place in 1787, induced the people to refuse to pay taxes either to North Carolina, or to the local government, until the supremacy of one or the other should be more generally acknowledged. In this state of affairs, and with his government tottering to its downfall, Sevier earnestly appealed to North Carolina for a ratification of the independence of the state of Franklin, and to Franklin himself, and the governors of Georgia and Virginia, for counsel and assistance. Disappointed on all sides, he finally rested for support upon his immediate friends, conscious of the rectitude of his own intentions, and jutifying the origin of the separation by the cession which North Carolina at first made to the general government.

But the people were already weary of a feud which threatened, at every fresh outbreak, to end in bloodshed. In 1787 the last legislature of the state of Franklin held its session at Greenville. North Carolina had offered terms of compromise, which tended greatly to soften the asperities of those who had hitherto resisted her jurisdiction. The growing desire to restore peace and order in the revolting counties was exhibited in the election of the new delegates, a majority of those chosen being favourable to a reunion with the parent state. Meeting in this frame of mind, they presently authorized the election of representatives to the legislature of North Carolina, an action which was subsequently endorsed by the people, who once more recognised the maternal authority by choosing members to the general assembly as of old. Sevier still held out, but his partisans were gradually deserting him. The conciliatory measures of North Carolina presently disarmed the malecontents of all further argument for opposing the reunion; and in February, 1788, the state of Franklin ceased to exist.

Unhappily, the progress of the late events had not tended to lessen the personal animosity existing between Sevier and Tipton. Both were brave men, and both believed they were actuated only by principles of patriotism and honour. An occurrence took place about this time which brought them into collision. Under an execution issued against the estate of Sevier, the sheriff, acting by the authority of the state of North Carolina, had levied upon his negroes, and conveyed them for safe-keeping to the house of Colonel Tipton. This intelligence reaching Sevier while on the frontiers, he determined, as governor of the state of Franklin, to resist a jurisdiction which he had not yet acknowledged; to retake his negroes by force of arms, and to punish those who, he contended, had acted illegally. He accordingly put himself at the head of one hundred and fifty men, and hastening to the house of Tipton, summoned the latter to surrender. Meeting with a firm refusal, he invested the house within which Tipton had hastily collected a garrison of fifteen men, equally bold and determined as himself. Some shots were exchanged, by which one man was killed, and a man and woman wounded. During the second night of the siege, while the followers of Sevier were gathered round their watch fires, Tipton was reinforced by troops from Sullivan county. Making an unexpected sally upon the camp of Sevier, he succeeded in putting his assailants to a complete route, killing the sheriff of Washington county, and making prisoners of the two sons of Sevier, whom he was only prevented from immediately executing by the earnest entreaties of his friends. In October, Sevier was himself arrested for high treason, and carried, first to Jonesborough, and subsequently to the jail at Morgantown, from whence, by the assistance of his sons, he escaped. Notwithstanding these excesses, the courage, patriotism and generosity of Sevier were warmly recognised. His services were remembered, and his faults forgotten. Being chosen the following year to represent Greene county in the senate of North Carolina, the act disqualifying him from holding office under the state government was repealed; and with the renewal of his oath of allegiance, the whole dispute was amicably closed.

CHAPTER XIV.

Robertson's colony on the Cumberland—Increase in population—Hostility of the Indians—Keywood and Hay killed—Freeland's station attacked—The settlers take refuge in block-houses—Cause of Indian hostility—Settlement on Red River broken up—Donaldson's party attacked—Panic among the settlers—Robertson's resolute advice—Freeland's station surprised—Repulse of the Indians—Desultory warfare—Robertson's fort at the Bluff invested—Eight of the garrison killed by a stratagem—Custom of the country—Close of Revolutionary war—Temporary cessation of hostilities—Indian council at the Bluff—Spanish intrigues—Renewal of Indian incursions—Desperate skirmishes—Treaty of Hopewell—Continuance of hostilities—Robertson's expedition—Attack on Hay at the mouth of Duck River—Surprise of Indian village by Robertson, and capture of traders—Capture of French trading boats—Division of the spoils.

IT will be remembered that, in 1779, a party of emigrants under James Robertson first commenced a settlement on the Cumberland. To these was subsequently added a party under Colonel Donaldson. As the reports of the fertility of that region became more disseminated, other emigrants made their appearance in the new settlement; which, as it grew in population, aroused the hostility of the Upper Creeks and Cherokees, whose war-parties were constantly on the alert to cut off all stragglers, and to lay waste those plantations that were either badly defended or too remote from timely assistance. To the sufferings and privations of a winter peculiarly severe was added the constant dread of assassination. In the spring of 1780, Keywood, a hunter, fell a victim to outlying savages on Richland Creek, a few miles only from the station at the Bluff. Soon after this a Mr. Hay was killed on the Lick Branch. Freeland's station was invested; and from this time small bands of warriors pursued their sanguinary career, murdering the settlers, burning their houses, and laying waste their crops, whenever an opportunity offered. Being weak in numbers, and too far distant from the Holston and Watauga to receive assistance from their countrymen, the Cumberland emigrants were obliged to abandon such of their farms as were most exposed to the ravages of the enemy, and fly with their families to the shelter of a few forts and block-houses. The cause of this implacable warfare may be found in the encroachments of the whites.

General George Rogers Clarke, by whose bold and romantic exploits the British forts in Illinois had been captured, undertook to overawe the Chickasaws by building Fort Jefferson, on the east bank of the Mississippi, eighteen miles below the mouth of the Ohio. A few plantations had also been opened on Red River; and, as the Chickasaws claimed all the territory west of the

Tennessee, they resolved to resist these intrusions by force of arms. The emigrants on Red River were the first to feel the effects of their enmity. The settlement was broken up, two of the men killed, and the remainder compelled to fly for refuge to the fort at the Bluff. Even the latter, though better protected, was not secure from Indian depredations. A party under Colonel Donaldson, which had ascended the Cumberland for the purpose of freighting two boats with corn, was intercepted by the Indians, who killed three persons, and wounded and took prisoners several others. Among the killed was a son of Captain Robertson.

Disheartened by the pertinacity with which the Indians continued their attacks, and by the loss of the greater portion of the corn upon which they had relied for their winter supplies, a large number of inhabitants abandoned the country, and sought safety in Kentucky and Illinois. Others, more daring or more hopeful, unwilling to lose the result of their labours, resolved to remain and defend themselves in the best manner they could. The leader and adviser of these resolute men was Captain James Robertson. About the middle of January, a few hours only after the return of the latter from Kentucky, the station at Freelands was surprised by an armed band of Indians. Their success was only partial. Roused from their slumbers by the vigilant Robertson, the garrison, eleven in number, repelled the assailants, with the loss, during the attack, of Major Lucas, and a negro belonging to Captain Robertson. This repulse only stimulated the revengeful savages to commit other outrages in quarters more defenceless. Being joined by reinforcements of Cherokees, they cut off many of the inhabitants who had not yet abandoned their plantations, drove in the garrison at Mansco's station, killed two of the men who had loitered behind their companions, and, lying ambushed in the woods, shot down many who were seeking safety in flight.

Early in April a large body of Cherokee warriors secretly invested the fort at the Bluff. Nineteen of its garrison, drawn out by a stratagem, were surrounded and eight of them killed—the remainder, many of whom were grievously wounded, succeeded in fighting their way back to the fort. Frustrated in their main design, the Indians presently retired; but throughout the summer of this year, and the whole of 1782, they kept up their desultory attacks until nearly all the isolated stations were broken up, and the remaining inhabitants had taken refuge at the Bluff or had abandoned the territory in despair. Those who still sturdily sought to maintain possession of a soil already ensanguined with the blood of their kindred and friends, were compelled to exercise a constant vigilance. "It became a custom of the country for one or two persons to stand as watchmen or sentinels, while others laboured in the field; and even while one went to a spring to drink, another stood on the watch with his rifle ready to protect him by shooting a creeping Indian or one rising from the thickets of canes and brush that covered him from view; and wherever four or five were assembled together at a spring, or other place where business required them to be, they held their guns in their hands, and with their backs turned to each other, one faced the north, another the south, another the west—watching in all directions for a lurking or creeping enemy."

During the period when most harassed by their subtle enemies, and consequently least able to pursue their customary labours without exposing themselves to the utmost danger, the inhabitants at the Bluff seriously contemplated the abandonment of a territory they were too few in number adequately to defend. But the design being strenuously opposed by Captain Robertson, they yielded to his mature experience, and finally concluded to remain where they were. Happily for the safety of this little community the Revolutionary war was terminated soon after, and the Indians, no longer instigated by British agents, began to relax in their hostility, while the increase of emigration from the older states rendered the settlement upon the Cumberland better able to meet and retaliate upon their enemies the outrages they were still disposed to commit. During the year 1783 some few settlers lost their lives; but events were now assuming a more pacific aspect. The Chickasaws, responding to overtures made them by commissioners appointed for that purpose, held in the spring of this year a council at the Bluff, which terminated in the cession to North Carolina of all that region, "extending nearly forty miles south of the Cumberland River to the ridge dividing the tributaries of that river from those of Duck and Elk."

But Spain, whose possessions in Florida and Louisiana were menaced by the advance of American settlers, was not disposed to permit the latter to maintain peaceful possession of the territory they occupied. Spanish agents were accordingly sent among the southern Indians to provoke them to a renewal of hostilities; and in this they were so far successful as to induce various small war parties to take up the hatchet and lay waste those portions of the frontiers which were most open to attack. In this way various hunters, stragglers, and exploring parties were surprised and killed. Impressed with the belief that these incursions were encouraged by the Spanish authorities, Robertson, during the year 1784, wrote to M. Portell, an officer of that government, expressing his desire to maintain amicable relations; but though he received a friendly response, the Indians continued their incursions. They fired upon Philip Trammell and Philip Mason while in the act of skinning a deer at the head of White's Creek; Mason was wounded, but both the men succeeded in reaching Eaton's station, from whence they obtained a reinforcement of volunteers, and set out in pursuit of the marauders. The Indians being overtaken, a skirmish ensued, wherein Mason received a second wound which proved mortal. Trammell killed two of the Indians, but the latter being reinforced, compelled the Americans to retreat. These in their turn receiving an accession to their force again started in pursuit of their enemies, and brought on the fight anew. Trammell and an associate named Hopkins threw themselves into the midst of the Indians, and fell fighting gallantly to the last. The contest was kept up by the survivors until both parties were weary, and separated by common consent. Another skirmish, in which equal bravery was exhibited, took place at the head waters of Drake's Creek. In the latter contest a man named Aspie received a wound which completely disabled him. At the same time Andrew Lucas was shot through the throat. Johnson and Spencer, the only two remaining unhurt, stood their ground with great determination, but were at length compelled to give way and leave Aspie to his fate. Lucas, who had fallen behind a bush, escaped the search of the Indians, and reached his home soon after the battle. But though parties of Chickasaw and Cherokee warriors continually hovered around the settlement, waylaying and murdering small bands of hunters and emigrants almost with impunity, their ceaseless hostility did not deter pioneers from spreading themselves over the territory and taking up such lands as promised to yield the best return for their labours. The constant peril to which these hardy borderers were exposed at length induced the United States government to send commissioners to the Chickasaws, by whose exertions a council was held at Hopewell on the 10th of January, 1786. It resulted in a treaty, defining the boundary of the lands belonging to the Chickasaws, and confirming the treaty made in 1783 with the commissioners of North Carolina.

But treaty stipulations were not likely to be kept by savage warriors who daily saw their hunting-grounds restricted by the steady increase of a white population; and in 1787 their inroads became so frequent that the assembly of North Carolina authorized the organization of a battalion for the protection of the frontiers. From some cause or other this necessary measure was delayed, and Robertson, finding his colony continued to be harassed by the Creeks and Cherokees, determined to assume the offensive and march against the nearest of their towns. He was the more disposed to adopt this resolution from the belief that hostilities were now fomented by French traders from the Wabash, who supplied the Indians with arms, and found their own aggrandizement in fostering a hostile feeling against the Americans. On the 1st of June, 1787, he placed himself at the head of one hundred and thirty mounted volunteers, who had assembled at his station from different parts of the Cumberland region. Accompanied by Colonels Hays and Ford, he set out for the Tennessee River, piloted by two Chickasaws. At the same time Captain David Hay, with his company and three boats freighted with supplies, left Nashville for the muscle shoals. While passing up the Tennessee River the flotilla was suddenly attacked by a party of Indians ambushed among the cane at the mouth of Duck River, who killed several of the crew, and wounded so many others, that Hay was compelled to return to Nashville for surgical assistance.

This unfortunate occurrence reduced the troops under Robertson to great straits, by depriving them of provisions upon which they had relied.

After a long and fatiguing march, Robertson struck the Tennessee River at the lower end of the muscle shoals, where the troops concealed themselves until night. Having discovered several Indian cabins on the opposite side of the river, seven men crept down the bank, and secreting themselves in the canes below, kept up a keen watch upon the southern shore. Presently some Indians made their appearance, who, after looking cautiously around them, entered a canoe and paddled out some distance into the stream. Seemingly satisfied by this reconnoissance that no enemies were near, they returned from whence they had started. Desirous of capturing an Indian alive, Robertson despatched Captain Rains with fifteen men up the river for that purpose; but after ascending nearly to the mouth of Blue Water, the party returned without succeeding in their object. It being determined to cross the river under cover of the night, soon after sunset the seven men in ambush below swam to the opposite shore. Approaching noiselessly the cabins, they found them deserted; but they returned to their companions with an immense canoe having a hole in its bottom. Stopping the leak with their shirts, forty men embarked with their firearms. The crazy vessel had scarcely left the shore before it began to fill, and they were compelled to put back. After this mishap the design was abandoned until daylight, when the hole was covered with a piece of linn bark, and some forty or fifty men succeeded in reaching the southern shore, leaving their companions to swim the river with the horses. A heavy rain coming on, they took shelter in the deserted cabins until the clouds dispersed, when they mounted their horses, and, taking a well-beaten path leading westwardly, pressed rapidly forward. After riding some five miles they passed some cornfields, and came soon after to Cold Water Creek, which the greater portion of the troops crossed in single file. On the low grounds, within three hundred yards of the river, stood a number of cabins.

Surprised by this unexpected invasion, the people of the town fled hastily to their boats; but being closely followed by the main body of the troops under Robertson, suffered severely during their flight. Such as crossed the river fell under the fire of a detachment headed by Captain Rains, which had been left on the other side of the creek for the purpose of intercepting the fugitives. Twenty-six Indians, accompanied by three French traders and a white woman, sought to effect their escape in a boat. Refusing to surrender, they were fired upon and every one killed. The principal trader and several other Frenchmen were made prisoners. In the town the Americans made prize of large stores of taffai, arms and ammunition, and a great variety of articles adapted to Indian traffic. After collecting all the canoes upon the river and placing a guard over them, the troops killed all the live stock they could capture, and set fire to the town. The following morning they buried the whites, and having liberally rewarded their Chickasaw guides, loaded several of the boats with the remainder of the captured stores and despatched them down the river in charge of three men. Robertson, marching by land, overtook the boats during the second day, and crossing the Tennessee near Colbert's Ferry, encamped on the north shore.

At this encampment all the wearing apparel belonging to the French prisoners was restored to them. Being set at liberty, and provided with a canoe and a liberal supply of provisions, they presently took their departure. When the remainder of the sugar and coffee had been divided among the troops, the boats containing the merchandise were sent round to Nashville, while the mounted men struck across the country in the direction of the Cumberland. As the boats descended the Tennessee, the men in charge of them met a party of French traders with additional supplies of goods. The latter mistaking the boatmen for their own countrymen, saluted them by firing off their guns, and before they could reload the Americans boarded the boats and made them prisoners.

In due time the daring voyagers reached the

Cumberland settlement, and the merchandise being sold soon after at Eaton's station, the proceeds were divided among the troops.

CHAPTER XV.

Desultory Indian warfare continued—American attempts at retaliation—Robertson and Bledsoe remonstrate with McGillivray—Death of Colonel Bledsoe—Robertson's negotiations with the Creeks—Hostilities continue—Increase of emigration—Causes which influenced it—State grants and reservations—District of Morgan established—Courts of law—Davidson county established—Nashville receives its name—Partial cessation of hostilities—Road opened through the wilderness—Sumner and Tennessee counties established—Voyage of Colonel Brown down the Tennessee—Massacre of his party by the Chickamauga Indians—Captivity of Mrs. Brown and the younger children—Their release—North Carolina cedes her western lands to the United States.

THE relief afforded by the destruction of the Indian town at Coldwater was but temporary. Exasperated by the losses experienced on that occasion, numerous small bands of warriors presently attacked all the weak points along the frontiers, carrying terror and devastation wherever they went. In the fall, a war-party under Blackfoot was pursued by a company of mounted men under Captain Shannon. They came up with them on the bank of the Tennessee River, and, after a desperate conflict, during which

Blackfoot and five of his followers were killed, succeeded in putting them to flight. This success stimulated the Americans on the Duck and Elk Rivers to form themselves into parties to retaliate the murders which had been committed. The security of the frontiers was further promoted by the arrival of a battalion of mounted men under Major Evans, by reinforcements of emigrants, and by the formation of a company of rangers whose duty it was to traverse the forest in all directions, and afford timely warning to the settlers of the approach of their insidious enemies. In this service Captain Rains was particularly conspicuous. Notwithstanding, however, all the precautions which had been taken, the savages penetrated into the settlement, and killed several persons near the mouth of the Harper and in the vicinity of the Bluff. Being hotly pursued by Rains, with a body of mounted men, they were overtaken at Rutherford's Creek, and dispersed with the loss of one of their number. On a second occasion Rains succeeded in putting another war party to the route, after killing four men and capturing an Indian boy. Several other excursions were made toward the close of 1787, which resulted in a similar manner; but they only afforded a partial relief. In 1788 the war broke out afresh, and a number of settlers were killed; among the slain was a son of Colonel Robertson.

Believing that the Spanish authorities in Florida encouraged the Creeks to persevere in their repeated attacks upon the American frontiers, Colonels Robertson and Bledsoe addressed a remonstrance to Colonel McGillivray, a half-blood chief, who exercised almost unlimited influence over the Creek nation; but though the response was couched in pacific language, the sanguinary excesses of the savages were not abated.

Colonel Bledsoe was slain soon after in a midnight attack upon his brother's station. Repressing his resentment at the inestimable loss which the colony had sustained by the death of his able and energetic associate, Robertson continued his negotiations with McGillivray, and earnestly called upon him to restrain the ferocious incursions of his warriors. "It is a matter of no reflection," wrote Robertson sorrowfully, "to a brave man, to see a father, a son, or a brother fall in the field of action; but it is a serious and melancholy incident to see a helpless woman or an innocent child tomahawked in their own houses." But though he appealed thus earnestly to the better feelings of McGillivray, and though Congress attempted to open negotiations, that wily chieftain listened alike to the Americans and the Spaniards, and while professing to the one a desire for peace, was covertly intriguing with the other to prosecute the war.

Growing more wary, but not less active, his

warriors continued to murder the settlers wherever an opportunity offered, and by taking to flight immediately after very generally escaped their pursuers. During the month of June, 1780, they attempted to surprise Robertson's station in open day, while the men were at work in the fields. Being foiled in their design, they retreated rapidly, and though hotly pursued, escaped with only the loss of one man killed and six wounded.

But the danger to which the Cumberland people were so constantly exposed did not deter emigrants from joining them in large numbers. Guarded by a strong escort, they passed safely through the perils of the intervening wilderness, and were presently to be found assisting to repel the pertinacious attacks of their ubiquitous enemy.

Other causes operated largely at this time in increasing the population on the south-western frontier, the chief of which was the bounty in lands granted during this year by North Carolina to her officers and soldiers of the continental line. In favour of the earlier settlers on the Cumberland, an act was passed in 1782, by which rights of pre-emption were given to each head of a family and each single man who had been in the country since 1780; but the state reserved to herself the salt springs and licks and the section of land adjoining them. These lands, together with twenty-five thousand acres granted to General Nathaniel Greene for his eminent services in the South, were presently laid off by commissioners; and the whole of the territory which was subsequently to become the State of Tennessee was formed into one district, which took the name of Morgan. Courts of law, established by the parent state, now began, for the first time, to exercise jurisdiction over the settlers on the Cumberland.

In 1783 the county of Davidson was established in honour of the brave General Davidson, who fell at Cowan's ford while endeavouring to cover the retreat of Morgan, when pursued by Cornwallis after the battle of Cowpens.

Robertson's settlement at the Bluff took the name of Nashville during the succeeding year, in commemoration of the patriotic services of Colonel Francis Nash, who at the outbreak of the Revolutionary war was a member of the Carolina legislature; but subsequently accepted a commission in the continental line, and fell at the head of his brigade in the battle of Germantown.

The contest with Great Britain was virtually closed by the surrender of Cornwallis at Yorktown, but the proclamation of peace did not take place until the spring of this year. The frontiers, however, had already been benefited by the cessation of the war with England. Indian depredations became less frequent, and, at length, for several years, the inhabitants of middle Tennessee pursued their avocations without experiencing any very serious molestation. But as population increased, the angry feeling which arose with regard to the lands reserved to the Cherokees by the treaty at Hopewell, led to some minor assaults and reprisals, and finally threatened to result in a new border war.

To provide for the defence of the frontier settlements, the legislature of North Carolina, during the session of 1785, authorized the enrolment of three hundred men, whose duty it was made to open a military road from the lower end of Clinch Mountain to Nashville. A part of this work being accomplished the following year, the facilities it afforded to emigrants increased so largely the population of Davidson county as to call for its division, and the new county of Sumner was accordingly established. By the exertions of the militia of Davidson and Sumner counties, other roads were opened during the years 1787 and 1788. Emigrants flocking in by these routes rendered the division of Davidson county again necessary, and the county of Tennessee was accordingly established.

At this time an incident occurred which exhibited, in a striking degree, the deep-rooted hostility of the inhabitants of the Nick-a-jack towns. Desirous of avoiding the long and difficult land route through the wilderness, Colonel James Brown, a veteran officer of the continental line, of North Carolina, resolved to descend the Tennessee to the Ohio, and ascending the latter stream, reach Nashville by way of the Cumberland.

Constructing a boat on the Holston below Long Island, he embarked with his family, which consisted of his wife, five sons, and four daughters. Two of his sons had reached the age of manhood. Accompanied also by five young men, and several negro servants, Colonel Brown commenced his voyage on the 4th of May, and after floating down the river for five days, approached, on the morning of the 9th, the Chickamauga towns. At the Tuskigagee Island town several Indians came on board, who, after being treated kindly, returned to the shore and despatched a messenger to the lower towns, calling on the warriors to intercept the Americans. Responding to this treacherous summons, twelve canoes, filled with savages whose arms were carefully secreted, ascended the river, and approaching the boat, threw its defenders off their guard by a perfidious stratagem, and then, suddenly assaulting them, killed Colonel Brown, his two eldest sons, and the young men by whom they were accompanied. Mrs. Brown, the younger children, and the negroes, were hurried off into captivity. Joseph Brown, after remaining one year a prisoner in the Nick-a-jack towns, bearing with such fortitude as a child might the most dreadful hardships, was surrendered to Governor Sevier, whose expedition from Frankland has already been mentioned. The other survivors of this terrible massacre were subsequently released.

The condition of the United States, at the period when peace was declared, was such as demanded a speedy relief from the pressure of a heavy and almost unsupportable debt, and from civil disturbances which the general government, as then constituted, were not able to control. To provide for the national debt, amounting to forty millions of dollars, it was proposed to vest in Congress the power to levy a tax of five per cent. on foreign goods; but to this project New York and Rhode Island refused their assent. All other suggestions being received with similar tokens of popular disfavour, and the general government not being vested with power to act in the matter, the adoption of new articles of confederation became necessary. Accordingly, delegates from all the states, Rhode Island excepted, met in convention at Philadelphia, and after a stormy and protracted session adopted the present constitution of the United States, which was ratified by North Carolina on the 13th of November, 1789. At the same session, conscious of the difficulty of adequately defending the remote settlements on the Cumberland, the legislature ceded to the United States the territory which now forms the State of Tennessee, subject to the land warrants already issued, and on the condition "that no regulation made or to be made by Congress shall tend to the emancipation of slaves."

CHAPTER XVI.

Territorial government formed—Blount appointed governor—Difficulty with Spain—Instructions to Mr. Jay—Indignation of the western people—Instructions rescinded—Unpopularity of the Federal government—Intrigues of Spain—Activity of Governor Blount—Indian hostilities—Campaigns of Harman and St. Clair—Restlessness of the Cherokees—Treaty of Holston—Depredations by the Creeks—Knoxville founded—The lower Cherokees declare war—Attack on Buchanan's station—Capture of Captain Handly—Captain Beard surprises Hiwassa—Is court-martialed—Hostile movements of the Creeks and Cherokees—Massacre at Cavet's station—Sevier's expedition—Defeat of the Indians—The Nick-a-jack expedition.

CONGRESS having accepted the deed of cession from North Carolina, William Blount was appointed governor of the territory south-west of the Ohio. "Of this new territory, coincident with the present State of Tennessee, the greater part, at this time, was in possession of the Indians. To only two detached portions had the

Indian title been extinguished; one of four or five thousand square miles—the late State of Franklin—the north-east corner of the present State of Tennessee; the other, an oblong tract of some two thousand square miles around the town of Nashville, on both sides of the Cumberland River." The new governor, a native of North Carolina, and one of the delegates from that state to the convention, which framed the Federal constitution, had already recommended himself to the people over whom he was commissioned to preside by his services at the treaty of Hopewell.

In the meanwhile, however, a difficulty had arisen between Spain and the Federal government, in which the western people were particularly interested. Spain, occupying Florida and Louisiana, claimed not only to extend her territory back to the head-waters of the Clinch River, a region already partially settled by Americans, but she also asserted her right to the exclusive navigation of the Mississippi River from its mouth to the thirty-first degree of latitude. Against any such restrictions, the inhabitants of Virginia, Kentucky, and the southwest territory loudly protested.

Negotiations were accordingly entered into with Spain, which resulted in the adoption of instructions, authorizing Mr. Jay, the American minister at Madrid, to consent to the introduction of an article into the treaty then pending, yielding to Spain for twenty years the full control of the navigation of the Mississippi River, from where it crossed the northern boundary of the Spanish American possessions to its confluence with the ocean.

Against this unjust concession, Virginia strongly remonstrated. Supported by the other southern states, and by the clamorous outcries of the people of the Ohio valley, the obnoxious instructions were rescinded. All further negotiation proving ineffectual, Spain continued to tax heavily all American commodities which sought an outlet by way of the Mississippi. The hardy western men, who knew but little of commercial restrictions and liked them still less, after bearing for some time to have their rude flotillas boarded by revenue officers, and their agricultural products or peltry subjected to a heavy impost, resolved to open the navigation of the Mississippi in their own fearless way. Believing that the failure of the Federal government to obtain the right to an unrestricted navigation of the Mississippi evinced a disregard for the prosperity of the West, they entertained, at one period, a serious design of separating from the Atlantic States, and of organizing an independent expedition against the Spanish posts in Louisiana. But the esteem in which Governor Mero was personally held, and the efforts which he made through his emissaries to bring his government into favour with the western people, averted, for a season, the impending storm.

Conscious of her inability to control the navigation of the Mississippi, or to resist the advance of the American settlers, Spain, fearful of the growing power of the United States, determined to use every effort to separate the inhabitants west of the mountains from the Federal union, her final purpose being to draw them under her own jurisdiction. These intrigues were so far successful as to increase the disaffection against the Federal government; but the louder the angry pioneers denounced the Union, the more averse they became to detach themselves from it.

On the Holston and Cumberland there were other matters demanding the attention of the people. In addition to his executive office, Governor Blount had been appointed Indian superintendent for the southern tribes, a position demanding great firmness of character conjoined to a wise prudence and forbearance.

The occasion, however, always found him equal to its demands; and whether building forts along the frontiers, corresponding with the Spanish authorities, or treating with the Indians in council, his zeal and ability were alike conspicuous.

Repeated efforts, on the part of commissioners appointed by the general government, having failed to put an end to Indian depredations, especially throughout Kentucky and the North-West Territory, General Harmar was authorized to proceed with the militia of Pennsylvania and Virginia against the Miami towns. The force assembled at Fort Washington during the month of September, 1790; but their efforts to chastise the hostile tribes proved singularly disastrous. After suffering two defeats, by which the militia suffered great loss, and the regulars were almost annihilated, Harmar returned with his dispirited troops to the Ohio, and there disbanded them.

The unfortunate result of this campaign influenced the general government to project an expedition upon a more imposing scale; the command of which was given to General St. Clair. Already unpopular in the West, St. Clair found great difficulty in obtaining from Kentucky and Tennessee their respective quotas of militia; the latter being desirous of fighting the Indians in their own way, and regarding the services of regulars as perfectly useless. In order to meet the requisition of the president, Governor Blount was compelled to resort to a draft. This mode of raising troops was indignantly resisted by men whose actions had hitherto been free and unshackled; and for a time considerable disaffection evinced itself throughout the province. Two hundred men were, however, sent under Major Rhea to Fort Washington, a portion of whom shared in the terrible defeat of St. Clair on the 4th of November, 1791.

At this time the Cherokees were growing very restless, but were at length induced, mainly by the influence of Robertson, to meet Governor Blount in council on the banks of the Holston. The result of this meeting was a further cession of territory, in consideration of a large amount to be paid in goods, and an annual stipend of one thousand dollars.

But while the Cherokee delegates were formally placing their people under the protection of the United States, the Creeks were again committing serious depredations on the Cumberland. Some of the settlers, attributing these outrages to the Cherokees, were disposed to break the treaty just concluded, and commence a war of retaliation; but by the exertions of Blount and Robertson, the malecontents were finally pacified. The dense population around White's station, the site of the late council, pointing it out as a favourable position for the seat of the territorial government, a town was presently laid off at that point, which received the name of Knoxville, in honour of Major-General Knox, at that time secretary of war under President Washington.

But however desirous of remaining at peace with the surrounding Indians, the intrigues of Spain and the shameful rout of St. Clair led the confederated warriors to indulge the hope that it might yet be possible to recover all the territory occupied by the Americans south of the Ohio River, and west of the Cumberland Mountains. It was not long before the Cherokees began to exhibit the effects of the influence which had been brought to bear upon them. Murders and depredations recommenced; and although McGillivray still expressed a desire to preserve pacific relations with the Americans, the conduct of his warriors gave just cause for alarm. Governor Blount exerted himself with great activity to avert the peril impending over the settlements. He held a council at Coyatee with the chiefs of the lower towns, and received from them assurances of peace. He crossed the mountain, and met the Chickasaw and Choctaw delegates in conference at Nashville. These also disclaimed all hostile feeling toward the Americans. But the Creeks and Cherokees were still active with the hatchet and the brand. The five lower Cherokee towns boldly declared war against the United States, and sent out armed bands of warriors to ravage the frontiers. In anticipation of this outbreak, Governor Blount had placed the frontier settlements of the Cumberland under the protection of Major Sharpe. Scouts and reconnoitering parties were ordered to patrol from station to station, with instructions to shoot down any Creeks or Cherokees who might be found lurking in the forest.

Notwithstanding these precautions, Buchanan's station, four miles south of Nashville, was attacked on the night of the 30th of September, 1792. But though the enemy numbered some seven hundred warriors, and the garrison consisted but of fifteen effective men, the strength of the works and the courage of the defenders sufficed to baffle the assault of the Indians, and compelled them to retreat with considerable loss.

This daring incursion called out the troops under General Sevier, who, stationing his main body at the mouth of the Clinch River, sent off detachments to assist in garrisoning the chain of fortified stations which had been erected for the protection of Washington district. By this judicious measure, the inhabitants of East Tennessee were secured from any serious attack. But the activity of roving bands of warriors often baffled the utmost vigilance of the whites. On the Cumberland, a party of Creeks, Cherokees, and Shawanese, attacked and put to flight a company of forty-two men under Captain Handley, taking the latter prisoner to Willstown, where the Indians debated for several days whether to put him to death, or suffer him to live. After forcing him to run the gauntlet, and practising many other barbarities, they finally concluded, at the intercession of two British traders in the Spanish interest, to adopt the captive into their tribe.

Being liberally supplied with the necessary arms by the Spanish governor, John Watts, a half-breed chief of the lower Cherokees, had latterly increased the military efficiency of his warriors by the formation of three companies of mounted men, and it soon became evident that all the southern tribes were preparing for a bold and bloody struggle.

With the commencement of the year 1793, the attacks on the frontier stations, within which the more exposed settlers presently took refuge with their families, increased in number and daring. Kentucky also felt very severely the effects of Indian hostility; and a party of volunteers was organized under General Logan for the purpose of invading the lower Creek towns. But the expedition was deprecated by Governor Blount, who feared it would only exasperate the Indians to commit greater excesses. Though some of the Indians were bitterly hostile, others were known to be friendly; and as but little discrimination is exercised usually in case of an attack upon towns so divided, it was more than probable that the innocent would have been confounded with the guilty. Indeed, this soon showed itself to be the case. On the 13th of June, Captain Beard, with a company of mounted men, fell suddenly upon the friendly town of Hiwassa, wounded Hanging Maw the chief, killed his wife, Scantee a Chickasaw chief, and a number of other Indians of consequence. The neighbouring warriors immediately rose in arms to the number of two hundred, repulsed Beard and his followers, and assumed an attitude of determined hostility. When this occurrence took place, Governor Blount was absent. His secretary, General Smith, took such steps as resulted in bringing Beard to trial by a court-martial; but, in the disturbed state of the frontier, and from the revengeful feelings by which the borderers were animated against the Indians, there was no possibility of bringing Beard to punishment.

Indeed the hostility of the southern tribes was now becoming so manifest as to repress all sympathy for the outrage which had been committed. The territorial authorities, acting under the advice of the general government, still endeavoured to restrain the people from pursuing retaliatory measures; but they could not always be brought to withhold their hands while their friends were being murdered around them.

On the 24th of September, one thousand Creek and Cherokee Indians, commanded by John Watts and Double Head, crossed the Tennessee with the intention of attacking Knoxville; but disputes between the leaders prevented the assault from being made under cover of the darkness. The customary firing of the morning gun by the garrison at Knoxville being mistaken by the Indians as an indication that their approach was discovered, they suddenly turned aside and wreaked their vengeance upon the garrison of a small block-house then within sight. This station, known as Cavet's, contained thirteen inmates, three only of whom were gun men; but, notwithstanding the immense superiority of the besiegers, this slender garrison resolved to defend themselves as well as they were able. Two of the assailants were presently killed, and several others being wounded, the Indians fell back beyond rifle-shot while they sent forward a messenger proposing conditions of surrender. The terms were accepted, but the savages proved treacherous, and barbarously murdered all their prisoners with the exception of Alexander Cavet, a youth whose life was saved by the interposition of Watts.

This perfidious massacre, within eight miles of the seat of government, roused the entire population of the Holston. Governor Blount ordered General Sevier to take the field. Placing himself at the head of six hundred mounted men, the latter, after crossing the Tennessee and making some prisoners on the Oostanaula, marched to the Etowah, on the opposite bank of which, he discovered the Indians intrenched. Crossing the river by a ford above, the troops bore down upon the disconcerted enemy, and after an hour's hard fighting, succeeded in gaining a complete victory.

Notwithstanding this reverse, war-parties still continued to harass the settlements to such a degree that, in spite of a direct prohibition from the general government, a number of the settlers on the Cumberland, aided by volunteers from Kentucky, led by the gallant Colonel Whitley, and, by a detachment of mounted men under Major Ore, who was chosen to command in chief, marched from Nashville against the Nick-a-jack towns. On the 13th of September, 1794, this party fell upon the savages by surprise, slew a large number of them, and made prisoners of nineteen women and children. On his return-march up the Tennessee, Ore was attacked at the narrows; but he beat back his assailants, and pursued them to the Running Water town, which was captured and destroyed. In this important expedition, Andrew Jackson served as a volunteer; the complete success which attended the assault on Nick-a-jack being attributed to his judicious suggestions.

CHAPTER XVII.

Organization of a territorial assembly—Congress petitioned to declare war against the Creeks and Cherokees—Colleges established at Greenville and Knoxville—Washington college established—Convention at Knoxville and adoption of a Constitution for the State of Tennessee—Sevier elected Governor—Blount and Coxe chosen Senators of the United States—Their election declared invalid—Subsequent action of the legislature of Tennessee—Andrew Jackson appointed a member of Congress—His personal appearance—Indian difficulties—Blount expelled the Senate—Appointment of Jackson to fill the vacancy—Reception of Blount in Tennessee—Chosen a senator of the State—His trial and acquittal—His death—Roane elected governor—Prosperity of Tennessee.

In 1793, the number of free white male inhabitants of the South-West Territory being found to exceed five thousand, Governor Blount, in accordance with the provisions of the ordinance of 1787, authorized the election of delegates to a territorial assembly, which met at Knoxville on the fourth Monday of February, 1794, for the purpose of choosing ten persons, from whom five were to be selected by Congress as a legislative council. A committee was also appointed to draw up an address to Congress, petitioning for a declaration of war against the Creeks and Cherokees. In this temperately worded and well written document it was stated that, since the treaty of Holston, two hundred citizens of the South-West Territory had fallen victims to Indian barbarity, and a number of others had been carried into captivity; that property to the amount of one hundred thousand dollars had been stolen from them, independent of the slaves which from time to time had been carried off; that the Creeks and Cherokees, within the past two years, had twice invaded the territory in force, and that their ravages had been so universally felt that there was not a single member of the assembly but could "recount a dear wife or child, an aged parent or near relative massacred in their houses or fields by the hands of these blood-thirsty nations."

Painfully impressed with the necessity of affording more efficient protection to a people who had already suffered but too severely, the congressional committee to whom the subject was referred, recommended "that the President should be authorized to call out an adequate military force to carry on offensive operations against any hostile tribe, and to establish such posts and defences as would be necessary for the permanent security of the frontier settlers."

The first legislative council commissioned by the President of the United States, consisted of Griffith Rutherford, John Sevier, James Winchester, Stockley Donaldson, and Parmenas Taylor: these, with the governor and the members of the house of delegates, constituted the general assembly for the South-West Territory.

One of the earliest measures adopted by the new assembly was to pass an act establishing a college at Greenville. At the same session another institution for educational purposes was provided for in the vicinity of Knoxville. The latter, which received the name of Blount College in honour of the governor, still exists under the title of the University of East Tennessee. The details of the tax-bill having been adjusted, though not without some discordant feeling between the upper and lower branches of the legislature, and another memorial to Congress drawn up, asking protection from Indian inroads, the assembly finally requested the governor "to direct that, when the census is taken next June, the sense of the people may at the same time be inquired into how far it may be their wish for admission into the Union as a State." The business of the session being thus completed, the two houses were prorogued, at their own request, until the 1st of October, 1795. Governor Blount, however, thought fit to summon them to meet again at Knoxville on the 29th of June. The session only lasted thirteen days, but during this period an act was passed incorporating Washington College, and provision made for calling a convention of delegates from the people to adopt a constitution for the new State, in the event of its being ascertained that the population of the territory exceeded sixty thousand. The census returns made in the autumn of the same year showing sixty-seven thousand free white inhabitants and ten thousand slaves, a convention was held at Knoxville on the 11th of January, 1796, and a constitution adopted for the State of Tennessee.

The territorial government being thus abrogated, fresh writs of election were issued, which resulted in the choice of General John Sevier as governor of the new state. The delegates of the state legislature, who had been voted for at the same time, assembled at Knoxville on the 28th of March, and presently elected ex-Governor Blount and William Cocke senators of the United States. To the reception of the latter, however, Congress raised objections. It was argued that the authority for taking the census, and for establishing the new state, ought to have emanated from Congress. The report of the committee in favour of admitting the new state finally passed the house. The senate was less compliant. The new state was, however, after considerable opposition, admitted into the Union; but when the senators elect presented their credentials and claimed their seats, it was decided that their election was invalid, because "their credentials were of a date prior to the act admitting the state into the Union."

It was not long before this objection was removed. The legislature of Tennessee, in obedience to a summons from Governor Sevier, met at Knoxville toward the close of July, and very early the following month re-elected their senators to Congress, taking occasion, at the same time, to correct certain errors in the enactments of the previous session, by providing for the election of a single member to Congress instead of two, and for the choice of three presidential electors instead of four. When these amendments had been made, Andrew Jackson, a young lawyer of Davidson county, who had already distinguished himself by his firmness in the discharge of his professional duties, and his courage in defending the frontiers from the predatory incursions of the savages, was chosen to represent the State of Tennessee in the Congress of the United States.

At this period Jackson was about thirty years of age. He is remembered by Gallatin "as a tall, lank, uncouth-looking personage, with long locks of hair hanging over his face, and a cue down his back, tied in an eel skin: his dress singular, his manners and deportment that of a rough backwoodsman.

Re-elected governor in 1798, Sevier found himself under the necessity of restraining the encroachments of the people upon the Indian lands. The Cherokees were especially desirous that the integrity of their boundaries should be respected, but they addressed their complaints to men accustomed to perfect freedom of action, and but little likely to observe a courteous forbearance toward those from whom they had suffered so much in times past. The general government, however, evinced a proper regard for the rights of the Indians, by instructing Colonel Butler, who was in command of the United States troops on the frontiers of Tennessee, to order all the squatters upon Indian lands to recross the boundary. But imperative as this mandate was, it was found impossible to enforce it. The people to whom it was especially addressed indignantly refused to recede a single step; and as the affair presently assumed a threatening aspect, the legislature amicably interposed.

Commissioners having already been appointed by the United States to obtain a cession of the lands illegally occupied, Governor Sevier was authorized to apply to the President for a temporary suspension of the obnoxious order. The effect of this application is not recorded, but it may be presumed to have been favourable, as the trespassers were unmolested.

In the early part of the following July a council was held at Tellico; but the chiefs manifesting a reluctance to part with any portion of their territory, the negotiation was postponed until September, when Colonel Butler, on the part of the United States, assisted by Governor Sevier, who attended the conference to watch over the interests of Tennessee, succeeded in extinguishing the Cherokee claim to certain lands between the Tennessee and Clinch Rivers, and embracing those already settled upon.

In the mean time Senator Blount had been expelled from the Senate of the United States, on a charge of conspiring to set on foot a military expedition against the Spanish territory in Florida and Louisiana. Andrew Jackson was elected to fill the vacancy. Blount returned to Tennessee before articles of impeachment were preferred against him. His arrest being ordered, the sergeant-at-arms repaired to Knoxville for the purpose of taking him prisoner to Philadelphia; but though this official was courteously received by Blount, and hospitably entertained by the citizens of Knoxville, so great was the popularity of the accused that the sergeant-at-arms, finding it impossible to obtain the co-operation of the state authorities, was compelled to return home without executing his mission. As an evidence they regarded that project as praiseworthy which Congress had denounced as criminal, the inhabitants of Knox county prevailed upon General White to resign his seat in the senate of Tennessee in favour of Mr. Blount, who, on taking his seat in that body at the ensuing session, was unanimously chosen its presiding officer.

But while he was thus honoured at home the charges against him were brought to a trial in the Senate of the United States. On the 18th of December, Jared Ingersoll and A. J. Dallas appeared as his counsel and objected to the jurisdiction of the court. After considerable discussion this objection was admitted to be valid, and on the 14th of January, 1799, the Vice-President declared the opinion of the court, dismissing the impeachment.

It needed not this decision to increase the popularity which Blount enjoyed in Tennessee. Having won the good opinion of the inhabitants while governor of the territory, it was now thought they would manifest their regard for his previous services, and their emphatic disapproval of the indignity which had been put upon him, by choosing him governor of the state, but his death in the spring of 1800 put an end to the project. The following year Archibald Roane was elected chief magistrate, and was continued in that office until 1809, when he was succeeded by Willie Blount, a younger brother of the deceased senator.

The perfect quiet and prosperity which prevailed for several years subsequent to the election of Roane, render the history of Tennessee during that period barren of incidents sufficiently striking to be worthy of record. Emigrants continued to pour into the territory in such numbers that the census of 1800 exhibited a population of one hundred and five thousand six hundred and eighty-two, of which thirteen thousand five hundred and eighty-four were slaves.

The rich valleys of East Tennessee and the fertile plains of the Cumberland bountifully repaid the labours of the husbandman. The hardy and courageous race which had grown to manhood amid the horrors of an unceasing warfare now exchanged the rifle for the plough, and found leisure almost for the first time to cultivate the amenities of life. The earlier borderers were rough uneducated men, careless of danger from being inured to its constant presence, and enjoying a precarious existence with a keener zest from a knowledge of its uncertain tenure. But as the cluster of log cabins, originally built around or connected with the old picketed stations, gave place to the neat and well-ordered village, as the village became a town of some consequence, as the mechanic arts began to flourish, and education extended itself to that class which had hitherto remained in ignorance, the nomadic-habits of the people were gradually subdued, local attachments sprang up, domestic comforts increased, the manners and habits of the people experienced insensibly a change, and luxuries hitherto unattainable became requisites in every respectable household.

But this happy improvement in the social condition of the people did not tend to lessen in any marked degree their original force of character; for when, at a later day, a formidable Indian conspiracy threatened to devastate their fertile and well-cultivated fields, and a foreign invader disembarked an army of veteran soldiers upon the southern coast, they manifested the same martial ardour, power of endurance, elasticity of spirit and sturdy courage which so eminently distinguished their progenitors.

CHAPTER XVIII.

Aaron Burr—His duel with Hamilton—His journey to the West—Account of his projects against Spain and the United States—Co-operation of Blennerhasset—Burr publicly welcomed at Nashville—Becomes the guest of Andrew Jackson—Descends the Mississippi—Returns to Philadelphia—Intrigues with Eaton, Truxton, and Decatur—Eaton's visit to Jefferson—Reappearance of Burr in the West—Military preparations in the Ohio valley—Burr's correspondence with Wilkinson—Denounced by the latter—Jackson's warning to the Governor of Louisiana—Jefferson's proclamation—Arrest of Burr in Kentucky—His acquittal—Suddenly appears at Nashville—Frustration of his schemes—Burr descends the Cumberland—Encamps on the west bank of the Mississippi—His arrest, trial and acquittal—His subsequent fortunes.

IN 1804, having lost the confidence of the republican party of which he had been a distinguished leader, Aaron Burr, a native of New Jersey, a graduate of Princeton, a colonel in the War of Independence, an eminent lawyer, a prominent legislator of New York, a senator and subsequently a Vice-President of the United States, determined, in default of a regular nomination, to run independently for the office of governor of New York. Depraved in morals yet artful and dissembling, with brilliant talents, a fascinating address and polished manners, Burr still possessed many warm friends among the young and enthusiastic of his own party. He greatly depended for success, however, upon the votes of the Federalists, who had not considered it worth while to nominate a candidate. Failing to be elected, the disappointed office-seeker attributed his defeat to the influence of the great federal leader Alexander Hamilton, whom he deliberately forced into a duel and killed. To avoid the first outbreak of public indignation, Burr fled to South Carolina, but presently returned to Washington and served out his unexpired term as Vice-President.

When Congress closed its session in March, 1805, Burr, not venturing to return to New York, set out for the West. He had several ostensible objects in view, one of which was to offer himself as a candidate for Congress from Tennessee, where no previous residence was required. Suggested by Matthew Lyon, a Kentucky congressman, whose district adjoined Tennessee, the proposition had been supported by a former companion-at-arms, General Wilkinson, who feared that if some legitimate field of action was not thrown open to him, he would betake himself to unlawful and desperate courses.

Already, however, as subsequently appeared, Burr was contemplating far other than the innocent objects which he pretended to have in view.

To a considerable portion of the southern and western people Spain had become particularly odious, partly on account of the difficulties which she had for so long continued to throw in the way of navigating the Mississippi, and partly from her intrigues with the southern Indians. Aware of this feeling, and ready himself for any enterprise, however repugnant to common justice, in which he might hope to better his present fortunes, Burr meditated the organization of a military force in the West, to descend the Mississippi and wrest from Spain a portion of her territory bordering on the Gulf of Mexico. As the execution of this scheme could not but implicate the whole South-West, it was contemplated, in the expected event of a dismemberment of this portion of the country from the Union, to establish New Orleans as the capital of a new empire. Of this, either as dictator or president as circumstances might determine, Burr was to be made the chief.

With this scheme yet dimly shadowed out in his mind, Burr started on his voyage down the Ohio, during which he stopped for some time at the island of Blennerhasset, subsequently so called from the name of its wealthy proprietor and occupant, Herman Blennerhasset. This warm-hearted but impulsive and visionary Irishman, the artful adventurer found little difficulty in winning over to his vaguely defined but ambitious purposes.

At the Falls of the Ohio Burr met Lyon, by whom he had been preceded. From him he learned that his delay had proved fatal to his prospect of being elected from Tennessee. Nevertheless he accompanied Lyon to his home at Eddyville, on the Cumberland, whence he journeyed on horseback to Nashville. Here he was honoured by a public welcome, hearty and enthusiastic, and remained for several days under the hospitable roof of General Andrew Jackson. Of this gentleman, with whom he had become acquainted while both were in Congress, Burr at this time remarked, in a journal which he kept for the entertainment of his gifted but unfortunate daughter, that he "was once a lawyer, afterward a judge, and now a planter, a man of intelligence, and one of those prompt, frank, ardent souls whom he loved to meet."

Returning down the Cumberland to Fort Massac, Burr there met Wilkinson, through whose influence he was provided with a well-manned officer's barge, in which he proceeded to New Orleans, where he arrived late in June. After a brief stay in the Orleans Territory, where he found the authorities highly unpopular, he re-ascended the Mississippi to Natchez, whence he travelled by land to Nashville. Again complimented with a public reception, he enjoyed the hospitalities of Jackson for another week, and then proceeded through Kentucky and the Indiana Territory to St. Louis.

It was here that Wilkinson, according to his own story, first suspected Burr of meditating a desperate and illegal enterprise. Assuming an air of mystery, the artful plotter hinted at some glorious undertaking favoured by the general government. Yet that government he asserted was imbecile, and darkly spoke of the western people as being ripe for revolt.

Returning to the east, Burr spent the ensuing winter, spring, and summer in Washington and Philadelphia. Mystery still attended all his proceedings. Nevertheless he began to talk more boldly, and to tamper with prominent public men at Washington, assuring some of them that Wilkinson was a party to his enterprise. But from such men as Eaton, Truxton, and Decatur he received no countenance; though to the two latter he represented his project to be merely the establishment of an independent government in Mexico in the event of a war between Spain and the United States, which then seemed by no means improbable. Speaking more freely of his designs to Eaton, that officer visited the president and suggested Burr's appointment to a foreign mission, declaring it to be his belief that a revolution in the West would thus be prevented. Jefferson, however, expressing his firm confidence in the patriotism of the western people, demanded no further explanation, and Eaton did not feel authorized to give it unasked.

Late in August, 1806, Burr again made his appearance in the West, and began to make active preparations to carry out his designs. In company with Blennerhasset, he contracted for the building of fifteen boats on the Muskingum; authority was given to a mercantile house at Marietta to purchase provisions; a kiln was erected on Blennerhasset's island to dry corn for shipment; and numbers of the young and adventurous were enlisted to participate in some splendid enterprise, of the true nature of which they were told little or nothing.

In the mean time Wilkinson had taken command at Natchitoches. While at this point there came to him a messenger bearing a letter in cipher from Burr. This letter, in disjointed phrases and a tone of mystery, announced that Burr had nearly completed his arrangements for some enterprise, which, judging from the tenor of the communication, Wilkinson was tolerably cognizant of, and in which he was expected to engage. How far the latter was implicated in the conspiracy it is difficult to determine. Subsequently Burr charged him with having carried on a correspondence in regard to the expedition, and with being privy to his designs. But admitting the fact of the correspondence, Wilkinson alleged that it was continued solely for the purpose of drawing Burr out. However this may have been, the course he now adopted left no room for suspicion. Gathering from Burr's messenger all the particulars he could of the projected enterprise, he sent the intelligence in a letter to the president; despatched an order to the commanding officer at New Orleans to put the place in the best state of defence; warned Claiborne, the governor of the Louisiana Territory, that his government was threatened by a secret plot; made a requisition upon the acting governor of the Mississippi Territory for a reinforcement of five hundred militia to proceed to New Orleans; and, in short, did all that it was possible for activity and energy to accomplish.

Meanwhile it had been widely rumoured that Wilkinson himself was concerned in the scheme of Burr—a fact that caused the former no little embarrassment, and for which as we have seen his conduct had afforded no slight ground. Writing to Governor Claiborne, General Jackson warned that gentleman of an enterprise being on foot against his territory, and advised him to guard against internal as well as external danger—as well against Wilkinson as against Burr. "For my own part, I hate the Dons," continued Jackson; "I would delight to see Mexico reduced; but I would die in the last ditch before I would see the Union disunited."

At length, on the 29th November, finding it impossible any longer to doubt the dangerous and unlawful character of Burr's projected enterprise, President Jefferson issued a proclamation calling upon all in authority to exert themselves for its suppression and for the arrest of the parties concerned in it.

A few days previous to the issuing of this proclamation, however, Burr had been arrested at Lexington, upon the affidavit of the United States district-attorney for Kentucky. But having all the influence of the district-judge in his favour, the conspirator was acquitted, and his triumph was celebrated by a ball at Frankford.

After the ball, Burr suddenly departed for Nashville. Scarcely had he gone when the President's proclamation arrived. Its effect was completely destructive to Burr's plans. His boats on the Muskingum were seized; Blennerhasset was compelled to fly down the river at the head of a few followers; and every arrangement was made by the authorities of Kentucky and

Ohio to intercept all suspicious parties descending the river.

Meanwhile, having reached Nashville, Burr departed thence with a few followers and two boats down the Cumberland. On an island at the river's mouth he was joined by Blennerhasset. Finding that the whole number of those who still adhered to his desperate fortunes was less than two hundred, he endeavoured to draw recruits from the garrison of Fort Massac, in the neighbourhood of which he was encamped. His efforts proving signally unsuccessful, Burr once more took to his boats, and proceeded down the Mississippi to Chickasaw Bluff, now Memphis, the only military station between Fort Massac and Natchez. Here the conspirator endeavoured again to raise recruits. The commanding officer of the fort so far yielded to his seductions as to promise to join him after he had visited his friends; but neither the arts nor the tempting offers of Burr had any effect on the soldiers of the garrison.

Resuming his voyage, Burr, before reaching New Orleans, upon which his sole hope now depended, became acquainted with the revelations made by Wilkinson. He saw at once that his whole project was baffled. Withdrawing from the jurisdiction of the Mississippi Territory, he formed an encampment on the west bank of the river, some thirty miles above Natchez. But he was not secure even here. Influenced by the president's proclamation, the governor of Mississippi sent a detachment of militia to arrest him. Surrounded, and hopeless of escape, he was at length induced to yield.

Thus once more a prisoner, Burr was taken to Washington, the capital of the Mississippi Territory, where he easily found sureties for his appearance at court. When the court met on the 5th of February, 1807, he appeared with his counsel, and demanded his release on the ground that the attorney-general had given it as an official opinion that his offences did not come within the jurisdiction of the Mississippi Territory. His application for a discharge being overruled by the judges, Burr fled the same evening. A reward was immediately offered for his capture. For nearly two weeks nothing was heard of him; but at length, on the 17th of February, he was arrested, in mean clothes, while travelling with a single companion through the westernmost settlements of what is now Alabama.

Of Burr's subsequent history, of his trial at Richmond, of his acquittal on account of the informality of the evidence brought against him, of his wandering career in Europe and obscure and lonely life in New York, where he died at the advanced age of eighty years—it does not seem necessary to give any further account in a volume like the present.

CHAPTER XIX.

Difficulties with Great Britain and France—Action of Congress—Increase of popular indignation against Great Britain—Congress declares war—Disastrous issue of the campaign at the north—Naval victories—Wilkinson calls on Tennessee for volunteers—Prompt response—Reach Natchez under Jackson and Coffee—Ordered to be disbanded—Conduct of Jackson—Return to Nashville—Tecumseh—His attempt to form an Indian confederacy—Effect of his visit to the southern tribes—The Creeks become hostile—Massacre of Fort Mimms—Jackson reassembles the militia of Tennessee—Battle of Tallasehatche—Battle of Talladega—Successes of the Georgians and Mississippians.

During the progress of the events narrated in the foregoing chapter, the relations of the United States with the governments of Great Britain and France had been growing less and less friendly.

Engaged in war with each other, the two latter powers, in 1806, issued certain orders and decrees, by which American or other neutral vessels, having on board British or French merchandise, or trading to French or English ports, were rendered liable to seizure and confiscation by the naval forces of Great Britain or France. Upon the United States the effect of these orders and decrees was to check, and wellnigh to destroy a commerce hitherto thriving, and fast rising to the first importance.

In the expectation of bringing both England and France to terms, by cutting off a considerable source of their necessary supplies, Congress, in 1807, declared an embargo to prevent the sailing of American vessels to British or French ports. This measure, however, operating seriously to the disadvantage of the commercial states, was, in 1809, abandoned, and an act passed in its stead, to prohibit all intercourse with Great Britain, France, and their dependencies.

In the mean time other questions had arisen to complicate and increase the existing difficulties between the United States and Great Britain. Among these were the rights of search and impressment, claimed and exercised by the latter government, and under color of which thousands of our seamen, native-born as well as adopted citizens, on the pretence that they were British subjects, had been dragged from the protection of their own flag to the galling servitude of the English navy.

The patience of the country having been exhausted, at length, in unavailing protests against these various aggressions upon our commerce and the rights of our seamen, it was determined, as a last resort, to try the effect of an appeal to arms. Accordingly, on the 18th of June,

1812, Congress issued a formal declaration of war against Great Britain. As France had just signified her willingness to enter into an amicable arrangement of difficulties, it was not deemed advisable or necessary to include that government in the proclamation of hostilities.

At the north, the early operations of the first campaign resulted in a series of disasters—the loss of Mackinaw, the abandonment of Chicago, the ignominious surrender of Hull at Detroit, and the capture of a thousand American troops at Queenstown Heights. On the ocean, however, the navy of the United States proudly sustained the honour of our arms, and dissipated in a great degree the gloom occasioned by the untoward course of events on land.

The war had raged for some time along the Canadian frontier, when Wilkinson, in command at New Orleans, made a call upon the militia of Tennessee to march to the protection of that important post. In answer to this summons the gallant Tennesseeans, heedless of driving snow storms and the severity of an unprecedented winter, assembled at Nashville, on the 10th of December, to the number of fifteen hundred foot and four hundred horse—all volunteers.

Headed by General Andrew Jackson, whose previous application for a regular commission had been rejected, the foot soldiers descended in boats to Natchez. Here a junction was formed with the horse, who, under the lead of General Coffee, had marched four hundred and fifty miles through the Indian country.

Remaining at Natchez during the winter, Jackson, early in the spring of 1813, received an order from the Secretary of War to disband his troops, and deliver over all the stores and other public property to Wilkinson. The reason alleged for this order was, that as the services of the militia were very expensive, it had been determined to dispense with them as far as possible. Jackson, however, shrewdly suspected that the real motive for disbanding them at Natchez was to facilitate their enlistment into the army of Wilkinson, whose recruiting officers had already appeared in the camp. Two hundred of the men were sick, and very few had means of their own to return home. Consequently, in the event of their discharge, many of them would be compelled by their necessities to enter the regular service, however unwilling they might otherwise be to do so.

Deeming himself responsible to the brave men who had followed him so far, for their safe return to their homes and families, Jackson did not long hesitate as to what should be his proper course, under the circumstances. That course, though in direct opposition to the orders of the war department, he pursued with the fearless resolution which formed a prominent trait in his character. Driving away the recruiting officers of Wilkinson, in spite of warnings, threats, and efforts to embarrass his action, he procured wagons for his sick and disabled, and, heading his troops, marched them through the wilderness again to Nashville, the point where they had been originally mustered, and disbanded them.

The patriotism of Jackson could not be doubted; his services had already proved valuable and important. The motive for his conduct was one that did honour to his heart. The government did not deem it advisable, therefore, to take any notice of his disobedience of orders, but silently paid the expenses it had incurred.

Previous to the declaration of hostilities, it had been urged as a cause for war on the part of the United States, that agents of the British government were actively engaged in inciting the animosity of the north-western Indian tribes against the American frontier settlements. However this may have been, no sooner was war proclaimed than the most of those tribes became the open allies of Great Britain. The moving spirit, by whose influence they had been in a great measure swayed to such a course, was Tecumseh, the celebrated chief of the Shawanese.

From his boyhood this remarkable man had been an active and unrelenting foe of the

Americans. Sagacious and observant, he early saw that their encroachments could be stayed only by the combination, in one friendly league, of all the various contending tribes of his race. To effect such a union became the grand aim of his existence. Of a dignified and commanding appearance, an eloquent orator, a brave warrior, crafty, resolute, and capable of bearing every extreme of wilderness life, he possessed all the qualities held in esteem by the Indians. Thus endowed, and aided by the arts of his brother, the Prophet, who claimed to hold a mysterious intercourse with the Great Spirit, Tecumseh had acquired an extraordinary influence over the various savage tribes of the north-west. How that influence was exerted on the breaking out of the war between England and America has already been noticed.

After having held repeated conferences with the British at Detroit, Tecumseh, in the spring of 1812, attended by thirty mounted warriors, left the North-West Territory, and moving rapidly southward, penetrated the country as far down as Florida, where he succeeded in persuading the Seminoles to join his standard. Returning northward, some time during the autumn he made his appearance among the Creeks of Alabama. Passing from town to town, he exerted all his fiery eloquence, creating wherever he went a fierce feeling of animosity to the Americans.

He entreated his hearers to become again what they had formerly been—hunters and warriors, and the foes of the white man and his civilization. Their ancient allies, the English, he told them, had sent him from the great lakes to procure their aid in expelling the Americans from every foot of Indian soil; and he assured them that the King of England would reward well every one that should take up arms in his cause.

Departing in December for the North, Tecumseh left the Creek nation in a state of fearful excitement. Two parties had arisen; the one, comprising the wealthy and more intelligent chiefs, anxious to maintain peace; the other, composed of the young and ardent clamorous for the immediate destruction of the American settlements. Stimulated continually by the prophet, whom Tecumseh had appointed to disseminate his doctrines, the war feeling continued to grow more and more violent, until it broke out in murderous attacks, not upon whites only, but also upon such of the Creeks as desired to continue at peace with the United States.

At length the surprise and capture of Fort Mimms by a band of the war faction, under the lead of Weatherford, a noted half-breed chief, brought affairs to a crisis. On this occasion nearly four hundred whites and friendly Creeks were either slain in the fight or massacred after the capture of the fort.

Reaching Nashville on the 25th September, 1813, the tidings of this sanguinary affair created an intense excitement. Scarcely had Governor Blount time to summon out the militia, before General Jackson, having assembled the volunteers of his late Natchez expedition, was on his march to the "Hickory Ground," the chief seat of the hostile Creeks, embracing the entire district between the Coosa and Tallapoosa Rivers. Crossing the Tennessee at Ritter's landing, Jackson with difficulty cut his way over the intervening ridges to Mill's Creek, where he remained for several days encamped, until his foragers had collected provisions, in want of which the army suffered a great deal.

While waiting at this place the commander-in-chief despatched General Coffee, with two divisions of five hundred men each, to attack the town of Tallasehatche, some thirteen miles distant, where a considerable body of the enemy had assembled. Having forded the Coosa a short distance above the Ten Islands, Coffee directed one of his divisions to scour the neighbouring country, while he led the other in person against Tallasehatche. The sun was just rising on the 3d of November when the Tennesseeans, approaching the town on two sides, began the attack. Not wholly unprepared, the savages, headed by their prophets, with fierce yells and the beating of drums rushed furiously upon the advancing lines. A brief but sanguinary struggle put an end to the action, in which, scorning to beg for life, few Indians escaped destruction. Nearly two hundred warriors lay dead on the field, and eighty-four women and prisoners remained in the hands of the victorious Tennesseeans, whose loss was but five killed and eighteen wounded. Recrossing the Coosa, Coffee reached the main camp late in the evening.

Jackson now pushed forward over the mountains. Arriving at the Ten Islands of the Coosa, he there established a depot for provisions, protected by strong pickets and block-houses, to which he gave the name of Fort Strother.

While these events were transpiring, a small band of friendly Creeks, having taking refuge in a fort at the town of Talladega, had been closely besieged there by a large party of "Red Sticks," as the hostile Indians were called, in allusion to the colour of their war-clubs. Aware that Jackson was on the Coosa, the besieged for a time vainly endeavoured to convey to him some intelligence of their alarming situation. Not a single warrior could leave the fort unseen. At length a crafty chief, clothing himself in the skin of a large hog, with the head and legs attached, crawled out of the fort one night on his hands and knees, and, thus disguised, grunting occasionally and rooting in the earth, managed to pass unsuspected through the enemy's camps. Once beyond arrow-shot, he threw off his disguise, and sped like a deer to the head-quarters of Jackson, who immediately prepared to march to the relief of the fort.

General White, with a detachment of General Cocke's East Tennesseeans, being some distance higher up the river, Jackson despatched a messenger to him with orders to hasten to Fort Strother, and protect it in his absence. Leaving a small guard to watch over the sick and wounded, he crossed the Coosa at midnight, and moved rapidly down the southern bank toward Talladega, within six miles of which the troops encamped, late in the evening of November the 8th.

Scarcely had the tents been pitched, when Jackson received the irritating intelligence that White, instead of marching to Fort Strother, had complied with an order from Cocke to retrace his steps to the mouth of the Chattanooga, and there join the main body of the Eastern volunteers. Fearing for the feeble garrison of Fort Strother, Jackson nevertheless determined, before hastening back to its protection, to make a desperate effort to relieve the beleaguered Creeks at Talladega.

In the gray of the following morning the Tennesseeans moved to the attack of the Red Sticks, who, more than a thousand in number, were posted in a dense thicket, along the margin of a shallow rivulet, in the immediate vicinity of the fort. This position, as well as that of the beleaguered fort, Jackson's line, composed of twelve hundred infantry, and eight hundred horse, encompassed in an almost unbroken circle. About eight o'clock the American advance came in contact with the Indians. Though taken by complete surprise, the savages fought bravely, and with terrific yells and screams threw themselves against the fiery circle by which they were surrounded. At one point the militia momentarily gave way to the impetuosity of their charge. Being quickly rallied, however, the whole line rushed in upon the savages. The fight now became general. Flying, at length, the Red Sticks were hotly pursued through the forests, and many shot down as they fled. Their total destruction seemed inevitable. But taking advantage of an unavoidable break in the line the main body, the survivors effected their escape to the mountains, leaving more than three hundred of their number dead.

By this victory, in which the Tennesseeans lost but fifteen killed and eighty-five wounded, one hundred and sixty friendly Creek warriors, with their wives and children, were saved from the slaughter that would have otherwise overtaken them.

Having buried his dead, Jackson, whose provisions threatened to fail him, hastened back to

Fort Strother. Here he was presently joined by Cocke, who, having formed a junction with White, had penetrated the Creek country, destroying three villages, killing sixty warriors, and taking two hundred and fifty prisoners, without the loss of a man.

In the mean time two other columns of troops, one of the Georgia militia and friendly Creeks, the other of Mississippi volunteers, regulars, and Choctaws, had advanced from different points against the hostile district. Both gained important victories; the Georgians, at Autosee, on the Tallapoosa; and the Mississippians at Holy Ground, above the mouth of the Catawba.

These successes against the Creeks, and the recapture of Detroit, formed almost the only encouraging events in the second year of the war.

CHAPTER XX.

Jackson's difficulties at Fort Strother—Arrival of fresh troops—Jackson marches toward the centre of the Creek country—Battle of Emuckfau—Repulse of the Red Sticks—Return of the army toward Fort Strother—Battle of Enitachopeo—Gallant conduct of Constantine Perkins and Craven Jackson—Defeat of the Indians—Volunteers discharged—Jackson marches from Fort Strother with a new army—Battle of Cholocco Litahixee—Terrible slaughter of the Red Skins—Anecdote of Jackson—Submission of the Indians—Weatherford surrenders to Jackson—His speech—West Tennessee volunteers ordered home.

SHORTLY after his return to Fort Strother Jackson became involved in difficulties of a most discouraging character. In consequence of the remissness of his contractors, his provisions, at no time plenty, now threatened to fail entirely. Already restive under short allowance, the troops soon found cause for open dissatisfaction in a difference of opinion as to their legal period of service. Repeated mutinies broke out, and at length the whole expedition seemed on the point of breaking up in an armed struggle between Jackson and a few faithful followers on the one hand, and the discontented militia and volunteers on the other. Entreating, commanding, and threatening, by turns, the general finally induced about a hundred men to adhere to him until the arrival of reinforcements. The rest, claiming that the period of their service had expired, persisted in returning home.

At this critical juncture, on the 13th of January, 1814, eight hundred and fifty fresh volunteers, sent forward by Governor Blount, made their appearance at Fort Strother. Immediately advancing toward the heart of the Creek country, Jackson at Talladega received a further addition to his force of two hundred friendly Indians.

In the afternoon of the 21st, the army fell in with numerous fresh trails. These indications of the proximity of a large body of the enemy being presently confirmed by the reports of his spies, Jackson, encamping on the high grounds of Emuckfau, made every preparation to meet a sudden attack. It was well he did so. The morning of the 22d was just beginning to dawn, when his left wing was startled by the furious assault of a swarm of savages. For half an hour the attack was maintained stubbornly, and as stubbornly resisted. Daylight at length disclosing the position of their assailants, the Tennesseeans, charging in a body, drove them through the woods with great slaughter.

Though thus repulsed the Red Sticks were not discouraged. In the course of the morning they boldly advanced a second time, and attacked the right of the encampment. Charged by Coffee's cavalry and a few friendly Creeks, they were at length forced from their position into a reedy swamp, where they lay concealed and unassailable.

While Coffee was thus engaged, the main body of the enemy had attacked Jackson's left, pouring from behind logs, trees, and shrubbery, an irregular but deadly fire. This the Tennesseeans, though mostly raw troops, sustained with the greatest firmness, until Jackson, who commanded in person at this point, finally ordered a charge. Led by the impetuous Colonel Carroll, the whole line now advanced, driving the enemy before them with the bayonet.

In the mean time the Red Sticks on the right, issuing from their swampy fastnesses, had turned on Coffee, who, though severely wounded, remained at the head of his troops, and kept the assailants at bay. Reinforced by Jackson, he ordered a charge. Once more the savages gave way, and the fight was ended.

Though repulsed, the Creeks had displayed a ferocious courage that commanded the serious consideration of Jackson, whose force was weaker than he desired. His provisions were scarce, his wounded numerous, and the enemy would doubtless soon be reinforced. He determined, therefore, to return to Fort Strother with all possible despatch.

At ten o'clock the next day, the army began its retrograde march, the wounded being borne on litters made of the hides of the slain horses. Enitachopeo creek was reached that evening. Knowing that the Red Sticks had been hanging on his rear during the preceding day's march, Jackson, on the morning of the 24th, fearing an ambuscade at the usual crossing-place, determined to pass the creek some six hundred yards lower down.

The wounded and the front guard had just crossed, and Jackson, upon the eastern bank, was superintending the operations of the army, when an alarm gun was heard, followed immediately by a fierce attack of the savages upon Captain Russell's company of spies, who gradually retired, fighting gallantly, till they reached the rear-guard. Colonel Carroll, commanding the centre column, ordered his men to halt and form. Struck with sudden panic, the right and left columns fled without firing a gun, with their officers foremost in the flight. Colonel Stump, who came plunging down the bank, near the exasperated commander-in-chief, narrowly escaped being cut down by his sword. Sharing the panic of the two others, the centre column also plunged into the creek, leaving Carroll, supported by Captain Quarle's company, Russell's spies, and the artillery under Lieutenant Armstrong—in all scarcely a hundred men—to check the enemy's advance.

While the infantry and a portion of the artillery, mounting to the top of the bank, there held the Indians at bay, Armstrong, with a few assistants, succeeded in dragging his solitary six-pounder from the bed of the creek to an eminence that commanded the approach to the ford. In the hurry of unlimbering the gun, the rammer and picker had been left on the carriage. With wonderful presence of mind, and while Indian bullets rattled like hail around them, Constantine Perkins and Craven Jackson, two of the gunners, supplied the deficiency; Perkins, by removing his bayonet, and ramming the charges home with his musket, and Jackson by using his ramrod as a pricker, and priming with a musket cartridge. Thus loading their piece, this gallant little band, pouring grape among the savages, kept them in check until Jackson and his staff were enabled, by great exertions, to rally the flying troops, and recross the creek. At the same time Gordon's spies, in front when the alarm was given, having made a circuit through the forest, fell upon the left flank of the Indians; who, finding that the whole army was now moving against them, threw away their packs, blankets, and whatever seemed likely to retard their flight, and fled precipitately from the field.

The loss of the Tennesseeans in the battles of Emuckfau and Enitachopeo, was seventy killed and seventy wounded. Of Indians, one hundred and eighty-nine dead bodies were counted on the two fields. How many of those who escaped were wounded there is no means of knowing.

Continuing their march without further interruption to Fort Strother, Jackson's volunteers became entitled to their discharge, and were sent home.

New calls for militia had meanwhile been made. They came in slowly; but, through the exertion of Governor Blount, Jackson was enabled to leave Fort Strother, on the 15th of March, at the head of thirty-five hundred men, including, besides Tennesseeans, a regiment of regulars and many friendly Indians. Pushing with this force fifty miles down the Coosa, he built and garrisoned Fort Williams, on that river. He then again directed his march through the mountain wilderness for the great bend of the Tallapoosa, some seventy miles above the present town of Dadeville, in Alabama.

At this point—Cholocco Litahixee, or the Great Horse-shoe Bend—the main body of the Red Sticks, some twelve hundred strong, had assembled to make a desperate stand. Surrounded almost entirely by the river, whose windings here assume the figure of an immense horse-shoe, enclosing a peninsula of about a hundred acres, the position of the Indians was accessible only by a narrow neck of land, across which they had thrown up a strong breastwork of huge logs, so arranged as to expose assailants to a cross fire. The houses of the village stood upon some low grounds at the extremity of the peninsula, where hundreds of canoes were tied to the river bank.

Determined to carry the breastwork, Jackson, early in the morning of the 27th of March, despatched General Coffee with the mounted men and friendly Indians to ford the river some two miles below, and line the opposite bank of the bend, so as to prevent the enemy from escaping in their canoes. Signalized by Coffee that he had taken his position, Jackson marched the remainder of his force toward the breastwork, planted his cannon on an eminence about eighty yards from its nearest face, and at ten o'clock opened a brisk but ineffectual fire.

Meanwhile some of Coffee's Cherokees, swimming the river, took possession of the canoes, upon which the Red Sticks had relied for escape, in the event of their being defeated. Employing the means thus offered, Coffee immediately sent a considerable force across the river.

Headed by Colonel Morgan and Captain Russell, this adventurous detachment, not without loss, reached the Indian village, and in a few moments wrapped it in flames.

This new and unexpected attack, throwing the Red Sticks into partial confusion, afforded Jackson an opportunity of which he was not slow to take advantage. He immediately gave the order, impatiently waited for, to storm the breastwork. Rushing forward with loud shouts, the men fought their way through a deadly fire to the ramparts. Here an obstinate and sanguinary conflict ensued. At length Major Montgomery, of the regulars, mounting the logs, called upon his men to follow; but he had scarcely spoken when a rifle ball pierced his brain, and he fell lifeless. Undaunted by the fall of their leader, the troops, imitating his example, scaled the breastwork and, after a desperate hand to hand struggle, finally forced their way within the enemy's line.

Coffee's troops, hurrying from the destruction of the village, now attacked the unfortunate savages in the rear. Thus hotly assailed, they fought with the courage of desperation, none asking for quarter, but each man selling his life as dearly as possible. After a lengthened struggle some fled to the river and, attempting to swim it, met death from the unerring rifles of the Tennesseeans. Many betook themselves to the western angle of the breastwork, where, screened by heaps of timber and treetops, they maintained a spirited fire upon Jackson's line. Desiring to save the lives of those brave men, the commander-in-chief despatched a messenger to them, telling them of the uselessness of further resistance, and assuring them of his clemency provided they would surrender. Shouting defiance, they replied by firing upon the messenger, who received a severe wound in the breast. An attempt was then made to dislodge them with the artillery. This failing, fire was applied to their covert, and as they fled they were shot down without mercy. Night only put an end to this scene of blood, during which five hundred and fifty-seven Indians left their bodies on the field of battle. Besides these, many were slain while crossing the river; and it is conjectured that not more than two hundred survived, and under cover of the darkness of night made good their escape. Two hundred and fifty were taken prisoners; all men and women except two or three. The loss of Jackson, when compared with that of the enemy, was small. Including the friendly Indians it was but fifty-five killed and one hundred and forty-six wounded.

After the battle an interesting incident occurred. Moved by the wail of an Indian infant found upon the field, the mother of which had perished during the confusion of the battle,

Jackson endeavoured to persuade some nursing women among the captives to suckle it. "Its mother is dead," was the stoical answer; "let the child die too." Without children himself, the general then undertook the duties of a nurse, feeding the forsaken infant with some brown sugar, which formed part of his private stores. Subsequently carried home by Jackson, the poor orphan thus provided for grew to be an intelligent lad, learned the trade of a saddler, and coming to manhood was comfortably established at Nashville.

The battle of the Horse-shoe brought the war nearly to an end. Entirely broken in spirit, the Red Sticks made but few efforts to rally, and presently began to come into Fort Jackson, built since the fight, four miles above the confluence of the Coosa and Tallapoosa.

Among the most conspicuous of the chiefs who thus submitted themselves and their people to the terms of peace offered by Jackson, was Weatherford, the half-breed, who, leading the Indians at Fort Mimms, had opened the war. Riding up to the general's marquee, Weatherford was met by Jackson, who passionately inquired,—

"How dare you, sir, to ride up to my tent after having murdered the women and children at Fort Mimms?"

"General Jackson"—so he replied—"I am

not afraid of you. I fear no man, for I am a Creek warrior. I have nothing to ask for myself. Kill me if you desire. I come to beg you to send for the women and children of the war party, who are now starving in the woods. Their fields and their cribs have been destroyed by your people, who have driven them to the woods without an ear of corn. I exerted myself in vain to prevent the massacre of women and children at Fort Mimms. I fought there. I fought the army of Georgia. I did you all the injury I could. I am now done fighting. My warriors are all killed, and I can fight no longer. I look back with sorrow that I have brought destruction upon my nation. Send for the women and children. They never did you any harm. But kill me if the white people want it done."

When this speech was concluded, the throng that had gathered around the marquee began to cry out, "Kill him! kill him! kill him!" Commanding silence, "Any man," exclaimed Jackson, "who would kill so brave a man as this, would rob the dead!" The men murmured, but Weatherford's life was spared, and he took no further part in the war except to influence his warriors to surrender.

By the establishment of Fort Jackson a line of posts was now formed from Tennessee and from Georgia to the Alabama river. The lenient policy of the general having induced most of the Red Sticks to submit, it was not deemed necessary to maintain a large army longer in the field. Garrisoning the different posts with the East Tennesseeans of General Dougherty, General Pinckney, the senior officer of the southern army, on the 21st of April, ordered the West Tennessee troops to march home. Two hours after the order was issued they were in motion. Reaching Camp Blount, near Fayetteville, they were there discharged by Jackson, who, before parting with them, spoke gratefully of their gallant conduct and of the patience with which they had borne the privations and hardships of war.

CHAPTER XXI.

Jackson appointed a major-general—He negotiates a treaty with the Creeks—The British at Pensacola—Jackson's correspondence with the Spanish governor—His project for the reduction of Pensacola—He calls upon Tennessee for volunteers—Fort Bowyer attacked—Repulse of the British—They take refuge at Pensacola—Jackson determines to attack that place—Arrival of volunteers from Tennessee—Jackson marches upon Pensacola—Unsuccessful negotiations—Americans attack the town—Submission of the Spanish governor—Escape of the British—Indians driven off—Jackson resurrenders Pensacola—He proceeds to New Orleans.

HAVING been elevated to the rank of major-general in the United States army, Jackson once more left the retirement of the Hermitage, and early in July proceeded to the fort called by his name, where during the following month he successfully negotiated a treaty with the conquered Creeks. Through this treaty an assurance of safety was given to the frontiers of Tennessee, by the cession to the United States of all the Indian territory lying along the Tennessee River.

In the mean time, a considerable number of the Red Sticks refusing to submit to the terms offered them, had fled to the Floridas, which at this period belonged to Spain. Already preparing for an energetic attack upon the southwest when the northern campaign should close, the British, landing a large quantity of military stores at the mouth of the Apalachicola River, began to reassemble and arm the fugitive Creeks. Of this fact, and of the succour and protection afforded the savages by the Spanish authorities at Pensacola, rumours reached Jackson while he was still employed in negotiating the treaty of which mention has already been made. He immediately despatched a letter to Manriquez, the governor of Pensacola, remonstrating against the conduct of the Spanish authorities toward the United States, with which power Spain professed to be at peace. In reply, Manriquez denied that the fugitive Creeks were then with him. If they were, he continued, hospitality would forbid him to surrender them, or to refuse them assistance in their distress. Admitting that the English still possessed and used certain posts in the Floridas, he attempted to show that they did so by right of a treaty which existed between Great Britain and the Indians previous to the conquest of the country by Spain.

Not at all pleased with the reply to his first note, Jackson despatched to Manriquez a second, sharp and energetic in its tone and quite characteristic. "I have the honor," so he wrote, "of being intrusted with the command of this district. Charged with its protection and the safety of its citizens, I feel my ability to discharge the task, and trust your excellency will always find me ready and willing to go forward in the performance of that duty whenever circumstances shall render it necessary. . . . . Your excellency has been candid enough to admit your having supplied the Indians with arms. In addition to this, I have learned that a British flag has been seen flying on one of your forts. All this is done while you are pretending to be neutral. You cannot be surprised then, but will provide a fort in your town for my soldiers and Indians, should I take it into my head to pay you a visit."

In this last sentence, Jackson hinted at what he had more than once previously urged upon the federal authorities, the necessity of accomplishing the reduction of Pensacola. Returning from that place, the messenger who had carried the general's second letter to Manriquez, reported that he had there seen from one hundred and fifty to two hundred soldiers, and about five hundred Indian warriors, under the drill of British officers, armed with new muskets, and dressed in the English uniform.

This information Jackson immediately despatched to the government, and again urged his favourite project—the reduction of Pensacola. Orders to take possession of that post had already been sent to him, but he did not receive them till six months afterward.

At length, having finished his business with the Indians at Fort Jackson, the commander-in-chief, on the 11th of August, departed for Mobile, which it was expected that the British would soon attack. Here he found himself at the head of three thin regiments of regulars. In view of the preparations which the enemy were making at Pensacola, he presently hurried off despatches to Tennessee, with pressing calls for volunteers. These despatches had scarcely reached Nashville, when, on the 15th of September, Fort Boyer was attacked by the British. This post, the possession of which would greatly facilitate the proposed operations of the enemy against New Orleans, was built on the eastern point of Mobile Bay, thirty miles distant from the town, and commanding the approach to it. Garrisoned by one hundred and thirty regulars, the fort made so gallant a resistance that the British were at length forced to retire, with the loss of a sloop-of-war blown up, and of two hundred and thirty-two men killed and wounded.

After this repulse the enemy took refuge at Pensacola. Finding all his previous conjectures thus confirmed, Jackson, though without orders, determined to assume the responsibility and take possession of that place. Such a course he believed could not afford even a pretext for rupture between Spain and the United States. If the latter country through her agents gave assistance to our enemy, she deserved herself to be treated as a foe. On the other hand, if Spain, having but a small force in the Floridas, could not maintain her neutrality by expelling thence the troops of Great Britain, it would certainly be no just ground of complaint if the United States were to bring in an army to assist her. At any rate, so Jackson argued, should complaint be made, his government having never given him authority to do as he proposed might with propriety disavow the act, and by exposing himself to punishment sufficiently atone for whatever outrage he might thus inflict upon Spain. Accordingly he resolved to march upon Pensacola as soon as a sufficient force could be raised.

In the mean time, Jackson's call upon Tennessee had been responded to with spirit and alacrity. Only nineteen days after it had reached the state capital, Coffee was at Fayetteville with two thousand able-bodied troops, well equipped, and eager to advance. Joined during his rapid march by eight hundred additional volunteers, Coffee presently encamped on the western bank of the Tombigbee, a short distance above its confluence with the Alabama. Here on the 26th of October he was met by Jackson, who proceeded expeditiously to make the necessary arrangements for an immediate march.

Crossing the Tombigbee, Coffee's brigade pressed forward to Fort Montgomery. After a few days of repose at this place, Jackson took up his line of march for Pensacola, at the head of three thousand Tennesseeans, regulars, Mississippi mounted men, and friendly Indians. On the 6th of November he encamped within two miles of the Spanish town.

Before proceeding farther, Jackson determined to try once more the effect of peaceable negotiation, and endeavour to ascertain how far Manriquez felt disposed to preserve a good understanding between the two governments. Accordingly Major Pierre was despatched with a flag to make known the objects at which the Americans aimed, and to require that the different forts, Barrancas, St. Rose, and St. Michael, should be immediately surrendered, to be garrisoned by United States troops until Spain, by furnishing a sufficient force, might be able to protect the province and preserve her neutrality unimpaired.

Fired upon from Fort St. Michael's, Pierre was compelled to return without having accomplished his mission. Notwithstanding this outrage, Jackson still desired a peaceable understanding, and by a prisoner sent a letter to the Spanish governor, demanding an explanation for the insult that had been offered to his flag. In his reply, Manriquez disclaimed any participation in the affair, and expressed his perfect willingness to receive any overtures the American general might be pleased to make.

Confirmed in his opinion that what had been done was chargeable upon the English rather than upon the Spanish authorities, Jackson admitted himself satisfied with this explanation by immediately despatching Pierre a second time to the governor, with a message similar to the one previously attempted to be sent. "I come not," he wrote, "as the enemy of Spain, to make war, but to ask for peace; to demand security for my country, and that respect to which she is entitled and must receive. My force is sufficient, and my determination taken to prevent a future repetition of the injuries she has received. I demand, therefore, the possession of the Barrancas, and other fortifications, with all their munitions of war. If delivered peaceably, the whole will be receipted for, and become the subject of future arrangements by our respective governments; while the property, laws, and religion of your citizens shall be respected. But if taken by an appeal to arms, let the blood of your subjects be upon your own head. One hour is given you for deliberation. At the expiration of that hour your determination must be had."

Receiving the message at midnight, Manriquez immediately summoned a council, which decided that the American general's demands could not be acceded to. Assuring the governor that recourse would certainly be had to arms, Pierre returned to Jackson, who at once put his troops in motion toward the town.

Across the only street by which Jackson could enter Pensacola, without passing under the guns of Fort St. Michael, the Spaniards had planted several pieces of artillery. To remove this obstruction, Captain Laval, of the third regiment, was ordered forward with one hundred picked men. Regardless of a heavy cross-fire, poured in upon him from houses and gardens, Laval, early on the morning of November the 7th, advanced with a daring rapidity that carried him almost into the midst of the Spaniards before they had time to discharge their pieces. Though at this moment deprived of their leader, who fell with his leg shattered by a grape-shot, Laval's little band reaching the battery, carried it at the bayonet's point, and drove the Spaniards from their guns.

In this brief but spirited affair seven Americans were slain and eleven wounded. The loss of the Spaniards was four killed, six wounded, and several taken captive.

Forming in three columns, the main body of Jackson's troops now advanced along the beach eastward of the town. Here they were met by the terrified governor, bearing a flag of truce, and expressing his readiness to agree to the American commander's proposals. Ordering a cessation of hostilities, Jackson hurried to the Intendant's house, and there completed an arrangement by which the town-arsenals and munitions of war were to be immediately surrendered.

Leaving Major Pierre with eight hundred men to take possession of Fort St. Michael, Jackson withdrew the remainder of his troops to their camp outside the town. An attempt was made by the British, whose shipping still remained at anchor in the harbour, to intercept his return march. Aided by their boats, they were enabled to open a brisk fire upon the Americans as they passed along the principal streets, but Lieutenant Call hastening to the beach with a single piece of artillery, soon obliged them to disperse.

At six o'clock in the evening the commandant of Fort St. Michael declared that he could not evacuate before morning. Word was at once sent him that if the fort were not instantly delivered up it would be stormed and the garrison put to the sword. The American troops were immediately admitted.

Early in the following morning preparations were made to take possession of Fort Barrancas, seven miles from Pensacola, and which, commanding the entrance to the harbour, if once in the hands of Jackson, would enable him to cut off the retreat of the British shipping—an object he earnestly desired to accomplish. The order for its delivery had been signed by Manriquez and the line of march toward it already taken up, when a tremendous explosion, followed by two others in quick succession, was heard in that direction. Intelligence presently arrived that the fort had been blown up by the British, whose fleet, sailing by the yet smoking ruins, made good their escape to sea.

Having thus driven off the British, and compelled the fugitive Red Sticks to flee for shelter to the banks of the Apalachicola, Jackson, on the 9th of November, gave up Pensacola to the Spanish authorities, and marched his forces to Fort Montgomery. From this post, Coffee with his mounted Tennesseeans was ordered to proceed to the Mississippi, and to encamp on the borders of that stream as near New Orleans as a supply of forage could be obtained. Convinced that the British were preparing a formidable expedition against that city, Jackson himself hastened by way of Mobile to take command there in person.

CHAPTER XXII.

Jackson calls again for volunteers—Patriotism of the Tennesseeans—Disaffection at New Orleans—British forces under Packenham threaten that city—Difficulty with the Louisiana militia—Martial law proclaimed—Vanguard of the enemy encamp on the Mississippi—Night attack by Jackson and Coffee—Dilatory movements of the British—Destruction of the schooner Caroline—First repulse of the enemy—Jackson's difficulty with the Louisiana legislature—Battle of the 8th of January—Packenham slain—Final repulse of the British.

In consequence of communications from the Governor of Louisiana, Jackson seeing at once that for the defence of New Orleans he would have to rely mainly upon exterior resources, had already pressed the executives of the neighbouring states to hasten forward bodies of militia to his support.

Enthusiastic and active, Governor Blount had exerted all his authority and influence in compliance with Jackson's solicitations. By the 19th of November twenty-five hundred brave Tennesseeans, headed by the energetic Carroll, were assembled at Nashville. Eight days afterward they embarked on the Cumberland for New Orleans. Fortunately the river, usually low at this period of the year, was unexpectedly swollen by heavy rains, and the boats descended without obstruction to the Ohio.

Reaching New Orleans on the 1st of December, Jackson found that city illy prepared to meet an attack. The anxiously-expected troops from Tennessee and Kentucky had not as yet been heard from. A few regulars and the militia and volunteers of the city and its vicinity formed almost the sole force upon which Jackson could depend in the event of the enemy's sudden appearance. Already in session several weeks, the legislature of Louisiana had as yet resolved upon nothing. Despondency and discontent, and what was more alarming, disaffection were manifested on all sides. The arrival of Jackson, however, and the activity and energy which he immediately displayed, gave a more encouraging aspect to affairs and inspired even the desponding with hope.

On the 12th of December intelligence arrived at New Orleans of the appearance off the entrance to Lake Borgne of the long-looked-for English fleet, having on board, exclusive of sailors and marines, between ten and twelve thousand veteran troops, commanded by Sir Edward Packenham, a distinguished general of Wellington's late Peninsula army. Two days afterward, the American flotilla of gunboats, despatched to reconnoitre the enemy, having been becalmed on Lake Borgne, was there attacked by a greatly superior number of British barges, and after a hard struggle compelled to surrender.

Seriously concerned at this disaster, Jackson on the 15th hurried off expresses to obtain tidings, if possible, of Coffee's brigade and of the militia expected from Tennessee and Kentucky. "You must not sleep," so he wrote to Coffee, "until you arrive within striking distance. Your accustomed activity is looked for. Innumerable defiles present themselves where your services and riflemen will be all-important. An opportunity is at hand to reap for yourself and brigade the approbation of your country."

On the 16th, an aid-de-camp arrived with intelligence from Carroll, who wrote that the state of the weather, and high and contrary winds, greatly retarded his progress. To remedy this, the only steamboat then on the river having just arrived from Pittsburg, was sent to bring him down.

After encountering numerous hardships from heavy rains and a scarcity of supplies, Coffee reached Sandy Creek, a short distance above Baton Rouge, where he received Jackson's orders on the evening of the 17th of December. Leaving behind him the sick, three hundred in number, he set off at once with twelve hundred and fifty men. Pushing forward himself with eight hundred of the best mounted, he accomplished the distance of one hundred and twenty miles in two days, and on the third encamped within four miles of the city.

In the mean time, Jackson had been actively engaged in preparations to prevent surprise, and to meet the enemy promptly at every accessible point. In this, however, he encountered serious difficulties. His first effort to draw out the militia, among whom were many disaffected persons, met with resistance on their part, and that resistance was encouraged by the legislature then in session, who declared his requisition to be illegal, unnecessary, and oppressive. Thus supported, a considerable portion of the militia clung to the position they had taken, and resolutely refused to answer any call upon their services, except on conditions to which Jackson's unyielding disposition would not suffer him to consent.

In this emergency the commander-in-chief urged upon the legislature the necessity of suspending the writ of habeas corpus. Wearied at length with the dilatory, and perhaps justifiable cautiousness of the legislature in acting upon this subject, on the 20th of December he took the responsibility of closing their deliberations by proclaiming the city and environs of New Orleans under martial law. This rigid policy which, as will presently be seen, involved its author in considerable difficulty, was adopted "under a solemn conviction that the country committed to his care could by such a measure alone be saved from utter ruin. By it he intended to supersede such civil powers as in their operation interfered with those he was obliged to exercise. He thought that, at such a moment, constitutional forms should be suspended for the preservation of constitutional rights; and that there could be no question, whether it were better to depart for a moment from the enjoyment of our dearest privileges, or to have them wrested from us for ever."

Meanwhile, having been joined by the Tennesseeans under Carroll, and a body of Mississippi dragoons, Jackson, on the 21st, found himself at the head of five thousand men, less than one-fifth of whom were regulars. With the exception of the Kentucky troops all the forces expected had arrived.

On the 22d, the British vanguard, composed of three thousand men, led by General Keene, having passed, under the guidance of some Italian fishermen, from the head of Lake Borgne through the Bayou Bienvenu to within a short distance of the Mississippi, encamped on the left bank of that river, fifteen miles below New Orleans.

Concentrating his forces, Jackson determined to attack the enemy that evening. Marching from the city at the head of the regulars, Coffee's brigade, the city militia, and Hind's Mississippi dragoons, he arrived within view of the British camp a little before dark. Jackson's plans were speedily arranged. The schooner Caroline, dropping down the river, was to give the signal of attack, by opening a fire upon the British left, while Coffee's brigade, taking a circuitous route, was ordered to advance against and turn their right. The main body, under Jackson in person, pushed forward to assail them in front.

It was dark night, when the Caroline, floating quietly down the stream, anchored abreast of the enemy's watch-fires, and directed by their light poured a heavy and destructive fire upon the most crowded portion of the encampment. Having had no suspicions of the real character of the Caroline, the British were thrown into momentary confusion by this unexpected attack. Recovering, however, they extinguished their watch-fires, and retired a short distance into the open field; meanwhile answering the cannonade of the vessel by harmless volleys of musketry and discharges of Congreve rockets.

When the Caroline commenced firing, Coffee had reached a point which he believed to be in front of the centre of the enemy's right wing. Extending his own line parallel with the river, he marched directly toward the camp. He had scarcely advanced a hundred yards, when not knowing that the British had been forced back from the river, he was startled by encountering a sudden and heavy discharge of musketry.

The moon had now risen, but shone dimly through the gathering fog. Though fired upon, Coffee's riflemen could not mark their assailants with that distinctness which was necessary to the fatality of their aim, and consequently to the success of their movement. Ordered to advance, however, they moved forward bravely, utterly regardless of what might be the strength of the force opposed to them, and gaining a nearer position opened upon the enemy, who speedily gave way, retreated, rallied again, and were a second time forced back by the deadly fire of the Tennesseeans.

In the mean time, after a desperate struggle and a great deal of confusion on both sides, Jackson had broken the enemy's centre. Coffee again charging on their right, drove his opponents once more before him. Thus successfully assailed at three points, the British abandoning their original position at length stood firm in a very strong one, between an old levee, which sheltered them from the Caroline, and a new one, raised within, which covered them from the rifles of the Tennesseeans.

Finding that this position could not be carried, and that the enemy, reinforced during the contest, now greatly outnumbered him, Jackson remained inactive on the battle-field till day-break, and then withdrew to a strong stand-point, two miles closer to the city, where the Mississippi and the swamp approached nearest each other.

The loss of the British in this night attack was estimated at four hundred killed, wounded, and missing. That of the Americans was but twenty-four killed, one hundred and fifteen wounded, and seventy-four made prisoners.

Had the enemy advanced at once upon Jackson, the ultimate fortune of their expedition would probably have been different. But, as the American commander had foreseen, his spirited night assault threw them into alarm and rendered their subsequent operations cautious and slow. Ignorant of his strength, which the American prisoners exaggerated greatly, they waited to bring up reinforcements and artillery. Profiting by their delay, Jackson proceeded with almost incredible activity and labour to fortify his naturally strong position. Having deepened and widened the shallow ditch which stretched across his front from the Mississippi to the swamp, he formed a rampart along the line with bales of cotton, and covered it with earth.

On the 27th, a British battery, planted on the levee near the late battle-field, succeeded in setting fire to and destroying the Caroline. Gathering confidence from this slight success, the enemy, led by Packenham in person, the next day left their encampment in force, drove in Jackson's outposts, and approaching within half a mile of his lines, began a furious attack upon them with artillery, bombs, and Congreve rockets. Checked in their advance by Jackson's five pieces and by a raking fire from the Louisiana sloop-of-war, the British, after maintaining a continued cannonade of seven hours duration, finally withdrew with the loss of more than a hundred in killed and wounded.

During this attack a detachment of the enemy, moving against the extreme left of the American line, were there met by Coffee and his riflemen. Though greatly outnumbering the Tennesseeans, the British were driven back. Perceiving from this demonstration, however, that his left might be turned, Jackson immediately proceeded to strengthen his defences in that quarter by extending his rampart of cotton bales, logs, and earth into the swamp, an arduous task, which was intrusted to Coffee and his brigade. When completed, the new breastwork was left to be defended by the Tennesseeans, who hourly expecting an attack, maintained their post night and day, resting and sleeping on logs and brush, by which they were elevated above the waters that surrounded them.

Matters now approaching a crisis, Jackson began to be disturbed by apprehensions of internal treachery. Waited upon by a special committee of the Louisiana legislature, he was asked what his course would be if he were driven from his position. "If," replied the general, "if I thought the hair of my head could divine what I should do, I would cut it off. Go back with this answer. Say to your honourable body, that if disaster does overtake me, and I am driven from my line to the city, they may expect to have a very warm session." After the war, in answer to a question on this point, "I should have retreated to the city," such were Jackson's words, "fired it, and fought the enemy amidst the surrounding flames. There were with me men of wealth, owners of considerable property, who would have been among the foremost to apply the torch to their own dwellings."

A rumour flying about the city that Jackson had determined upon this course, the speaker of the Louisiana senate began to make inquiries of the general's aid, Major Butler, as to the foundation for it. From this and other more significant circumstances, it was conjectured that the legislature contemplated saving the city by offering to capitulate. Apprizing Governor Claiborne of his suspicions, Jackson directed him to keep a close watch upon the legislature, and should a motion be made to capitulate, to place a guard at the door and confine the members to the hall. Misinterpreting the general's orders, Claiborne, without waiting for the necessary contingency, placed an armed force at the door of the capital, and prevented the legislature from convening.

Instead of shutting the members in doors, as Jackson had desired, he turned them out.

At length, after a severe conflict on the 1st, in which Packenham had a second time failed in an attempt to batter down the American breastwork, the morning of the 8th of January, 1815, found both armies prepared for what proved to be a final struggle.

On the right of Jackson's line, which was strengthened by an advanced redoubt, were posted the regulars and Louisiana militia. Coffee's riflemen still held their position in the swamp on the left, while Carroll's Tennesseeans and the recently arrived Kentucky militia formed the centre. Along the line were judiciously disposed eight separate batteries, mounting in all twelve guns. On the right bank of the river, General Morgan, with fifteen hundred men, was stationed behind an intrenchment, defended by several brass twelves and by a battery of twenty-four pounders, under the direction of Commodore Patterson. As many of the Kentuckians and others were unprovided with arms, they were set to work at throwing up a second line of intrenchments, as a place of rally should the breastwork be carried.

A detachment having crossed the river to assail Morgan, the main body of the British, at the firing of two signal rockets, moved forward with steady rapidity to storm Jackson's position.

Through the dense fog that hung heavily over the plain, the regulated tramp of the middle column, led by Packenham in person, was heard plainly long before it appeared. Guided solely by the sound, the American batteries opened a destructive fire upon the approaching assailants; who, nevertheless, closing their ranks as fast as they were thinned, pressed forward with a steady and unshaken front.

It was not until the fog lifting disclosed them fully to view, and the ramparts before them blazed with a sheet of deadly flame from the rifles of the Tennesseeans, that these brave men began to show signs of wavering. Still they moved forward, only to fall by hundreds. A few gaining the ditch in front of the American works, remained there during the rest of the battle, and were afterward made prisoners. Their comrades, unable to endure the storm of balls and bullets that incessantly assailed them, fell back in disorder, meeting death even in retreat. Hastening to restore order, Packenham fell dead in the arms of his aid-de-camp. Generals Gibbs and Keene were next borne from the plain, the one mortally and the other severely wounded.

At this moment, General Lambert, the next in command, coming up with the reserve, met the retreating column and succeeded in rallying it for a second effort. Again the enemy moved forward only to encounter once more that succession of deadly volleys. A few reached the ditch, many fell riddled with rifle-bullets, the rest fled in confusion. A third time Lambert and his officers endeavoured to win victory and save their reputations. But threats and entreaties were equally vain. Not a man could be found willing to advance again upon what seemed to be certain and unavailing death.

Meanwhile the British column operating upon the American right, under the command of Lieutenant-Colonel Rennie, had met with temporary success. The redoubt, as yet unfinished, was carried, but with a fearful loss of life. Having crossed the ditch and mounted the wall, waving his sword and calling upon his men to follow, Rennie fell dead. Gaining the redoubt, the victors found themselves unable to advance farther, and exposed to a murderous fire from the breastwork, they with difficulty maintained the position they had purchased so expensively. Finally, the centre column being repulsed, they effected a disorderly retreat.

On the left, where Coffee's brigade awaited their assault, the British signally failed. The swamp and the stern resistance of the Tennesseeans were obstacles they were unable to overcome, or even to attack with spirit; and when the two other columns fell back they also withdrew with less confusion and with less loss, but not with less complete defeat than their companions.

In the mean time, the British detachment against Morgan on the opposite bank had met with entire success. But the failure of Packenham rendered that success of little value. Regarding the lost position as an important one, however, Jackson contemplated regaining it by force; but having alarmed Lambert by an ingenious stratagem, that general withdrew the victorious detachment, and hastened to abandon the whole enterprise. On the day after the battle, he commenced with great secrecy the preparation for re-embarking his troops, first falling back to his original landing-place at the head of Lake Borgne, from which point the army finally retired on the 27th.

With regard to the British loss on this fatal day there are many conflicting accounts. Their killed, wounded, and prisoners, according to the report of the American inspector-general, did not amount to less than twenty-five hundred. Lambert's account represented it at two thousand and seventy. The force of the enemy actually engaged on both banks of the river has been variously stated at from seven to nine thousand. That of the Americans numbered in all between four and five thousand, a considerable portion of whom were destitute of arms, and consequently unable to engage in the fight. Of the whole number, but seventy-one were killed and wounded on both sides of the river.

CHAPTER XXIII.

Return of Jackson to New Orleans—Opposition of the Citizens to the continuance of Martial Law—Imprisonment of a member of the legislature by order of Jackson—Arrest of Judge Hall—Intelligence of peace—Return of Hall to New Orleans—Arrest and trial of Jackson for contempt of court—A fine imposed—Demonstration of popular sympathy—Dismissal of the Tennessee volunteers—Honours awarded Jackson by Congress—McMimm elected governor—Difficulties with the Cherokees—With the Florida Indians—Jackson ordered to take the field—Tallahassee towns burned—Seizure of the Spanish fort at St. Mark's—Skirmishes with the Indians—Execution of Arbuthnot and Ambrister—Jackson takes possession of Pensacola—Protest of the Spanish minister—Execution of Arbuthnot and Ambrister discussed by Congress—Jackson sustained by the House of Representatives—Florida ceded to the United States.

WAITING until the greater part of the British had taken to their ships, Jackson returned with the main body of his troops to New Orleans. His entrance into the city was a scene of triumph and rejoicing.

Doubtful as to whether the enemy had wholly abandoned their enterprise, Jackson deemed it necessary to keep New Orleans a little longer under the restrictions of martial law. Now that danger seemed to have passed away, this state of things was not borne with very patriotic fortitude. Much discontent began to show itself.

An anonymous article on the subject, full of bitter complaints, and calculated to excite a bad feeling among the troops, having appeared in one of the city papers, Jackson compelled the publisher to disclose the name of its author. The latter, proving to be a member of the legislature, was forthwith committed to prison, with the prospect of being tried for his life by a military court. A writ of habeas corpus was immediately issued on his behalf by Judge Hall, of the United States District Court. But, determined to settle at once the question of authority which he believed the proceeding was intended to test, Jackson, instead of obeying the writ, arrested Hall and sent him out of the city.

Two days afterward, on the 13th of March, official intelligence arrived of the ratification of a treaty of peace between Great Britain and the United States. The aspect of affairs now changed. Martial law ceasing, Hall, returning to the city, resumed the exercise of his judicial office, and caused process to be served on Jackson to appear and show cause why an attachment should not issue against him for contempt of court in resisting the writ of habeas corpus.

Answering this summons, the general appeared at court on the 30th of March, and through his counsel offered a written statement in defence of what he had done. After considerable discussion the court permitted certain portions of this statement to be read. That part of it, however, in which Jackson gave his reasons for declaring martial law, Hall refused to hear, and ordered the issue of an attachment, returnable on the following day.

At the time appointed, assuming the dress of a civilian, Jackson entered the crowded court-room, and had nearly reached the bar when, being recognised, the whole audience saluted him with a loud and enthusiastic cheer. Restoring silence by a deprecating move of his hand, he sat down, whereupon Hall, rising, and intimating his fear of a popular outbreak, was about to order an adjournment.

"There is no danger," interrupted Jackson. "There shall be none. The same arm that protected this city from outrage will shield this court or perish in the effort."

Thus reassured, Hall proceeded to business, and called upon the general to answer certain interrogatories, by which his guilt or innocence was to be determined.

"You would not hear my defence"—such were Jackson's words—"although you were advised that it contained nothing improper. Under these circumstances I appear before you to receive the sentence of the court, having nothing further to offer. Your honour will not understand me as intending any disrespect to this court, but as no opportunity has been afforded me of explaining the reasons and motives by which I was influenced, so is it expected that censure or reproof will constitute no part of that sentence which you may imagine it your duty to pronounce."

This plain speaking brought the affair to a speedy termination. Giving his decision, Hall imposed a fine of one thousand dollars, for which amount the general's check was immediately tendered to the clerk. Again cheering, the excited throng in the court-room now hurried Jackson out of doors, forced him into a carriage from which the horses had been taken, and dragged him in tumultuous triumph to his hotel. Fearing, from this perhaps excusable but still dangerous demonstration of popular sympathy, that his over-earnest friends might commit some unpardonable excess in his name, Jackson, in a brief address proclaiming the " important truth that submission to the civil authority is the first duty of a citizen," was finally enabled to allay a feverish excitement that seemed to threaten personal injury to the judge whose decision had just been made.

Giving a more legitimate, or at least less extravagant turn to the expression of their regard, Jackson's friends in New Orleans immediately made up the amount of his fine by subscription, and placed it in bank to his account. The general would not accept it, however, and proposed that the sum should be disposed of for the benefit of those whose relatives had fallen in the late battle. As a matter of course his suggestion was promptly acceded to.

In the mean time the Tennessee volunteers, having been dismissed, had marched home by land, arriving at Nashville after a long and tedious journey, in which they suffered much more by sickness than they had done from the enemy. They were soon followed by Jackson, who met from his townsmen a reception of the most gratifying character. By Congress he was rewarded for his gallant service with a vote of thanks, a gold medal commemorative of the battle of the eighth of January, and by being retained as one of the two major-generals of the United States army under the new peace establishment.

At the election of this year—a year ever to be remembered with pride by the citizens of Tennessee—Willie Blount, of whose active and energetic patriotism remark has been more than once made in the course of this narrative, was succeeded, as chief executive of the state, by Joseph M'Mimm.

In 1816 considerable dissatisfaction was created throughout the state on account of a new treaty arranged by the general government with the Cherokees, whose claim was recognised to the country on the southern course of the Tennessee River, which had been recently yielded up by the conquered Creeks. In consequence of the murmurs thus excited fresh negotiations were presently entered into, and the Cherokees induced to limit themselves, on the south side of the Tennessee, to the parallel of Huntsville, in Alabama. Almost the whole of the present State of Alabama, and a large tract in southern Tennessee, were thus laid open to settlement.

In 1817, repeated depredations by the Indians of Florida having rendered a resort to arms unavoidable, Jackson, who still commanded in the south, was ordered to take the field, with authority to call for troops from Tennessee.

Immediately issuing a summons for two thousand Tennessee volunteers, Jackson hastened to Hartford, on the Ockmulgee river, in Georgia, there to organize the militia of that state. At the head of these he presently marched toward Fort Scott, built near the confluence of the Flint and Chattahooche Rivers, and where about a thousand regulars were assembled. The country being new and barren, it was only by his indefatigable personal exertions that the general kept the troops supplied with provisions. Reaching Fort Scott, he found the Tennesseeans not arrived, and being still without adequate means of subsistence, hurried forward to meet the provision boats expected from New Orleans. As a depot for these supplies he built Fort Gadsden, not far from the head of Apalachicola Bay.

Having been at length furnished with provisions, Jackson, on the 26th of March, 1818, advanced against the Seminole towns in the neighbourhood of what is now Tallahassee. During the march his force was augmented by a party of Creek warriors, and a portion of the Tennesseeans whose advance had been retarded by the difficulty of procuring supplies.

Having easily defeated the Indians, whose villages were burned and their fields destroyed, Jackson proceeded to St. Mark's, the only Spanish fort in this section of Florida, and demanded its surrender on the ground that the Seminoles had there received aid and comfort. The Spanish commandant hesitating, an American detachment entered the fort and took forcible but bloodless possession.

Though still scantily supplied, the general now marched from St. Mark's, through a region almost entirely under water, to attack an Indian town near the mouth of the Surranee. He had expected to surprise the enemy, but found them prepared for resistance—their women and children having been sent away—under the lead of one Ambrister, a British trader. It was through this man's partner, a Scotsman named Arbuthnot, whom Jackson had found at St. Mark's, that the Indians received notice of the approach of the Americans. But though thus forewarned, the savages were unable to cope with the superior force opposed to them; and, after two considerable skirmishes, they fled from their village, which was burned, leaving their white leader a prisoner.

His men being worn down with fatigue and beginning to suffer from a scarcity of provisions, Jackson thought it inadvisable to march against the more southern Seminole towns, and presently set out on his return to St. Mark's. Reaching that place, he put Arbuthnot and Ambrister on trial for their lives before a court-martial. The former, found guilty of exciting and stirring up the Indians to war with the United States, and of providing them with means to carry on hostilities, was sentenced to death. Similar charges were preferred against Ambrister, with the additional one of affording the savages his personal assistance. He, too, was found guilty, and sentenced to death; but, on reconsideration, this sentence was mitigated to stripes on the bare back, and imprisonment at hard labour for a year. Having reason to believe Ambrister quite as guilty as his partner, Jackson disapproving of this modification, took the responsibility of reinstating the original sentence, and ordered both the incendiaries to be executed.

Shortly subsequent to this affair, Jackson received intelligence that the Spaniards of Pensacola had been instigating, or encouraging at least, Indian depredations upon the settlers of Alabama. Immediately advancing against that place, he was met by a protest from the Spanish governor, who declared that he would forcibly resist any invasion of the territory under his jurisdiction. Jackson pushed forward notwithstanding, and the next day entered Pensacola unopposed, the governor having taken refuge in a fort some six or seven miles below the town. But the Americans erecting batteries and opening a cannonade, the garrison of this work finally capitulated.

Intelligence of this act reaching Washington some seventy days later, the Spanish minister warmly protested against it. In reply, Mr. Adams, the secretary of state, declared that, though Jackson had acted without orders, yet, considering the aid and encouragement afforded by the forts of St. Mark's and Pensacola to hostile savages, notwithstanding the existence of treaty obligations binding the Spanish authorities to restrain the Indians under their jurisdiction, the general was abundantly justified in all that he had done. Still as the Seminoles were now defeated, the United States offered to restore Pensacola immediately, and St. Mark's whenever Spain should have there sufficient troops to keep in check the surrounding Indians.

While negotiations were pending on this subject, and on the complete surrender of the Floridas to the United States, the limits of Tennessee, as well as those of Kentucky, were greatly enlarged by a cession from the Chickasaw Indians of all that territory embraced between the northern flow of the Tennessee river and the Mississippi.

In the mean time, the course pursued by Jackson in the late Seminole campaign, from the successful completion of which he presently returned, became an important topic of public consideration.

On the 12th January, 1819, the subject was brought before Congress by the report of a majority of the military committee of the house, expressly condemning the executions of Arbuthnot and Ambrister. At the same time a minority report, sustained by the administration, and regarding the whole matter in a favourable light, was introduced by Richard M. Johnson, of Kentucky. In a lengthened discussion of nearly a month both sides had an opportunity of being heard.

On the one hand, it was maintained "that the American government had been the aggressor in the whole business; that the power of Congress in the matter of making war had been usurped upon; that the trials by court-martial were a mere mockery, since the parties were not liable to trial in that way; and that the execution of the British and Indian prisoners was in every respect unjustifiable."

On the other hand, "it was urged, as an apology for the executions, that as the Indians kill their captives, it was but a just retaliation to kill Indian captives; nor could white men, fighting on the Indian side, expect any better treatment than the Indians themselves. Harrison, of Ohio, vindicated Jackson's course except in executing Ambrister, which he thought irregular, as not sustained by the sentence of the court."

At length, after an ineffectual effort to indefinitely postpone the whole subject—an effort which Jackson's friends in no way seconded—the vote stood, for disapproving the executions of Arbuthnot and Ambrister, sixty-two to one hundred and three; and for disapproving the seizure of Pensacola and St. Mark's, seventy to one hundred.

Notwithstanding this triumph of the general's friends in the popular branch of the national legislature, an attempt was made in the Senate, about a fortnight later, to condemn his conduct in the Seminole campaign as a most reprehensible usurpation of authority. But the report containing this condemnation was suffered to lie on the table without action.

In whatever light the energetic proceedings of Jackson may now be regarded, one thing is scarcely to be doubted—their good effect in bringing Spain to some definite action with regard to the cession of the Floridas—a cession hitherto vainly applied for, and which was deemed extremely necessary for the safety and repose of the adjoining States. While the general's conduct was being debated in Congress, the Spanish minister, newly instructed by his government, had at length signed a treaty by which the Floridas were to be surrendered to the United States, in consideration of their discharging certain claims, amounting to five millions of dollars, brought by American citizens against Spain. Though immediately ratified by the Senate, this treaty, was not fully arranged and completed, by the consent of both parties, until the 18th of February, 1821.

CHAPTER XXIV.

Statistics of Tennessee according to the census of 1850—Form of government, &c.—Conclusion.

THE state of Tennessee, as at present constituted, is bounded on the north by Kentucky and Virginia, on the east by North Carolina, from which it is separated by the Alleghany mountains; on the south by Georgia, Alabama, and Mississippi; and on the west by the Mississippi river, which divides it from Arkansas and Missouri. It lies between 35° and 36° 36' north latitude, and between 81° 40' and 90° 15' west longitude, and includes an area of twenty-nine million one hundred and eighty-four acres, of which, according to the census of 1850, only five million one hundred and seventy-five thousand are as yet under cultivation. It is divided into three sections, commonly designated as East, Middle, and West Tennessee, which are subdivided into seventy-nine counties; the population numbering, by the latest official returns, one million two thousand six hundred and twenty-five, of whom three hundred and ninety-two thousand two hundred and fourteen were white males, three hundred and seventy-four thousand five hundred and thirty-nine white females, three thousand one hundred and eight free coloured males, three thousand two hundred and ninety-three coloured females; one hundred and eighteen thousand seven hundred and eighty male and one hundred and twenty thousand six hundred and eighty female slaves. The representative population being nine hundred and six thouaand eight hundred and thirty.

The agricultural products have been estimated at 52,276 bushels of Indian corn; 7,703,086 of oats; 1,619,381 of wheat; 89,163 of rye; 1,067,844 of Irish, and 2,777,716 of sweet potatoes; 369,321 of peas and beans; 14,214 of grass seed; 18,906 of flax seed; 20,148,932 pounds of tobacco; 8,139,585 of butter; 77,812,800 of cotton; 1,364,378 of wool; 1,036,571 of beeswax and honey; 177,680 pounds of cheese; 368,131 of flax; 248,000 of cane, and 158,557 of maple sugar; 258,854 of rice, and 74,092 tons of hay. The live stock valued at $29,978,016; market goods $97,183; orchard products $52,894; and slaughtered animals $6,401,765.

There were in 1850, 2789 manufacturing establishments in the State, each producing $500 and upward annually. Among these were 33 cotton factories, with a capital amounting in the aggregate to $669,600, employing 310 male and 580 female operatives; consuming raw material worth $297,500, and manufacturing 363,250 yards of stuffs, and 2,326,250 pounds of yarn, the total value of which was $510,624. Four woollen establishments, with a capital of $10,900, gave employment to 15 males and two females, consumed raw material to the value of $1675, and fabricated 2220 hats worth $6310. Eighty-one furnaces and forges, with $1,915,950 capital and 2705 male hands, consumed raw material worth $730,551, and produced 44,152 tons of wrought, cast, and pig iron, the gross value of which was $1,611,043. In breweries and distilleries there was invested a capital of $66,125, giving employment to 159 hands, consuming

3000 bushels of barley, 258,400 of corn, and 5480 of rye, and producing 657,000 gallons of whisky, wine, &c. Of tanneries there was found to be 364, employing $490,320 capital, consuming raw material worth $396,159, and producing leather to the value of $746,484. In addition to these the value of home-made manufactures was estimated at $3,137,810—the highest in the Union.

The exports of Tennessee are principally live stock, pork, bacon, lard, butter, ginseng, cotton bagging, flour, Indian corn, fruits, tobacco, cotton, hemp, feathers, and saltpetre. The foreign imports of 1852 amounted to $252,504.

It has been seen that Tennessee at an early day provided liberally for the support of education. In 1850 there were nine colleges in the State, with an aggregate of 551 students, and libraries containing 27,056 volumes. There was also one theological school with 24 students, one law school with 56, and two medical schools with 590. The number of children in the State was 288,454, of public schools 2713, and 278 academies. The school fund amounted to 1,321,655, the annual expenditure being $114,718. The number of books in the various school libraries amounted to 5100 volumes.

There were in 1850 no less than 1939 churches in the State, 831 of which belong to the Methodists, 611 to the Baptists, 357 to the Presbyterians, 57 to the sect of Christians, 28 to the Free Church, 17 to the Episcopalians, 15 to the Union Church, 12 to the Lutherans, and 3 to the Roman Catholics. The remaining churches belonged to the Friends, the Protestant Evangelical, the Tunkers, and the Africans—making one church to every 517 inhabitants. The gross value of the church property was $1,208,276.

The public institutions consisted of 21 libraries, with an aggregate of 47,356 volumes; a State Penitentiary at Nashville, the present capital; and a Deaf and Dumb Asylum at Knoxville.

Under the constitution of Tennessee the governor is elected for two years by the popular vote, his salary being fixed at $2000 per annum. The Senate consists of twenty-five and the House of Representatives of seventy-five members, both elected by the people for two years. The Judiciary consists of a Supreme Court, presided over by three judges, elected for twelve years by a joint vote of the two houses of the legislature; of a Court of Chancery, presided over by four chancellors; and of fourteen Circuit Courts, presided over by as many judges. The judges of the inferior courts are elected by the legislature for eight years. Davidson county, in which the capital of the State is seated, has a special criminal court, and the city of Memphis has a Common Law and Chancery court. The salaries of the judges range from $1500 to $1800.

The actual State debt of Tennessee, in January, 1853, was $3,901,856.66; loan debt, $915,000; endorsed debt, $675,000—total, $5,491,856.66.

On the other hand the State was in possession of a school fund, amounting to $1,346,068, of productive property valued at $4,837,840, and of unproductive property worth $1,101,390. The annual expenses of the State, exclusive of the interest upon the public debt and the charge for educational purposes, did not much exceed $165,000.

In January, 1853, the aggregate capital of twenty-three banks chartered by the State, was $8,405,197; the circulation, $5,300,000; and the amount of coin in the vaults of the different institutions, $1,900,000.

Though prevented by their geographical position from engaging in those profitable commercial enterprises which have tended so largely to increase the wealth of the people inhabiting the Atlantic borders, the citizens of Tennessee have sought and found the means of prosperity on their own soil. Possessing immense tracts of fertile land, water power in abundance, navigable rivers which drain an area of forty-one thousand square miles, abundance of coal and other fuel for manufacturing purposes, a climate so various as to ripen in equal perfection the cereals of the North and the cotton of the South, they have already become the first State of the Union in the value of their domestic manufactures, the fourth in the production of tobacco, and the fifth in the scale of population.

THE END.

STEREOTYPED BY L JOHNSON AND CO.
PHILADELPHIA.

CATALOGUE
OF
VALUABLE BOOKS,
PUBLISHED BY
LIPPINCOTT, GRAMBO & CO.,
(SUCCESSORS TO GRIGG, ELLIOT & CO.)
NO. 14, NORTH FOURTH STREET, PHILADA.:

CONSISTING OF A LARGE ASSORTMENT OF

BIBLES, PRAYER-BOOKS, COMMENTARIES, STANDARD POETS, MEDICAL, THEOLOGICAL, AND MISCELLANEOUS WORKS, ETC.

PARTICULARLY SUITABLE FOR

PUBLIC AND PRIVATE LIBRARIES;

For Sale by Booksellers and Country Merchants generally throughout the United States.

THE BEST AND MOST COMPLETE FAMILY COMMENTARY.

The Comprehensive Commentary on the Holy Bible;
CONTAINING

THE TEXT ACCORDING TO THE AUTHORIZED VERSION,

SCOTT'S MARGINAL REFERENCES; MATTHEW HENRY'S COMMENTARY, CONDENSED, BUT CONTAINING EVERY USEFUL THOUGHT, THE PRACTICAL OBSERVATIONS OF

REV. THOMAS SCOTT, D.D.;

WITH EXTENSIVE

EXPLANATORY, CRITICAL, AND PHILOLOGICAL NOTES,

Selected from Scott, Doddridge, Gill, Adam Clarke, Patrick, Poole, Lowth, Burder, Harmer, Calmet, Rosenmueller, Bloomfield, Stuart, Bush, Dwight, and many other writers on the Scriptures.

The whole designed to be a digest and combination of the advantages of the best Bible Commentaries, and embracing nearly all that is valuable in

HENRY, SCOTT, AND DODDRIGE.
EDITED BY REV. WILLIAM JENKS, D.D.,
PASTOR OF GREEN STREET CHURCH, BOSTON.

Embellished with five portraits, and other elegant engravings, from steel plates; with several maps and many wood-cuts, illustrative of Scripture Manners, Customs, Antiquities, &c. In 6 vols. super-royal 8vo. Including Supplement, bound in cloth, sheep, calf, &c., varying in

Price from $10 to $15.

The whole forming the most valuable as well as the cheapest Commentary in the world.

The Companion to the Bible.

In one super-royal volume.

DESIGNED TO ACCOMPANY

THE FAMILY BIBLE;

OR,

HENRY'S, SCOTT'S, CLARKE'S, GILL'S, OR OTHER COMMENTARIES.

ILLUSTRATIONS OF THE HOLY SCRIPTURES,

In one super-royal volume.

DERIVED PRINCIPALLY FROM THE MANNERS, CUSTOMS, ANTIQUITIES TRADITIONS, AND FORMS OF SPEECH, RITES, CLIMATE, WORKS OF ART, AND LITERATURE OF THE EASTERN NATIONS:

EMBODYING ALL THAT IS VALUABLE IN THE WORKS OF

ROBERTS, HARMER, BURDER, PAXTON, CHANDLER,

And the most celebrated Oriental travellers. Embracing also the subject of the Fulfilment of Prophecy, as exhibited by Keith and others; with descriptions of the present state of countries and places mentioned in the Sacred Writings.

ILLUSTRATED BY NUMEROUS LANDSCAPE ENGRAVINGS,

FROM SKETCHES TAKEN ON THE SPOT.

EDITED BY REV. GEORGE BUSH,

Prof. of Hebrew and Oriental Literature in the N. Y. City University.

THE ILLUSTRATED CONCORDANCE,

In one volume, royal 8vo.

A new, full, and complete Concordance; illustrated with monumental, traditional, and oriental engravings, founded on Butterworth's, with Cruden's definitions; forming, it is believed, on many accounts, a more valuable work than either Butterworth, Cruden, or any other similar book in the language.

LIPPINCOTT'S STANDARD EDITIONS OF

THE BOOK OF COMMON PRAYER;

IN SIX DIFFERENT SIZES.

ILLUSTRATED WITH A NUMBER OF STEEL PLATES AND ILLUMINATIONS.

COMPREHENDING THE MOST VARIED AND SPLENDID ASSORTMENT IN THE UNITED STATES.

LIPPINCOTT'S EDITIONS OF
THE HOLY BIBLE,
SIX DIFFERENT SIZES.

Printed in the best manner, with beautiful type, on the finest sized paper, and bound in the most splendid and substantial styles. Warranted to be correct, and equal to the best English editions, at a much lower price. To be had with or without plates; the publishers having supplied themselves with over fifty steel engravings, by the first artists.

Baxter's Comprehensive Bible,

Royal quarto, containing the various readings and marginal notes, disquisitions on the genuineness, authenticity, and inspiration of the Holy Scriptures; introductory and concluding remarks to each book; philological and explanatory notes; tables of contents, arranged in historical order; a chronological index, and various other matter; forming a suitable book for the study of clergymen, Sabbath-school teachers and students.

The Oxford Quarto Bible,

Without note or comment, universally admitted to be the most beautiful family Bible extant.

Crown Octavo Bible,

Printed with large clear type, making a most convenient Bible for family use.

Polyglot Bible.

The Sunday-School Teacher's Polyglot Bible, with Maps, &c.

The Oxford 18mo. Bible.

This is an extremely handsome and convenient Pew Bible.

Agate 32mo. Bible,

Printed with larger type than any other small pocket edition extant.

32mo. Diamond Pocket Bible,

The neatest, smallest, and cheapest edition of the Bible published.

CONSTANTLY ON HAND,

A large assortment of BIBLES, bound in the most splendid and costly styles, with gold and silver ornaments, suitable for presentation; ranging in price from $10 00 to $100 00.

A liberal discount made to Booksellers and Agents by the Publishers.

ENCYCLOPÆDIA OF RELIGIOUS KNOWLEDGE;
OR, DICTIONARY OF THE BIBLE THEOLOGY, RELIGIOUS BIOGRAPHY ALL RELIGIONS, ECCLESIASTICAL HISTORY, AND MISSIONS.

In one volume, royal 8vo

JOSEPHUS'S (FLAVIUS) WORKS,

FAMILY EDITION.

BY THE LATE WM. WHISTON, A.M.

FROM THE LAST LONDON EDITION, COMPLETE.

One volume, beautifully illustrated with Steel Plates, and the only readable edition published in this country.

FAMILY PRAYERS AND HYMNS,

ADAPTED TO FAMILY WORSHIP,

AND

TABLES FOR THE REGULAR READING OF THE SCRIPTURES.

BY REV. S. C. WINCHESTER, A.M.

Late Pastor of the Sixth Presbyterian Church, Philadelphia; and the Presbyterian Church at Natchez, Miss.

One volume, 12mo.

The Clergy of America:

CONSISTING OF

ANECDOTES ILLUSTRATIVE OF THE CHARACTER OF MINISTERS OF RELIGION IN THE UNITED STATES.

BY JOSEPH BELCHER, D.D.,

Editor of "The Complete Works of Andrew Fuller," "Robert Hall," &c.

One volume, 12mo.

THE ERRORS OF MODERN INFIDELITY ILLUSTRATED AND REFUTED.

BY S. M. SCHMUCKER. A.M.

In one volume, 12mo.; cloth. Just published.

Burder's Village Sermons,

Or, 101 Plain and Short Discourses on the Principal Doctrines of the Gospel.

INTENDED FOR THE USE OF FAMILIES, SUNDAY-SCHOOLS, OR COMPANIES ASSEMBLED FOR RELIGIOUS INSTRUCTION IN COUNTRY VILLAGES.

BY GEORGE BURDER.

To which is added to each Sermon, a Short Prayer, with some General Prayers for Families, Schools, &c., at the end of the work.

COMPLETE, IN ONE VOLUME, OCTAVO.

SPLENDID LIBRARY EDITIONS.

ILLUSTRATED STANDARD POETS.

ELEGANTLY PRINTED, ON FINE PAPER, AND UNIFORM IN SIZE AND STYLE.

The following Editions of Standard British Poets are illustrated with numerous Steel Engravings, and may be had in all varieties of binding.

BYRON'S WORKS.
COMPLETE, IN ONE VOLUME, OCTAVO.

INCLUDING ALL HIS SUPPRESSED AND ATTRIBUTED POEMS; WITH SIX BEAUTIFUL ENGRAVINGS

THE POETICAL WORKS OF MRS. HEMANS.
COMPLETE, IN ONE VOLUME, OCTAVO; WITH SEVEN BEAUTIFUL ENGRAVINGS.

MILTON, YOUNG, GRAY, BEATTIE, AND COLLINS'S POETICAL WORKS.
COMPLETE IN ONE VOLUME, OCTAVO.

WITH SIX BEAUTIFUL ENGRAVINGS.

Cowper and Thomson's Prose and Poetical Works.
COMPLETE IN ONE VOLUME, OCTAVO.

Including two hundred and fifty Letters, and sundry Poems of Cowper, never before published in this country; and a new and interesting Memoir of Thomson, and upwards of twenty new Poems, printed for the first time, from his own Manuscripts, taken from a late Edition of the Aldine Poets, now being published in London.

WITH SEVEN BEAUTIFUL ENGRAVINGS.

THE POETICAL WORKS OF ROGERS, CAMPBELL, MONTGOMERY, LAMB, AND KIRKE WHITE.

COMPLETE IN ONE VOLUME, OCTAVO.

WITH SIX BEAUTIFUL ENGRAVINGS.

CRABBE, HEBER, AND POLLOK'S POETICAL WORKS.

COMPLETE IN ONE VOLUME, OCTAVO.

WITH SIX BEAUTIFUL ENGRAVINGS.

No Library can be considered complete without a copy of the above beautiful and cheap editions of the English Poets; and persons ordering all or any of them, will please say, LIPPINCOTT, GRAMBO & Co.'s illustrated edition.

A COMPLETE

Dictionary of Poetical Quotations:

COMPRISING THE MOST EXCELLENT AND APPROPRIATE PASSAGES IN THE OLD BRITISH POETS, WITH CHOICE AND COPIOUS SELECTIONS FROM THE BEST MODERN BRITISH AND AMERICAN POETS.

EDITED BY SARAH JOSEPHA HALE.

As nightingales do upon glow-worms feed,
So poets live upon the living light
Of Nature and of Beauty.
Bailey's Festus.

Beautifully illustrated with Engravings. In one super-royal octavo volume, in various bindings.

THE DIAMOND EDITION OF BYRON.

THE POETICAL WORKS OF LORD BYRON.

WITH A SKETCH OF HIS LIFE.

COMPLETE IN ONE NEAT DUODECIMO VOLUME, WITH STEEL PLATES.

THE POETICAL WORKS OF THOMAS MOORE,

COLLECTED BY HIMSELF.

COMPLETE IN ONE VOLUME.

This work is published uniform with Byron, from the last London edition and is the most complete printed in the country.

THE DIAMOND EDITION OF SHAKSPEARE.
(COMPLETE IN ONE VOLUME.)
INCLUDING A COPIOUS GLOSSARY.
UNIFORM WITH BYRON AND MOORE.

THE FOREGOING WORKS CAN BE HAD IN SEVERAL VARIETIES OF BINDING.

SCHOOLCRAFT'S GREAT NATIONAL WORK ON THE INDIAN TRIBES OF THE UNITED STATES.
WITH BEAUTIFUL AND ACCURATE COLOURED ILLUSTRATIONS.

HISTORICAL AND STATISTICAL INFORMATION
RESPECTING THE
HISTORY, CONDITION AND PROSPECTS
OF THE
Indian Tribes of the United States.

COLLECTED AND PREPARED UNDER THE DIRECTION OF THE BUREAU OF INDIAN AFFAIRS, PER ACT OF MARCH 3, 1847.

BY HENRY R. SCHOOLCRAFT, LL.D.

ILLUSTRATED BY S. EASTMAN, CAPT. U. S. A.

PUBLISHED BY AUTHORITY OF CONGRESS.

The Traveller's and Tourist's Guide
THROUGH THE UNITED STATES OF AMERICA, CANADA, ETC.

CONTAINING THE ROUTES OF TRAVEL BY STEAMBOAT, STAGE, AND CANAL, TOGETHER WITH DESCRIPTIONS OF, AND ROUTES TO, THE PRINCIPAL PLACES OF FASHIONABLE AND HEALTHFUL RESORT; WITH OTHER VALUABLE INFORMATION.

ACCOMPANIED BY

AN ENTIRELY NEW AND AUTHENTIC MAP OF THE UNITED STATES, INCLUDING CALIFORNIA, OREGON, &c., AND A MAP OF THE ISLAND OF CUBA.

BY W. WILLIAMS.

LIPPINCOTT, GRAMBO & CO.'S PUBLICATIONS.

THE POWER AND PROGRESS OF THE UNITED STATES.

THE UNITED STATES; Its Power and Progress.

BY GUILLAUME TELL POUSSIN,
LATE MINISTER OF THE REPUBLIC OF FRANCE TO THE UNITED STATES.

FIRST AMERICAN, FROM THE THIRD PARIS EDITION.

TRANSLATED FROM THE FRENCH BY EDMOND L. DU BARRY, M. D.
SURGEON, UNITED STATES NAVY.

IN ONE LARGE OCTAVO VOLUME.

BIGLAND'S NATURAL HISTORY.

OF ANIMALS, BIRDS, FISHES, REPTILES, AND INSECTS.

ILLUSTRATED WITH NUMEROUS AND BEAUTIFUL ENGRAVINGS.

BY JOHN BIGLAND,

Author of a "View of the World," "Letters on Universal History," &c.

Complete in one volume, 12mo.

GOLDSMITH'S ANIMATED NATURE

IN TWO VOLUMES, OCTAVO.

BEAUTIFULLY ILLUSTRATED WITH 385 PLATES.

CONTAINING A HISTORY OF THE EARTH, ANIMALS, BIRDS AND FISHES; FORMING THE MOST COMPLETE NATURAL HISTORY EVER PUBLISHED.

THE FARMER'S AND PLANTER'S ENCYCLOPÆDIA.

THE FARMER'S AND PLANTER'S ENCYCLOPÆDIA OF RURAL AFFAIRS.

BY CUTHBERT W. JOHNSON.

ADAPTED TO THE UNITED STATES BY GOUVERNEUR EMERSON.

Illustrated by seventeen beautiful Engravings of Cattle, Horses, Sheep, the varieties of Wheat, Barley, Oats, Grasses, the Weeds of Agriculture, &c.; besides numerous Engravings on wood of the most important implements of Agriculture.

IN ONE LARGE OCTAVO VOLUME.

LIPPINCOTT, GRAMBO & CO.'S PUBLICATIONS.

THE AMERICAN GARDENER'S CALENDAR,

ADAPTED TO THE CLIMATE AND SEASONS OF THE UNITED STATES.

Containing a complete account of all the work necessary to be done in the Kitchen Garden, Fruit Garden, Orchard, Vineyard, Nursery, Pleasure-Ground, Flower Garden, Green-house, Hot-house, and Forcing Frames, for every month in the year; with ample Practical Directions for performing the same

BY BERNARD M'MAHON.

Tenth Edition, greatly improved. In one volume, octavo.

MASON'S FARRIER AND STUD BOOK—NEW EDITION.

Price, $1.

THE GENTLEMAN'S NEW POCKET FARRIER:

COMPRISING A GENERAL DESCRIPTION OF THE NOBLE AND USEFUL ANIMAL,

THE HORSE;

WITH MODES OF MANAGEMENT IN ALL CASES, AND TREATMENT IN DISEASE.

BY RICHARD MASON, M.D.,

Formerly of Surry County, Virginia.

TO WHICH IS ADDED,

A PRIZE ESSAY ON MULES; AND AN APPENDIX,

Containing Recipes for Diseaes of Horses, Oxen, Cows, Calves, Sheep, Dogs, Swine, &c., &c; with Annals of the Turf, American Stud-Book, Rules for Training, Racing, &c., &c.

WITH A SUPPLEMENT,

BY J. S. SKINNER,

Editor of the Farmers' Library, New York, &c., &c.

MASON'S FARRIER—FARMERS' EDITION.

Price, 62 Cents.

THE PRACTICAL FARRIER, FOR FARMERS:

COMPRISING A GENERAL DESCRIPTION OF THE NOBLE AND USEFUL ANIMAL,

THE HORSE;

WITH MODES OF MANAGEMENT IN ALL CASES, AND TREATMENT IN DISEASE.

TO WHICH IS ADDED,

A PRIZE ESSAY ON MULES; AND AN APPENDIX,

Containing Recipes for Diseases of Horses, Oxen, Cows, Calves, Sheep, Dogs, Swine, &c.

BY RICHARD MASON, M.D.

FORMERLY OF SURRY COUNTY, VIRGINIA.

In one volume, 12mo.; bound in cloth, gilt

HINDS'S FARRIERY AND STUD-BOOK—NEW EDITION.

FARRIERY,

TAUGHT ON A NEW AND EASY PLAN:

BEING A

Treatise on the Diseases and Accidents of the Horse;

With Instructions to the Shoeing Smith, Farrier, and Groom; preceded by a Popular description of the Animal Functions in Health, and how these are to be restored when disordered.

BY JOHN HINDS, VETERINARY SURGEON.

With considerable Additions and Improvements, particularly adapted to this country,

BY THOMAS M. SMITH,

Veterinary Surgeon, and Member of the London Veterinary Medical Society.

WITH A SUPPLEMENT, BY J. S. SKINNER.

TO CARPENTERS AND MECHANICS.

JUST PUBLISHED.

A NEW AND IMPROVED EDITION OF

THE CARPENTER'S NEW GUIDE,

BEING A COMPLETE BOOK OF LINES FOR

CARPENTRY AND JOINERY;

Treating fully on Practical Geometry, Saffit's Brick and Plaster Groins, Niches of every description, Sky-lights, Lines for Roofs and Domes; with a great variety of Designs for Roofs, Trussed Girders, Floors, Domes, Bridges, &c., Angle Bars for Shop Fronts, &c., and Raking Mouldings.

ALSO,

Additional Plans for various Stair-Cases, with the Lines for producing the Face and Falling Moulds, never before published, and greatly superior to those given in a former edition of this work.

BY WM. JOHNSON, ARCHITECT,

OF PHILADELPHIA.

The whole founded on true Geometrical Principles; the Theory and Practice well explained and fully exemplified, on eighty-three Copper-Plates, including some Observations and Calculations on the Strength of Timber.

BY PETER NICHOLSON,

Author of "The Carpenter and Joiner's Assistant," "The Student's Instructor to the Five Orders," &c.

Thirteenth Edition. One volume, 4to., well bound.

SAY'S POLITICAL ECONOMY.

A TREATISE ON POLITICAL ECONOMY;
Or, The Production, Distribution and Consumption of Wealth.
BY JEAN BAPTISTE SAY.
FIFTH AMERICAN EDITION, WITH ADDITIONAL NOTES.
BY C. C. BIDDLE, Esq.
In one volume, octavo.

A BEAUTIFUL AND VALUABLE PRESENTATION BOOK.
THE POET'S OFFERING.
EDITED BY MRS. HALE.
With a Portrait of the Editress, a Splendid Illuminated Title-Page, and Twelve Beautiful Engravings by Sartain. Bound in rich Turkey Morocco, and Extra Cloth, Gilt Edge.

A Dictionary of Select and Popular Quotations,
WHICH ARE IN DAILY USE.
TAKEN FROM THE LATIN, FRENCH, GREEK, SPANISH AND ITALIAN LANGUAGES.

Together with a copious Collection of Law Maxims and Law Terms, translated into English, with Illustrations, Historical and Idiomatic.

NEW AMERICAN EDITION, CORRECTED, WITH ADDITIONS.
In one volume, 12mo.

The City Merchant; or, The Mysterious Failure.
BY J. B. JONES,
Author of "Wild Western Scenes," "The Western Merchant," &c.

ILLUSTRATED WITH TEN ENGRAVINGS.
In one volume, 12mo.

LAURENCE STERNE'S WORKS,
WITH A LIFE OF THE AUTHOR:
WRITTEN BY HIMSELF.

WITH SEVEN BEAUTIFUL ILLUSTRATIONS, ENGRAVED BY GILBERT AND GIHON, FROM DESIGNS BY DARLEY.

One volume, octavo; cloth, gilt.

RUSCHENBERGER'S NATURAL HISTORY.
COMPLETE, WITH NEW GLOSSARY

THE ELEMENTS OF NATURAL HISTORY,
EMBRACING ZOOLOGY, BOTANY, AND GEOLOGY;
FOR SCHOOLS, COLLEGES, AND FAMILIES
BY W. S. W. RUSCHENBERGER, M.D.
IN TWO VOLUMES.

WITH NEARLY ONE THOUSAND ILLUSTRATIONS, AND A COPIOUS GLOSSARY.

Vol I contains *Vertebrate Animals.* Vol II contains *Intervertebrate Animals, Botany, and Geology.*

The Mexican War and its Heroes;
BEING
A COMPLETE HISTORY OF THE MEXICAN WAR,
EMBRACING ALL THE OPERATIONS UNDER GENERALS TAYLOR AND SCOTT
WITH A BIOGRAPHY OF THE OFFICERS.
ALSO,
AN ACCOUNT OF THE CONQUEST OF CALIFORNIA AND NEW MEXICO,

Under Gen Kearney, Cols Doniphan and Fremont Together with Numerous Anecdotes of the War, and personal adventures of the Officers. Illustrated with Accurate Portraits and other Beautiful Engravings.

In one volume, 12mo.

A Book for every Family.

THE DICTIONARY OF
Domestic Medicine and Household Surgery.

BY SPENCER THOMPSON, M.D., F.R.C.S.,
Of Edinburgh.

ILLUSTRATED WITH NUMEROUS CUTS.

EDITED AND ADAPTED TO THE WANTS OF THIS COUNTRY, BY A WELL-KNOWN PRACTITIONER OF PHILADELPHIA.

In one volume, demi-octavo.

NEW AND COMPLETE COOK-BOOK.

THE PRACTICAL COOK-BOOK,
CONTAINING UPWARDS OF
ONE THOUSAND RECEIPTS,

Consisting of Directions for Selecting, Preparing, and Cooking all kinds of Meats, Fish, Poultry, and Game; Soups, Broths, Vegetables, and Salads. Also, for making all kinds of Plain and Fancy Breads, Pastes, Puddings, Cakes, Creams, Ices, Jellies, Preserves, Marmalades, &c., &c, &c. Together with various Miscellaneous Recipes, and numerous Preparations for Invalids.

BY MRS. BLISS.

In one volume, 12mo.

THE YOUNG DOMINICAN;
OR, THE MYSTERIES OF THE INQUISITION,
AND OTHER SECRET SOCIETIES OF SPAIN.
BY M. V. DE FEREAL.

WITH HISTORICAL NOTES, BY M. MANUEL DE CUENDIAS.
TRANSLATED FROM THE FRENCH.
ILLUSTRATED WITH TWENTY SPLENDID ENGRAVINGS BY FRENCH ARTISTS.
One volume, octavo.

TALES OF THE SOUTHERN BORDER
BY C. W. WEBBER.

ONE VOLUME OCTAVO, HANDSOMELY ILLUSTRATED.

Price $1 50.

Gems from the Sacred Mine;
OR, HOLY THOUGHTS UPON SACRED SUBJECTS
BY CLERGYMEN OF THE EPISCOPAL CHURCH.
EDITED BY THOMAS WYATT, A. M.
In one volume, 12mo.
WITH SEVEN BEAUTIFUL STEEL ENGRAVINGS.

DODD'S LECTURES.

DISCOURSES TO YOUNG MEN.

ILLUSTRATED BY NUMEROUS HIGHLY INTERESTING ANECDOTES.

BY WILLIAM DODD, LL. D.

CHAPLAIN IN ORDINARY TO HIS MAJESTY, GEORGE THE THIRD.

FIRST AMERICAN EDITION, WITH ENGRAVINGS.

One volume, 18mo.

THE IRIS:

AN ORIGINAL SOUVENIR.

WITH CONTRIBUTIONS FROM THE FIRST WRITERS IN THE COUNTRY.

EDITED BY PROF. JOHN S. HART.

With splendid Illuminations and Steel Engravings. Bound in Turkey Morocco and rich Papier Mache Binding.

IN ONE VOLUME, OCTAVO.

DAY DREAMS.

BY MISS MARTHA ALLEN.

ONE VOLUME 12mo.

Price, paper, 50 cents. Cloth, 75 cents.

LONZ POWERS; OR, THE REGULATORS.

A ROMANCE OF KENTUCKY.

FOUNDED ON FACTS.

BY JAMES WEIR, ESQ.

One vol. 12mo. Price $1 00.

A MANUAL OF POLITENESS,

COMPRISING

THE PRINCIPLES OF ETIQUETTE AND RULES OF BEHAVIOUR

IN GENTEEL SOCIETY, FOR PERSONS OF BOTH SEXES.

18mo., with Plates.

BOOK OF POLITENESS.

THE GENTLEMAN AND LADY'S BOOK OF POLITENESS AND PROPRIETY OF DEPORTMENT,

DEDICATED TO THE YOUTH OF BOTH SEXES,

BY MADAME CELNART.

TRANSLATED FROM THE SIXTH PARIS EDITION, ENLARGED AND IMPROVED.

FIFTH AMERICAN EDITION.

One volume, 18mo.

SENECA'S MORALS.

BY WAY OF ABSTRACT TO WHICH IS ADDED, A DISCOURSE UNDER THE TITLE OF AN AFTER-THOUGHT.

BY SIR ROGER L'ESTRANGE, KNT.

A new and fine edition; one volume, 18mo.

A copy of this valuable little work should be found in every family library.

Bennett's (Rev. John) Letters to a Young Lady,

ON A VARIETY OF SUBJECTS CALCULATED TO IMPROVE THE HEART, TO FORM THE MANNERS, AND ENLIGHTEN THE UNDERSTANDING.

"That our daughters may be as polished corners of the temple."

THE AMERICAN CHESTERFIELD:

OR, "YOUTH'S GUIDE TO THE WAY TO WEALTH, HONOUR, AND DISTINCTION," &c.

In one volume, 18mo.

CONTAINING ALSO A COMPLETE TREATISE ON THE ART OF CARVING.

NEW SONG-BOOK.

Grigg's Southern and Western Songster;

BEING A CHOICE COLLECTION OF THE MOST FASHIONABLE SONGS, MANY OF WHICH ARE ORIGINAL.

In one volume, 18mo.

The Daughter's Own Book:

OR, PRACTICAL HINTS FROM A FATHER TO HIS DAUGHTER.

In one volume, 18mo.

THE LIFE AND OPINIONS OF TRISTRAM SHANDY, GENTLEMAN

COMPRISING THE HUMOROUS ADVENTURES OF

UNCLE TOBY AND CORPORAL TRIM.

BY L. STERNE.

Beautifully Illustrated by Darley. Stitched.

A SENTIMENTAL JOURNEY.

BY L. STERNE.

ILLUSTRATED AS ABOVE BY DARLEY. STITCHED.

The beauties of this author are so well known, and his errors in style and expression so few and far between, that one reads with renewed delight his delicate turns, &c.

ROBOTHAM'S POCKET FRENCH DICTIONARY.

CAREFULLY REVISED,

AND THE PRONUNCIATION OF ALL THE DIFFICULT WORDS ADDED.

THE YOUNG CHORISTER;

A Collection of New and Beautiful Tunes, adapted to the use of Sabbath-Schools, from some of the most distinguished composers, together with many of the author's compositions.

EDITED BY MINARD W. WILSON.

THE GREEK EXILE:

Or, A Narrative of the Captivity and Escape of Christophorus Plato Castanis,

DURING THE MASSACRE ON THE ISLAND OF SCIO BY THE TURKS.

TOGETHER WITH VARIOUS ADVENTURES IN GREECE AND AMERICA.

WRITTEN BY HIMSELF.

One volume, 12mo.

APPLES OF GOLD.
(From Fenelon.)
32mo., CLOTH, GILT. PRICE 13 CENTS.

LIFE OF PAUL JONES.
In one volume, 12mo.
WITH ONE HUNDRED ILLUSTRATIONS
BY JAMES HAMILTON.

THE LIFE OF GENERAL JACKSON,
WITH A LIKENESS OF THE OLD HERO.
In one volume, 18mo.

LIFE OF GENERAL ZACHARY TAYLOR,
COMPRISING A NARRATIVE OF EVENTS CONNECTED WITH HIS PROFESSIONAL CAREER, AND AUTHENTIC INCIDENTS OF HIS EARLY YEARS.

BY J. REESE FRY AND R. T. CONRAD.

With an original and accurate Portrait, and Eleven Elegant Illustrations, by Darley.

In one handsome 12mo volume.

GENERAL TAYLOR AND HIS STAFF:
Comprising Memoirs of Generals Taylor, Worth, Wool, and Butler; Colonels May, Cross, Clay, Hardin, Yell, Hays, and other distinguished Officers attached to General Taylor's Army.

INTERSPERSED WITH

NUMEROUS ANECDOTES OF THE MEXICAN WAR,

AND PERSONAL ADVENTURES OF THE OFFICERS.

Compiled from Public Documents and Private Correspondence.

WITH ACCURATE PORTRAITS AND OTHER BEAUTIFUL ILLUSTRATIONS
In one volume, 12mo.

General Scott and his Staff:

Comprising Memoirs of Generals Scott, Twiggs, Smith, Quitman, Shields, Pillow, Lane, Cadwallader, Patterson, and Pierce; Colonels Childs, Riley, Harney, and Butler; and other distinguished Officers attached to General Scott's Army.

TOGETHER WITH

Notices of General Kearney, Col. Doniphan, Colonel Fremont, and other Officers distinguished in the Conquest of California and New Mexico; and Personal Adventures of the Officers. Compiled from Public Documents and Private Correspondence.

WITH

ACCURATE PORTRAITS AND OTHER BEAUTIFUL ILLUSTRATIONS.

In one volume, 12mo.

THE LEGISLATIVE GUIDE:

Containing directions for conducting business in the House of Representatives; the Senate of the United States; the Joint Rules of both Houses; a Synopsis of Jefferson's Manual, and copious Indices; together with a concise system of Rules of Order, based on the Regulations of the United States Congress. Designed to economise time, secure uniformity and despatch in conducting business in all secular meetings, and also in all religious, political, and Legislative Assemblies.

BY JOSEPH BARTLETT BURLEIGH, LL.D.

In one volume, 12mo.

This is considered by our Judges and Congressmen as decidedly the best work of the kind extant. Every young man in the country should have a copy of this book.

THE FAMILY DENTIST,

INCLUDING THE SURGICAL, MEDICAL, AND MECHANICAL TREATMENT OF THE TEETH.

Illustrated with Thirty-one Engravings.

BY CHARLES A. DU BOUCHET, M. D.,

DENTAL SURGEON.

In one volume, 18mo.

MECHANICS

FOR THE MILLWRIGHT, ENGINEER, AND MACHINIST CIVIL ENGINEER AND ARCHITECT:

CONTAINING

THE PRINCIPLES OF MECHANICS APPLIED TO MACHINERY

Of American Models, Steam-Engines, Water-Works, Navigation, Bridge building, &c., &c.

BY FREDERICK OVERMAN,

AUTHOR OF "THE MANUFACTURE OF IRON," AND OTHER SCIENTIFIC TREATISES.

Illustrated by 150 Engravings.

In one large 12mo. volume.

CALIFORNIA AND OREGON:

Or, Sights in the Gold Region, and Scenes by the Way.

BY THEODORE T. JOHNSON.

WITH A MAP AND ILLUSTRATIONS.

THIRD EDITION, WITH AN APPENDIX,

Containing Full Instructions to Emigrants by the Overland Route to Oregon.

BY HON. SAMUEL R. THURSTON,

Delegate to Congress from that Territory.

WILD WESTERN SCENES:

A NARRATIVE OF ADVENTURES IN THE WESTERN WILDERNESS.

Wherein the Exploits of Daniel Boone, the Great American Pioneer, are particularly described. Also, Minute Accounts of Bear, Deer, and Buffalo Hunts; Desperate Conflicts with the Savages; Fishing and Fowling Adventures; Encounters with Serpents, &c., &c.

BY LUKE SHORTFIELD,

Author of "The Western Merchant."

WITH SIXTEEN BEAUTIFUL ILLUSTRATIONS.

In one volume, 12mo.

POEMS OF THE PLEASURES:

CONSISTING OF

THE PLEASURES OF IMAGINATION, by Akenside; THE PLEASURES OF MEMORY, by Samuel Rogers; THE PLEASURES OF HOPE, by Campbell; and THE PLEASURES OF FRIENDSHIP, by M'Henry.

WITH A MEMOIR OF EACH AUTHOR,

Prepared expressly for this Work.

One volume, 18mo.

The Initials; A Story of Modern Life.

THREE VOLUMES OF THE LONDON EDITION COMPLETE IN ONE VOLUME, 12mo.

A new novel, equal to "Jane Eyre."

ARTHUR'S LIBRARY FOR THE HOUSEHOLD.

In Twelve handsome 18mo. volumes, bound in scarlet cloth, and each work complete in itself.

1. WOMEN'S TRIALS; OR, TALES AND SKETCHES FROM THE LIFE AROUND US.
2. MARRIED LIFE; ITS SHADOWS AND SUNSHINE.
3. THE TWO WIVES; OR, LOST AND WON.
4. THE WAYS OF PROVIDENCE; OR, "HE DOETH ALL THINGS WELL."
5. HOME SCENES.
6. STORIES FOR YOUNG HOUSEKEEPERS.
7. LESSONS IN LIFE, FOR ALL WHO WILL READ THEM.
8. SEED-TIME AND HARVEST; OR, WHATSOEVER A MAN SOWETH THAT SHALL HE ALSO REAP.
9. STORIES FOR PARENTS.
10. OFF-HAND SKETCHES, A LITTLE DASHED WITH HUMOR.
11. WORDS FOR THE WISE.
12. THE TRIED AND THE TEMPTED.

The above Series are sold together or separate, as each work is complete in itself. No family should be without a copy of this interesting and instructive Series. Price Thirty-seven and a Half Cents per Volume.

BALDWIN'S PRONOUNCING GAZETTEER.

A PRONOUNCING GAZETTEER:

Containing Topographical, Statistical, and other Information, of the more important Places in the known World, from the most recent and authentic Sources.

BY THOMAS BALDWIN,

Assisted by several other Gentlemen.

To which is added an APPENDIX, containing more than TEN THOUSAND ADDITIONAL NAMES, chiefly of the small Towns and Villages, &c., of the United States and of Mexico

NINTH EDITION, WITH A SUPPLEMENT,

Giving the Pronunciation of near two thousand names, besides those pronounced in the Original Work: Forming in itself a Complete Vocabulary of Geographical Pronunciation.

ONE VOLUME 12MO.—PRICE, $1 50.

FIELD'S SCRAP BOOK.—NEW EDITION.

Literary and Miscellaneous Scrap Book.

Consisting of Tales and Anecdotes—Biographical, Historical, Moral, Religious, and Sentimental Pieces, in Prose and Poetry.

COMPILED BY WM. FIELDS.

SECOND EDITION, REVISED AND IMPROVED.

In one handsome 8vo. Volume. Price, $2 00.

AUNT PHILLIS'S CABIN;

OR, SOUTHERN LIFE AS IT IS.

BY MRS. MARY H. EASTMAN.

PRICE, 50 AND 75 CENTS.

This volume presents a picture of Southern Life, taken at different points of view from the one occupied by the authoress of *"Uncle Tom's Cabin."* The writer, being a native of the South, is familiar with the many varied aspects assumed by domestic servitude in that sunny region, and therefore feels competent to give pictures of "Southern Life, as it is."

Pledged to no clique or party, and free from the pressure of any and all extraneous influences, she has written her book with a view to its truthfulness, and the public at the North, as well as at the South, will find in "Aunt Phillis's Cabin" not the distorted picture of an interested painter, but the faithful transcript of a Daguerreotypist.

THE CONFESSIONS OF A HOUSEKEEPER.
BY MRS. JOHN SMITH.
WITH THIRTEEN HUMOROUS ILLUSTRATIONS.

One Volume 12mo. Price 50 Cents.

THE HUMAN BODY AND ITS CONNEXION WITH MAN.
ILLUSTRATED BY THE PRINCIPAL ORGANS.
BY JAMES JOHN GARTH WILKINSON.
Member of the Royal College of Surgeons of England.

IN ONE VOLUME 12MO.—PRICE, $1 25.

WHEELER'S HISTORY OF NORTH CAROLINA.

Historical Sketches
OF NORTH CAROLINA,
From 1584 to 1851.

Compiled from Original Records, Official Documents, and Traditional Statements; with Biographical Sketches of her Distinguished Statesmen, Jurists, Lawyers, Soldiers, Divines, &c.

BY JOHN H. WHEELER,
Late Treasurer of the State.

IN ONE VOLUME OCTAVO.—PRICE, $2 00.

THE NORTH CAROLINA READER:
CONTAINING A HISTORY AND DESCRIPTION OF NORTH CAROLINA, SELECTIONS IN PROSE AND VERSE, (MANY OF THEM BY EMINENT CITIZENS OF THE STATE), HISTORICAL AND CHRONOLOGICAL TABLES,

And a Variety of Miscellaneous Information and Statistics.

BY C. H. WILEY.

"My own green land for ever!
Land of the beautiful and brave—
The freeman's home—the martyr's grave."

Illustrated with Engravings, and designed for Families and Schools.

One Volume 12mo. Price $1.00.

THIRTY YEARS WITH THE INDIAN TRIBES.

PERSONAL MEMOIRS OF A

Residence of Thirty Years with the Indian Tribes

ON THE AMERICAN FRONTIERS:

With brief Notices of passing Events, Facts, and Opinions.

A. D. 1812 TO A. D. 1842.

BY HENRY R. SCHOOLCRAFT.

One large 8vo. Volume. Price $3 00.

THE SCALP HUNTERS;

OR,

ROMANTIC ADVENTURES IN NORTHERN MEXICO.

BY CAPTAIN MAYNE REID,
Author of the "Rifle Rangers."

COMPLETE IN ONE VOLUME   PRICE FIFTY CENTS

BOARDMAN'S BIBLE IN THE FAMILY.

The Bible in the Family:

OR, HINTS ON DOMESTIC HAPPINESS

BY H. A. BOARDMAN.

PASTOR OF THE TENTH PRESBYTERIAN CHURCH, PHILADELPHIA.

One Volume 12mo.—Price One Dollar.

THE REGICIDE'S DAUGHTER:

A Tale of two Worlds.

BY W. H. CARPENTER,

AUTHOR OF "CLAIBORNE THE REBEL," "JOHN THE BOLD," &C., &C.

One Volume 12mo.   Price Thirty-seven and a Half Cents.

Splendid Illustrated Books, suitable for Gifts for the Holidays.

The Iris: An Original Souvenir for any Year.
EDITED BY PROF. JOHN S. HART.
WITH TWELVE SPLENDID ILLUMINATIONS, ALL FROM ORIGINAL DESIGNS.

THE DEW-DROP: A TRIBUTE OF AFFECTION.
WITH NINE STEEL ENGRAVINGS.

GEMS FROM THE SACRED MINE.
WITH TEN STEEL PLATES AND ILLUMINATIONS.

THE POET'S OFFERING.
WITH FOURTEEN STEEL PLATES AND ILLUMINATIONS.

THE STANDARD EDITIONS OF THE POETS.
WITH ILLUSTRATIONS.

LORD AND LADY HARCOURT
OR, COUNTRY HOSPITALITIES.
BY CATHARINE SINCLAIR,

Author of "Jane Bouverie," "The Business of Life," "Modern Accomplishments," &c., &c.

One Volume 12mo. *Price 50 cents, paper; cloth, fine, 75 cents.*

William's New Map of the United States,
ON ROLLERS.
SIZE TWO AND A HALF BY THREE FEET.

A new map of the United States, upon which are delineated its vast works o Internal Communication, Routes across the Continent, &c., showing also Canada and the Island of Cuba,

BY W. WILLIAMS.

This Map is handsomely colored and mounted on rollers, and will be foun a beautiful and useful ornament to the Counting-House and Parlor, as we as the School-Room. Price Two Dollars.

SCHOOLCRAFT'S GREAT NATIONAL WORK

ON THE

Indian Tribes of the United States.

PART SECOND—QUARTO.

WITH EIGHTY BEAUTIFUL ILLUSTRATIONS ON STEEL,

Engraved in the first style of the art, from Drawings by Capt. Eastman, U.S.A.

PRICE, FIFTEEN DOLLARS.

COCKBURN'S LIFE OF LORD JEFFREY.

LIFE OF LORD JEFFREY,

WITH

A SELECTION FROM HIS CORRESPONDENCE,

BY LORD COCKBURN,

One of the Judges of the Court of Sessions in Scotland.

2 vols. 12mo. Price, $2 50.

ROMANCE OF NATURAL HISTORY;

OR, WILD SCENES AND WILD HUNTERS.

WITH NUMEROUS ILLUSTRATIONS, ONE VOLUME OCTAVO, CLOTH.

BY C. W. WEBBER,

Author of "Old Hicks the Guide," "Shot in the Eye," &c.

PRICE, TWO DOLLARS.

THE LIFE OF WILLIAM PENN,

WITH

SELECTIONS FROM HIS CORRESPONDENCE AND AUTOBIOGRAPHY

BY SAMUEL M. JANNEY.

Second Edition, Revised. Price, Two Dollars.

LIPPINCOTT'S
CABINET HISTORIES OF THE STATES,

CONSISTING OF A SERIES OF

Cabinet Histories of all the States of the Union,

TO EMBRACE A VOLUME FOR EACH STATE.

We have so far completed all our arrangements, as to be able to issue the whole series in the shortest possible time consistent with its careful literary production. SEVERAL VOLUMES ARE NOW READY FOR SALE. The talented authors who have engaged to write these Histories, are no strangers in the literary world.

"These most tastefully printed and bound volumes form the first instalment of a series of State Histories, which, without superseding the bulkier and more expensive works of the same character, may enter household channels from which the others would be excluded by their cost and magnitude."

"In conciseness, clearness, skill of arrangement, and graphic interest, they are a most excellent earnest of those to come. They are eminently adapted both to interest and instruct, and should have a place in the family library of every American." —*N. Y. Courier and Enquirer.*

New Themes for the Protestant Clergy;

CREEDS WITHOUT CHARITY, THEOLOGY WITHOUT HUMANITY, AND PROTESTANTISM WITHOUT CHRISTIANITY;

With Notes by the Editor on the Literature of Charity, Population, Pauperism, Political Economy, and Protestantism.

PRICE, ONE DOLLAR.

SIMPSON'S MILITARY JOURNAL.

JOURNAL OF A MILITARY RECONNOISSANCE FROM SANTA FE NEW MEXICO, TO THE NAVAJO COUNTRY,

BY JAMES H. SIMPSON, A. M.,

FIRST LIEUTENANT CORPS OF TOPOGRAPHICAL ENGINEERS.

WITH 75 COLOURED ILLUSTRATIONS.

One volume, octavo. Price, Three Dollars.

TALES OF THE SOUTHERN BORDER.
BY C. W. WEBBER.
ONE VOLUME OCTAVO, HANDSOMELY ILLUSTRATED.

The Hunter Naturalist, a Romance of Sporting;
OR, WILD SCENES AND WILD HUNTERS.
BY C. W. WEBBER,
Author of "Shot in the Eye," "Old Hicks the Guide," "Gold Mines of the Gila," &c.

ONE VOLUME, ROYAL OCTAVO.

ILLUSTRATED WITH FORTY BEAUTIFUL ENGRAVINGS,
FROM ORIGINAL DRAWINGS, MANY OF WHICH ARE COLORED.
Price, Five Dollars.

NIGHTS IN A BLOCK-HOUSE;
OR, SKETCHES OF BORDER LIFE.
Embracing Adventures among the Indians, Feats of the Wild Hunters, and Exploits of Boone, Brady, Kenton, Whetzel, Fleehart, and other Border Heroes of the West.

BY HENRY C. WATSON,
Author of "Camp-Fires of the Revolution"

WITH NUMEROUS ILLUSTRATIONS.
One volume, 8vo Price, $2 00.

HAMILTON, THE YOUNG ARTIST.
BY AUGUSTA BROWNE.
WITH AN ESSAY ON SCULPTURE AND PAINTING, BY H. C. BROWNE.
1 vol 18mo Price, 37 1-2 cents.

SIMON KENTON: OR, THE SCOUT'S REVENGE.
AN HISTORICAL ROMANCE.
BY JAMES WEIR.
Illustrated, cloth, 75 cents. Paper, 50 cents.

MARIE DE BERNIERE, THE MAROON,
AND OTHER TALES,
BY W. GILMORE SIMMS.
1 vol. 12mo, cloth. Price $1 25

In Press,
A NEW AND COMPLETE
GAZETTEER OF THE UNITED STATES.

It will furnish the fullest and most recent information respecting the Geography Statistics, and present state of improvement, of every part of this great Republic, particularly of

TEXAS, CALIFORNIA, OREGON, NEW MEXICO,

&c. The work will be issued as soon as the complete official returns of the present Census are received

THE ABOVE WORK WILL BE FOLLOWED BY
A UNIVERSAL GAZETTEER,
OR GEOGRAPHICAL DICTIONARY,

of the most complete and comprehensive character. It will be compiled from the best English, French, and German authorities, and will be published the moment that the returns of the present census of Europe can be obtained.

History of the Mormons
OF UTAH,
THEIR DOMESTIC POLITY AND THEOLOGY,
BY J. W. GUNNISON,
U. S. CORPS TOPOGRAPHICAL ENGINEERS.
WITH ILLUSTRATIONS, IN ONE VOLUME DEMI-OCTAVO.

REPORT OF A GEOLOGICAL SURVEY OF WISCONSIN, IOWA, AND MINNESOTA,

AND INCIDENTALLY OF A PORTION OF NEBRASKA TERRITORY,
MADE UNDER INSTRUCTIONS FROM THE U. S TREASURY DEPARTM'T

BY DAVID DALE OWEN,
United States' Geologist.
WITH OVER 150 ILLUSTRATIONS ON STEEL AND WOOD.
TWO VOLUMES, QUARTO. PRICE $10 00.

MERCHANTS' MEMORANDUM BOOK,
WITH LISTS OF ALL GOODS PURCHASED BY COUNTRY MERCHANTS, &c.
One volume, 18mo, Leather cover. Price, 50 cents.

THE ABBOTSFORD EDITION

OF

The Waverley Novels,

Printed upon fine white Paper, with new and beautiful Type,

FROM THE LAST ENGLISH EDITION,

EMBRACING

THE AUTHOR'S LATEST CORRECTIONS, NOTES, ETC.,

Complete in 12 volumes, demi-octavo, neatly bound in cloth,

With Illustrations,

FOR ONLY TWELVE DOLLARS,

CONTAINING

WAVERLEY, or 'Tis Sixty Years Since...THE FORTUNES OF NIGEL.
GUY MANNERING..............................PEVERIL OF THE PEAK.
THE ANTIQUARY................................QUENTIN DURWARD.
THE BLACK DWARF ....ST. RONAN'S WELL.
OLD MORTALITY................................REDGAUNTLET.
ROB ROY ....THE BETROTHED.
THE HEART OF MID-LOTHIAN..........THE TALISMAN.
THE BRIDE OF LAMMERMOOR..........WOODSTOCK.
A LEGEND OF MONTROSE ....THE HIGHLAND WIDOW, &c.
IVANHOE..THE FAIR MAID OF PERTH.
THE MONASTERY..............................ANNE OF GEIERSTEIN.
THE ABBOT..COUNT ROBERT OF PARIS.
KENILWORTH ....CASTLE DANGEROUS.
THE PIRATE.......................................SURGEON'S DAUGHTER, &c.

Any of the above Novels sold, in Paper Covers, at Fifty Cents each.

ALSO,

THE SAME EDITION

OF

THE WAVERLEY NOVELS,

In Twelve Volumes, Royal Octavo, on Superfine Paper, with

THREE HUNDRED CHARACTERISTIC AND BEAUTIFUL ILLUSTRATIONS.

ELEGANTLY BOUND IN CLOTH, GILT.

Price, Only Twenty-Four Dollars.

FROST'S JUVENILE SERIES.

TWELVE VOLUMES, 16mo, WITH FIVE HUNDRED ENGRAVINGS.

WALTER O'NEILL, OR THE PLEASURE OF DOING GOOD. 25 Engravings.
JUNKER SCHOTT, and other Stories. 6 Engravings.
THE LADY OF THE LURLEI, and other Stories. 12 Engravings.
ELLEN'S BIRTHDAY, and other Stories. 20 Engravings.
HERMAN, and other Stories. 9 Engravings.
KING TREGEWALL'S DAUGHTER, and other Stories. 16 Engr's.
THE DROWNED BOY, and other Stories. 6 Engravings.
THE PICTORIAL RHYME-BOOK. 122 Engravings.
THE PICTORIAL NURSERY BOOK. 117 Engravings.
THE GOOD CHILD'S REWARD. 115 Engravings.
ALPHABET OF QUADRUPEDS. 26 Engravings.
ALPHABET OF BIRDS. 26 Engravings.

PRICE, TWENTY-FIVE CENTS EACH.

The above popular and attractive series of New Juveniles for the Young, are sold together or separately

THE MILLINER AND THE MILLIONAIRE.
BY MRS. REBECCA HICKS,

(Of Virginia,) Author of "The Lady Killer," &c. 1 vol. 12mo. Price, 37 1-2 cents.

STANSBURY'S
EXPEDITION TO THE GREAT SALT LAKE.

AN EXPLORATION
OF THE VALLEY OF THE GREAT SALT LAKE
OF UTAH,

CONTAINING ITS GEOGRAPHY, NATURAL HISTORY, MINERALOGICAL RESOURCES, ANALYSIS OF ITS WATERS, AND AN AUTHENTIC ACCOUNT OF

THE MORMON SETTLEMENT.

Also, A Reconnoissance of a New Route through the Rocky Mountains, with Seventy Beautiful Illustrations, from Drawings taken on the spot, and two large and accurate Maps of that region.

BY HOWARD STANSBURY,
Captain Topographical Engineers. 2 vols. royal octavo. Price $5 00.

ARTHUR'S
New Juvenile Library.
BEAUTIFULLY ILLUSTRATED.

1. WHO IS GREATEST? and other Stories.
2. WHO ARE HAPPIEST? and other Stories.
3. THE POOR WOOD-CUTTER, and other Stories.
4. MAGGY'S BABY, and other Stories.
5. MR. HAVEN'T-GOT-TIME AND MR. DON'T-BE-IN-A-HURRY.
6. THE PEACEMAKERS.
7. UNCLE BEN'S NEW-YEAR'S GIFT, and other Stories.
8. THE WOUNDED BOY, and other Stories.
9. THE LOST CHILDREN, and other Stories.
10. OUR HARRY, and other Poems and Stories.
11. THE LAST PENNY, and other Stories.
12. PIERRE, THE ORGAN BOY, and other Stories.

EACH VOLUME IS ILLUSTRATED WITH

ENGRAVINGS FROM ORIGINAL DESIGNS BY CROOME,

And are sold together or separately.

LIBRARY EDITION OF SHAKSPEARE.
(LARGE TYPE.)

THE DRAMATIC WORKS OF WILLIAM SHAKSPEARE,

WITH A LIFE OF THE POET,

AND NOTES ORIGINAL AND SELECTED, TOGETHER WITH A COPIOUS GLOSSARY.

4 VOLUMES OCTAVO. WITH ILLUSTRATIONS.

STYLES OF BINDING:

Cloth, extra	$6 00
Library style	7 00
Half-Turkey morocco	9 00
Half-calf and Turkey, antique style	12 00
Full calf and Turkey, antique style	15 00

HISTORY OF THE NATIONAL FLAG OF THE U. STATES.
WITH COLOURED ILLUSTRATIONS.
BY SCHUYLER HAMILTON,
CAPTAIN BY BREVET, U. S. A.

One vol., crown 8vo. Price $1 00.

ANNA BISHOP'S TRAVELS.

TRAVELS of ANNA BISHOP in MEXICO (1849).
WITH TWELVE BEAUTIFUL ILLUSTRATIONS.

Price, paper, 50 cents. Cloth, 75 cents.

POLITICS FOR AMERICAN CHRISTIANS;
A WORD UPON OUR EXAMPLE AS A NATION, OUR LABOUR, &c.

TOGETHER WITH THE

POLITICS OF THE NEW TESTAMENT.

BY THE AUTHOR OF

"NEW THEMES FOR THE PROTESTANT CLERGY."

One vol 8vo, half cloth. Price 50 cents.

ANCIENT CHRISTIANITY EXEMPLIFIED,

In the Private, Domestic, Social, and Civil Life of the Primitive Christians, and in the Original Institutions, Offices, Ordinances, and Rites of the Church.

BY REV. LYMAN COLEMAN, D.D.

In one volume 8vo. Price $2 50.

CPSIA information can be obtained
at www.ICGtesting.com
Printed in the USA
BVHW08s2153050818
523607BV00003B/80/P